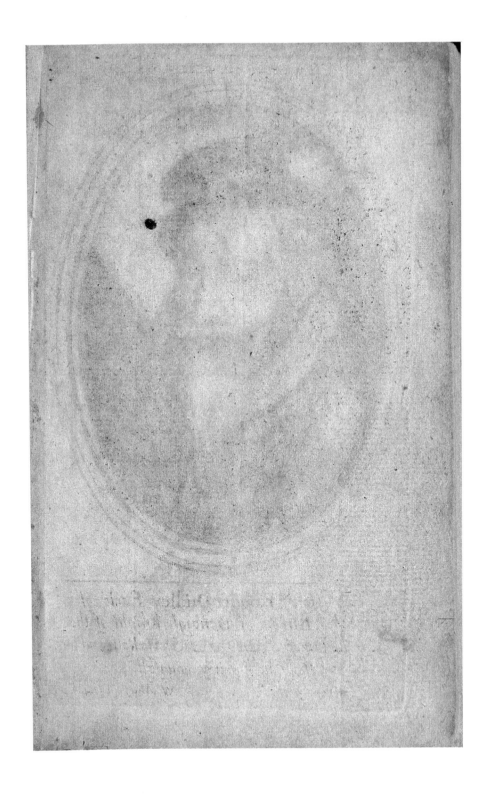

The right Honble Robert Dudley Earle of
Leicester, Baron of Denbigh, knight of the
noble order of St George & St Michall, and late
one of her Maties ho^ble privy counsell etc.

W Marshall sculpsit.

LEICESTER'S
COMMON-WEALTH.

Conceived, spoken and
published with most earnest
protestation of dutifull goodwill and affection towards
this Realme.

By
R O B E R T P A R S O N S
Jesuite.

WHEREUNTO IS ADDED
Leicesters-Ghost.

JOB, 20. 27.
The Heavens shall reveale his Iniquitie,
and the Earth shall rise up against him.

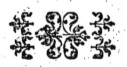

LONDON,
Printed *Anno Dom.* MDCXLI.

THE EPISTLE
DIRECTORY,
TO

M. G. M. In Gratious
Street in *London*.

 *Eare and loving friend, I recei-
ved about tenne daies agon your
letter of the* 9. *of this present :
wherein you demand and foli-
cite againe the thing , that I fo flatly denied
you , at my late being in your chamber : I
meane to put in writing the relation which
then I made unto you, of the fpeech had this
laft Chriftmas in my prefence, betweene my.
right worfhipfull good friend and patron ,
and his gueft the old Lawyer, of fome matters
in our ftate and country. And for that you
preffe me very ferioufly at this inftant, both
by requeft and many reafons, to yeeld to your
defire herein , and not only this, but alfo to
give my confent for the publifhing of the
fame, by fuch fecret meanes as you affure me*

you

you can there find out : I have thought good
to confer the whole matter with the parties
themſelves , whom principally it concerneth
(who at the receipt of your letter were not
far from me :) And albeit at the firſt I
found them averſe and nothing inclined to
grant your demand : yet after upon conſideration of your reaſons, and aſſurance of ſe-
creſie (eſpecially for that there is nothing in
the ſame contained, repugnant to charity or
to our bounden duty towards our moſt gratious Princes or Countrey, but rather for the
ſpeciall good of them both , and for the fore-
warning of ſome dangers imminent to the
ſame) they have referred over the matter to
mee, yet with this Proviſo , that they will
know nothing, nor yet yeeld conſent to the publiſhing hereof , for feare of ſome future flou-
riſh of the ragged Staffe to come hereafter a-
bout their eares, if their names ſhould breake
forth : which (I truſt) you will provide, ſhall
neuer happen, both for their ſecurity, and for
your own. And with this I will end, aſſuring
you that within theſe five or ſix dayes , you
ſhall receive the whole in writing by another
way and ſecret meanes , neither ſhall the
bearer ſuſpect what he carrieth : wherof alſo
I thought good to premoniſh you. And this
ſhall ſuffice for this time.

THE

THE
PREFACE OF THE
CONFERENCE.

Ot long before the laſt *Scholar.*
Chriſtmaſſe, I was
requeſted by a letter
from a very worſhipful
and grave Gentleman,
whoſe ſonne was then
my pupill in *Cambridge*, to repaire with
my ſaid Scholar to a certaine houſe of
his neare *London*, and there to paſſe over
the Holy-dayes in his company : for The occaſion
that it was determined that in *Hillary* of this confe-
tearme following, his ſaid ſonne ſhould rence and
be placed in ſome Inne of Chancery, to meeting.
follow the ſtudy of the Common-law,
and ſo to leave the Vniverſity. This re-
queſt was gratefull unto mee in reſpect
of the time, as alſo of the matter, but
eſpecially of the company. For that, as
I love much the yong Gentelman, my
pupill, for his towardlines in religion,
learning, and vertue : ſo much more I
doe reverence his Father, for the riper
A 3 poſſeſſion

poſſeſſion of the ſame ornaments, and for his great wiſedome, experience, and grave judgement in affaires of the world that do occurre : but <u>namely</u> touching our own Country, wherin truly I do not remember to have heard any man in my life, diſcourſe more ſubſtantially, indifferently, and with leſſe paſſion, more love and fidelity, then I have heard him. Which was the cauſe that I tooke ſingular delight to be in his company, and refuſed no occaſion to enjoy the ſame. Which alſo he perceiving, dealt more openly and confidently with me, then with many other of his friends, as by the relation following may well appeare.

The perſons and place of this conference.

When I came to the foreſaid Houſe by *London*, I found there among other friends, an ancient man that profeſſed the law, and was come from *London* to keepe his Chriſtmas in that place, with whom at divers former times I had been well acquainted, for that he haunted much the company of the ſaid Gentleman my friend, and was much truſted and uſed by him in matters of his profeſſion, and not a little beloved alſo for his good converſation, notwithſtanding ſome difference in religion between us. For albeit, this Lawyer was inclined to

be

be a Papiſt, yet was it with ſuch moderation and reſervation of his duty towards his Prince and Countrey and proceedings of the ſame : as he ſeemed alwaies to give full ſatisfaction in this point to us that were of contrary opinion.

Neither did he let to proteſt oftentimes A temperate Papiſt. with great affection, that as he had many friends & kinsfolk of contrary religion to himſelfe : ſo did he love them nevertheleſſe for their different conſcience, but leaving that to God, was deſirous to doe them any friendſhip or ſervice that he could, with all affection, zeale, and fidelity. Neither was he wilfull or obſtinate in his opinion, and much leſſe reproachfull in ſpeech (as many of them be) but was content to heare whatſoever we ſhould ſay to the contrary (as often we did :) and to read any booke alſo that we delivered him, for his inſtruction.

Which temperate behaviour, induced this Gentleman and me, to affect the more his company ; and to diſcourſe as freely with him in all occurrents, as if he had been of our own religion.

A 4　　THE

THE ENTRANCE
TO THE MATTER.

Ne day then of the Chriſtmaſſe, we three retiring our ſelves after dinner, into a large Gallery, for our recreation, (as often wee were accuſtomed to doe, when other went to cards & others paſtimes:) this Lawyer by chance had in his hand a little booke, then newly ſet forth, containing *A defence of the publique Juſtice done of late in England, upon divers Prieſts and other Papiſtes for treaſon*: Which book, the Lawyer had read to himſelfe a little before, and was now putting it up into his pocket; But the Gentleman my friend, who had read over the ſame once or twice in my company before, would needs take the ſame into his hand againe, and asked the Lawyer his judgement upon the booke.

The Lawyer anſwered: That it was evill penned in his opinion to prove the guiltines of ſome perſons therin named in particular, as alſo to perſwade in generall, that the Papiſtes both abroad and at home, who meddle ſo earneſtly with defence and increaſe of their religion (for theſe are not all, ſaid he) doe conſequently wiſh and labour ſome change in the ſtate: but yet whether ſo farre forth, and in ſo deepe a degree of proper treaſon, as here in this booke both in gene-

The booke of Iuſtice.

[handwritten marginalia: Lawyer. fol well v. 5699. el. 2. 15—18.]

generall and particular is prefumed and inforced, that (quoth he) is fome what hard (I weene) for you or me (in refpect of fome other difference between us) to judge or difcerne with indifferency.

Gentleman.

Nay truly faid the Gentleman, for my part I thinke not fo, for that reafon is reafon in what religion foever. And for my felfe, I may proteft, that I beare the honeft Papift (if there be any) no malice for his deceived confcience, wherof among others, your felfe can be a witnes: mary his Practifees againft the ftate, I cannot in any wife digeft: and much leffe may the Common-wealth beare the fame (wherof we all depend,) being a finne of all other, the moft hainous, and leaft pardonable. And therfore feeing in this, you grant the Papift both in generall abroad, and at home, and in particular fuch as are condemned, executed and named in this booke to be guilty: how can you infinuate (as you doe) that there is more prefumed or enforced upon them by this booke, then there is juft caufe fo to doe?

u. 4. 12, 3, 4.

The Papifts practices againft the ftate.

Lawyer.

Good Sir, faid the other, I ftand not here to examine the doings of my fuperiours, or to defend the guilty, but with hartily rather their punifhment that have deferved the fame. Only this I fay, for explication of my former fpeech: that men of a different religion from the ftate wherin they live, may be faid to deale againft the fame ftate in two forts: the one, by dealing for the increafe of their faid different religion, which is alwaies either directly, or indirectly againft the ftate, (Dreclly) when the faid religion containeth any point or article directly impugning the faid ftate, (as perhaps you will fay that the Roman Religion doth againft the prefent ftate of England in the point of Supremacy:) and (Indirectly) for that every different religion divideth in a fort and

Two forts of dealing againft the ftate.

Directly.

Indirectly.

draw-

draweth from the state, in that there is no man
who in his heart would not wish to have the chief
Governour and state to be of his religion; if he
could: and consequiently misliketh the other in respect of that: and in this kind, not only those
whom you call busie Papists in England, but
also those whom we call hot Puritans among you,
(whose difference from the state especially in matters of governement is very well known) may be
called all traytors, in mine opinion: for that every
one of these indeed, do labour indirectly, (if not
more) against the state, in how much soever each
one endeavoureth to increase his part or faction
that desireth a Governour of his own religion.

And in this case also, are the Protestants in **The state of all**
France and Flanders under Catholike Princes: **Subiects in a state**
the Calvinists (as they are called;) under the **of different reli-**
Duke of Saxony, who is a Lutheran: the Lutherans **gion.**
under *Casimere*, that favoureth Calvinists: the Grecians and other Christians under the Emperor of
Constantinople, under the Sophy, under the great
Chame of Tartary, and under other Princes that
agree not with them in religion. All which Subjects doe wish (no doubt) in their hearts, that
they had a Prince and state of their owne religion, instead of that which now governeth them:
and consequently in this first sense, they may be
called all traytors, and every act they doe for advancement of their said different religion (di- *v. 2. ult, 3. l.*
viding between the state and them) tendeth to
treason: which their Princes supposing, do sometimes make divers of their acts treasonable or
punishable for treason. But yet so long as they **The second kind**
breake not forth unto the second kind of treason **of treason.**
which containeth some actuall attempt or treaty
against the life of the Prince, or state, by rebellion
or otherwise: Wee doe not properly condemne
them

them for traytors, though they doe some acts of
their religion made treason by the Prince his
lawes, who is of a different faith.

The application
of the former
example. And so to apply this to my purpose : I thinke,
Sir, in good sooth, that in the first kind of treason, as well the zealous Papist, as also the Puritans in England, may well be called and proved
traytors; but in the second sort (whereof wee
speake properly at this time) it cannot be so precisely answered, for that there may be both guilty and guiltles in each religion. And as I cannot
excuse all Puritans in this point, so you cannot
condemne all Papists, as long as you take me and
some other to be as we are.

Gentleman. I grant your distinction of treasons to be true,
(said the Gentleman,) as also your application
thereof to the Papists and Puritans (as you call
them,) not to want reason, if there be any of
them that mislike the present state (as perhaps
there be :) albeit for my part, I thinke these
two kinds of treasons, which you have put down,
be rather divers degrees then divers kinds : wherin I will refer mee to the judgement of our
Cambridge friend here present, whose skill is
more in logicall distinctions. But yet my reason
is this, that indeed the one is but a step or degree
to the other, not differing in nature, but rather in
time, ability or opertunity. For if (as in your
former examples you have shewed) the Grecians
under the Turke, and other Christians under o-
ther Princes of a different religion, and as also
the Papists and Puritans (as you tearme them)
in England (for now this word shall passe betweene us for distinction sake,) have such alienation of mind from their present regiment, and doe
Two degrees of
treason. covet so much a governour and state of their
owne religion : then no doubt but they are also
resol-

resolved to imply their forces for accomplishing
and bringing to passe their desires, if they had o-
portunity: and so being now in the first degree or
kind of treason, doe want but occasion or ability,
to breake into the second.

True Sir, said the Lawyer, if there be no o- **Lawyer.**
ther cause or circumstance that may withhold
them.

And what cause or circumstance may stay them **Gentleman.**
I pray you (said the Gentleman) when they shall
have ability and oportunity to doe a thing which
they so much desire?

Divers causes (quoth the Lawyer) but especi- **Lawyer.**
ally and above all other (if it be at home in their
owne Country) the fear of servitude under forraine nations, may restraine them from such attempts: as we see in Germany that both Catholiques and Protestants would joyne together, a-
gainst any stranger that should offer danger to
their liberty. And so they did against *Charles* the
fifth. And in France not long agoe, albeit the Protestants were up in armes against their King, and
could have been content, by the help of us in England, to have put him down, and placed another
of their own religion: yet when they saw us once
seazed of New-haven, and so like to proceed to **France.**
the recovery of some part of our states on that side
the Sea: they quickly joyned with their owne
Catholiques againe to expell us.

In Flanders likewise, though Monsieur were **Flanders.**
called thither by the Protestants, especially for defence of their religion, against the Spaniard: yet
we see how dainty divers chief protestants of Ant-
werp, Gaunt, and Bruges were, in admitting him,
and how quick in expelling, so soon as he put them
in the least feare of subjection to the French.

And as for Portugall, I have heard some of the **Portugal.**
chiefest

chiefest Catholiques among them say, in this late contention about their Kingdome : that rather then they would suffer the Castilian to come in upon them, they would be content to admit whatsoever aids of a contrary religion to themselves ; and to adventure whatsoever alteration in religion or other inconvenience might befall them by that means rather then endanger their subjection to their ambitious neighbour.

The old hatred of East Grecians towards the West Latins. The like is reported in divers histories of the Grecians at this day, who doe hate so much the name and dominion of the Latines : as they had rather to endure all the miseries which dayly they suffer under the Turke for their religion and otherwise : then by calling for aid from the West to hazard the subjection to the said Latines. So that by these examples you see, that feare and horrour of externall subjection may stay men in states, and consequently also both Papists and Puritans in the state of England, from passing to the second kind or degree of treason, albeit they were never so deepe in the first, and had both ability, time, will, and oportunity for the other.

Scholar. Here I presumed to interrupt their Speech, and said : that this seemed to mee most cleare, and that now I understood what the Lawyer meant before, when he affirmed, that albeit the most part of Papists in generall might be said to deale against the state of England at this day, in that they deal so earnestly for the maintenance and increase of their religion, and so to incurre some kind of treason : yet (perhaps) not so far-forth nor in so deepe a degree of proper treason as in this booke is presumed or inforced : though for my part (said I) I do not see that the book presumeth or inforceth all Papists in generall to be pro-

Not all Papists properly traytors.

perly

perly traytors, but onely such as in particular are
therein named, or that are by law attainted, condemned or executed : and what will you say
(quoth I) to those in particular ?

Surely (quoth he) I must say of these, much **Lawyer.**
after the manner which I spoke before : that
some here named in this book are openly knowne
to have beene in the second degree or kind of
treason : as *Westmerland*, *Norton*, *Sanders*, and **The Priests and**
the like. But divers others (namely the Priests **Seminaries that**
and Seminaries that of late have suffered,) by **were executed.**
so much as I could see delivered and pleaded at
their arraignements, or heard protested by them
at their deaths, or gathered by reason and discourse of my selfe, (for that no forraine Prince
or wise councellor would ever commit so great
matters of state to such instruments :) I cannot (I say) but thinke, that to the wise of our
state, that had the doing of this busines, the
first degree of treason (wherein no doubt they
were) was sufficient to dispatch and make them
away : especially in such suspitious times as these
are : to the end that being hanged for the first,
they should never bee in danger to fall into the
second, nor yet to draw other men to the
same : which perhaps was most of all mis-
doubted.

After the Lawyer had spoken this, I held my **Gentleman.**
peace, to heare what the Gentleman would answer: who walked up and down two whole turnes
in the Gallery without yeelding any word again:
and then staying upon the sudden, cast his eyes
sadly upon us both, and said :

My masters, howsoever this be, which indeed ap-
pertaines not to us to judge or discus, but rather to
perswade our selves, that the state hath reason to
do as it doth, and that it must oftentimes as well
prevent

prevent inconveniences, as remedy the fame when they are happened : yet for my owne part I muft confeffe unto you, that upon fome confideration ons which ufe to come unto my mind, I take no fmall griefe of thefe differences among us (which you terme of divers and different religions) for which we are driven of neceffity to ufe difcipline toward divers, who poffibly otherwife would be no great malefactors. I know the caufe of this difference is grounded upon a principle not eafie to cure, which is the judgement and confcience of a man, whereunto obeyeth at length his will and affection, whatfoever for a time he may otherwife diffem ble outwardly. I remember your fpeech before of the doubtfull and dangerous inclination of fuch as live difcontented in a State of a different religion, efpecially, when either in deed, or in their owne conceipt, they are hardly dealt withall, and where every mans particular punifhment is taken to reach to the caufe of the whole.

The confidera- tions.

I am not ignorant how that mifery procureth amity, and the opinion of calamity moveth affection of mercy and compaffion, even towards the wicked: the better fortune alway is fubject to envie, and he that fuffereth, is thought to have the better caufe ; my experience of the divers reignes and proceedings of King *Edward*, Queene *Mary*, and of this our moft gracious Soveraigne hath taught me not a little , touching the fequell of thefe affairs. And finally (my good friends) I muft tell you plaine (quoth he, and this he fpake with great affeveration) that I could wifh with all my heart, that either thefe differences were not among us at all, or elfe that they were fo temperatly on al parts purfued, as the common ftate of our country, the bleffed reigne of her Majefty, and the common caufe of true religion were not endangered

Mifery moveth mercy.

A good wifh.

gered thereby. But now : and there he brake off, and turned aſide.

The Lawyer ſeeing him hold his peace and de-
part, he ſtepped after him, and taking him by the gowne, ſaid merrily ; Sir, all men are not of your complexion, ſome are of quicker and more ſtir-ring Spirits, and doe love to fiſh in water that is troubled, for that they doe participate the Black-
moores humour, that dwell in *Guinea* (whereof
I ſuppoſe you have heard and ſeene alſo ſome in
this Land) whoſe exerciſe at home is (as ſome write) the one to hunt, catch, and ſell the other, and alwayes the ſtronger to make money of the weaker for the time. But now if in England we ſhould live in peace and unity of the ſtate, as they doe in Germany, notwithſtanding their dif-ferences of Religion, and that the one ſhould not prey upon the other : then ſhould the great Faul-cons for the Field (I meane the favourites of the time) faile whereon to feed, which were an in-convenience as you know.

Truly Sir, ſaid the Gentleman, I thinke you
rove neerer the marke then you weene : for if I be not deceived; the very ground of much of theſe broiles whereof we talke, is but a very prey : not in the minds of the Prince or State (whoſe inten-tions no doubt be moſt juſt and holy) but in the greedy imagination and ſubtile conceit of him, who at this preſent in reſpect of our ſinnes, is per-mitted by God, to tyrannize both Prince and State : and being himſelfe of no religion, feedeth notwithſtanding upon our differences in religion, to the fatting of himſelfe and ruine of the Realm.
For whereas by the common diſtinction now re-
ceived in ſpeech, there are three notable differences of religion in the Land, the two extreams,
whereof are the Papiſt and the Puritan, and the

B   religi-

religious Proteſtant obtaining the meane : this fellow being neither, maketh his gaine of all : and as he ſeeketh a Kingdome by the one extreame, and ſpoile by the other : ſo he uſeth the authority of the third, to compaſſe the firſt two, and the counter mine of each one, to the overthrow of all three.

Scholar.

To this I anſwered : In good ſooth Sir, I ſee now where you are : you are fallen into the common place of all our ordinary talke and conference in the Univerſity : for I know that you meane my Lord of *Leiceſter*, who is the ſubject of all pleaſant diſcourſes at this day throughout the Realme.

The Earle of Leiceſter.

Gentleman.

Not ſo pleaſant as pittifull, anſwered the Gentleman, if all matters and circumſtances were wel conſidered, except any man take pleaſure to jeſt at our owne miſeries, which are like to be greater by his iniquity (if God avert it not) then by al the wickedneſſe of England beſides : he being the man that by all probability, is like to be the bane and fatall deſtiny of our State, with the everſion of true religion, whereof, by indirect meanes, he is the greateſt enemy that the Land doth nouriſh.

Lawyer.

Now verily (quorh the Lawyer) if you ſay thus much for the Proteſtants opinion of him, what ſhall I ſay for his merits towards the Papiſts ? who for as much as I can perceive, doe take themſelves little beholding unto him, albeit for his gaine he was ſome yeeres their ſecret friend againſt you : untill by his friends he was perſwaded, and chiefly by the Lord *North* by way of policy, as the ſaid Lord boſteth, in hope of greater gaine, to ſtep over to the Puritans, againſt us both, whom notwithſtanding it is probable, that he loveth as much, as he doth the reſt.

The Lord Norths policy.

You

You know the Beares love, said the Gentleman, which is all for his own panch, and so this Bear-whelp, turneth all to his own commodity, and for greedinesse thereof, will overturn all if he be not stopped or muzled in time.

Gentleman.

And surely unto me it is a strange speculation, whereof I cannot pick out the reason (but onely that I do attribute it to Gods punishment for our finnes) that in so wise and vigilant a State as ours is, and in a Countrey so well acquainted and beaten with such dangers; a man of such a Spirit as he is knowne to be, of so extreme ambition, pride, falshood and trechery; so borne, so bred up, so nozled in treason from his infancy, descended of a tribe of traytours, and fleshed in conspiracy against the Royall blood of King *Henries* children in his tender yeeres, and exercised ever since in drifts against the same, by the blood and ruine of divers others: a man so well knowne to beare secret malice against her Majesty, for causes irreconcileable, and most dradly rancour against the best and wifest Councellours of her Highnesse: that such a one (I say so hatefull) to God and man, and so markeable to the simplest Subject of this Land, by the publique ensignes of his tyrannous purpose, should be suffered so many yeeres without check, to aspire to tyranny by most manifest wayes, and to possesse himselfe (as now he hath done) of Court, Councell and Countrey, without controlement: so that nothing wanteth to him but onely his pleasure, and the day already conceived in his minde, to dispose as he list, both of Prince, Crowne, Realm and Religion.

It is much truly (quoth I) that you say, and it ministreth not a little mervaile unto many, whereof your Worship is not the first, nor yet the tenth person

The Queens Maiesties most excellent good nature.

person of accompt which I have heard discourse and complaine. But what shall I say hereunto? there is no man that ascribeth not this unto the singular benignity and most bountifull good nature of her Majesty, who measuring other men by her owne Heroicall and Princely sincerity; cannot easily suspect a man so much bounden to her grace, as he is, nor remove her confidence from the place, where she hath heaped so infinite benefits.

Gentleman.

No doubt (said the Gentleman) but this gracious and sweet disposition of her Majesty is the true originall cause thereof: which Princely disposition, as in her highnesse it deserveth all rare commendation, so lyeth the same open to many dangers oftentimes, when so benigne a nature meeteth with ingrate and ambitious persons: which observation perhaps, caused her Majesties most noble Grandfather and Father (two renowned wise Princes) to withdraw sometime upon the sudden, their great favour from certaine Subjects of high estate. And her Majesty may easily use her owne excellent wisdome and memory, to recall to minde the manifold examples of perilous haps fallen to divers Princes, by too much confidence in obliged proditours: with whom the name of a Kingdome, and one houres reigne, weyeth more, then all the duty, obligation, honesty, or nature in the world. Would God her Majesty could see the continuall feares that be in her faithfull Subjects hearts, whiles that man is about her noble person, so well able and likely (if the Lord avert it not) to be the calamity of her Princely blood and name.

Feares that subjects have of my Lord of Leicester.

The talke will never out of many mouthes and minds, that divers ancient men of this Realme, and once a wise Gentleman now a Councellour, had

Sir Francis Walsingham.

had with a certaine friend of his, concerning the
presage and deep impression, which her Majesties
Father had of the house of Sir *Iohn Dudley*, to be
the ruine in time of his Majesties royall house
and blood, which thing was like to have been ful-
filled soon after (as all the world knoweth) upon
the death of King *Edward*, by the said *Dudley*, this
mans Father: who at one blow, procured to dispatch from a possession from the Crown, all three
children of the said noble King. And yet in the
middest of those bloody practices against her Majesty that now is and her sister (wherein also this
fellowes hand was so far, as for his age he could
thrust the same) within sixteen dayes before King
Edwards death (he knowing belike that the King
should dye) wrote most flattering letters to the
Lady *Mary* (as I have heard by them who then
were with her) promising all loyalty and true service to her, after the decease of her brother, with
no lesse painted words, then this man now doth
use to Queene *Elizabeth*.

*Deepe dissimula-
tion.*

So dealt he then with the most deare children
of his good King and Master, by whom he had
beene no lesse exalted and trusted, then this man
is by her Majesty. And so deeply dissembled he
then when he had in hand the plot to destroy them
both. And what then (alas) may not we feare and
doubt of this his son, who in outragious ambition
and desire of reigne, is not inferiour to his Father
or to any other aspiring spirit in the world, but
far more insolent, cruell, vindicative, expert, potent, subtile, fine, and fox like then ever he was? I
like well the good motion propounded by the
foresaid Gentleman, to his friend at the same time,
and doe assure my selfe it would be most pleasant
to the Realme, and profitable to her Majesty, to
wit, that this mans actions might be called pub-

*Sir Francis Wal-
singham.*

B 3 liquely

liquely to triall, and liberty given to good subjects to say what they knew against the same, as it was permitted in the first yeer of King *Henry* the eight against his Grandfather, and in the first of Queen *Mary* against his Father: and then I would not doubt, but if these two his Ancestors were found worthy to lose their heads for treason; this man would not be found unworthy to make the third in kindred, whose treacheries doe farre surpasse them both.

After the Gentleman had said this, the Lawyer stood still, somewhat smiling to himselfe, & looking round about him, as though he had bin halfe afraid, and then said; My masters, doe you read over or study the Statutes that come forth? have you not heard of the *proviso* made in the last Parliament for punishment of those who speake so broad of such men as my Lord of *Leicester* is?

Yes, said the Gentleman, I have heard how that my Lord of *Leicester* was very carefull and diligent at that time to have such a Law to passe against talkers: hoping (belike) that his L. under that generall restraint might lye the more quietly in harbor from the tempest of mens tongus, which tatled busily at that time, of divers his Lordships actions and affairs, which perhaps himself would have wished to passe with more secresie. As of his discontentment and preparation to rebellion, upon *Monsieurs* first comming into the Land; of his disgrace and checks received in Court; of the fresh death of the noble Earle of *Essix*; & of this mans hasty snatching up of the widow, whom he sent up and downe the Countrey from house to house by privie wayes, thereby to avoid the sight & knowledge of the Queenes Majesty. And albeit he had not onely used her at his good liking before, for satisfying of his owne lust, but also married and

remarried

Marginal notes

Edmund Dudley

Robert Dudley.

Lawyer.

Gentlemen.

The Law against talking.

Actions of Leicester whereof he would have no speech.

remarried her for contentation of her friends : yet
denied he the same, by solemne oath to her Majesty, and received the holy Communion thereupon
(so good a conscience he hath) and consequently
threatned most sharp revenge towards all subjects
which should dare to speake thereof : and so for
the concealing both of this and other his doings,
which he desired not to have publike, no marvaile
though his Lordship were so diligent a procurer
of that law for silence.

Indeed (said I) it is very probable that his Lordship was in great distresse about that time, when
Monsieurs matters were in hand, and that he did
many things and purposed more, whereof he desired lesse speech among the people, especially afterwards, when his said designements tooke not
place. I was my selfe that yeer not far from Warwick when he came thither from the Court a full
Mile-content, and when it was thought most certainly throughout the Realm, that he would have
taken armes soon after, if the marriage of her Majesty with *Monsieur* had gone forward. The thing
in Cambridge and in all the Countrey as I rode,
was in every mans mouth : and it was a wonder to
see not onely the countenances, but also the behaviour, and to heare the bold speeches of all such as
were of his faction.

My Lord himselfe had given out a little before
at Killingworth, that the matter would cost many
broken heads before Michaelmasse day next; and
my Lord of *Warwick* had said openly at his table
in Greenwich, Sir *Thomas Hennige* being by (if I
be not deceived) that it was not to be suffered (I
meane the marriage) which words of his once
coming abroad (albeit misliked by his own Lady
then also present) every Serving man and common companion, tooke then up in defence of his

Scholar.

Leicesters prepa-
ratives to rebel-
on upon Monsi-
eurs marriage.

B 4   Lord-

Lordſhips part againſt the Queenes Majeſty. Such running there was, ſuch ſending and poſting about the Realme, ſuch amplification of the powers and forces of *Caſimere* and other Princes, ready (as was affirmed) to preſent themſelves unto his aid, for defence of the Realme and Religion againſt ſtrangers : (for that was holden to be his cauſe) ſuch numbring of parties and complices within the Realme, (whereof himſelfe ſhewed the Catalogue to ſome of his friends for their comfort) ſuch debaſing of them that favoured the marriage (eſpecially two or three Councellours by name, who were ſaid to be the cauſe of all, and for that were appointed out to be ſharply puniſhed to the terrour of all others :) ſuch letters were written and intercepted of purpoſe, importing great powers to be ready, and ſo many other things done and deſigned, tending all to manifeſt and open warre : as I began hartily to be afraid, and wiſhed my ſelfe backe at Cambridge againe, hoping that being there, my Scholars gowne ſhould excuſe me from neceſſity of fighting, or if not, I was reſolved (by my Lords good leave) to follow *Ariſtotle,* who preferreth alway the Lyon before the Beare; aſſuring my ſelfe withall, that his Lordſhip ſhould have no better ſucceſſe in this (if it came to triall) then his Father had in as bad a cauſe, and ſo much the more for that I was privie to the mindes of ſome of his friends, who ment to have deceived him, if the matter had broken out. And amongſt other, there was a certain Vice-preſident in the World, who being left in the roome and abſence of another, to procure friends; ſaid in a place ſecretly not far from Ludlow, that if the matter came to blowes, he would follow his Miſtreſſe, and leave his Maſter in the briars.

Marry

(marginal notes)

To Sir Thomas Layton.

L. Treaſurer.
L. Chamberlaine
M. Controler.

Sir Thomas Hibbot.

Marry fir (qd the Gentleman) and I trow many more would have followed that example. For albeit I know, that the Papifts were moft named and mifdoubted of his part, in that caufe, for their open inclination towards *Monfieur*, & confequently, for greater difcredit of the thing it felfe, it was given out every where by this Champion of religion, that her Majefties caufe was the Papifts caufe (even as his Father had done in the like enterprife before him, though all upon diffimulation, as appeared at his death, where he profeffed himfelf an earneft Papift :) yet was there no man fo fimple in the Realm, which defcried not this vizard at the firft : neither yet any good fubject (as I fuppofe) who feeing her Majefty on the one part, would not have taken againft the other part, what fo ever he had beene. And much more the thing it felfe in controverfie (I meane the marriage of her royall Majefty with the brother and heire apparant of France) being taken and judged by the beft, wifeft and faithfulleft Proteftants of the Realme, to be both honourable, convenient, profitable and needfull. Whereby onely, as by a moft foveraigne, and prefent remedy, all our maladies both abroad and at home, had at once been cured: all forraign enemies, and domeftical confpirators, all differences, all dangers, all feares had ceafed together : France had beene ours moft affured ; Spaine would not a little have trembled ; Scotland had been quiet ; our competitors in England would have quaked ; and for the Pope he might have put up his pipes. Our differences in religion at home, had been either leffe, or no greater then now they are, for that *Monfieur* being but a moderate Papift, and nothing vehement in his opinions was content with very reafonable conditions, for himfelfe and his ftrangers onely in ufe of their confci-

Gentleman.

Leicefters Father a traiterous Papift

The honour and commodities by the marriage with France.

conscience not unlikely (truly) but that in time he might by Gods grace, and by the great wisdome and vertue of her Majesty have been brought also to embrace the Gospell, as King *Ethelbert* an heathen was by noble Queen *Bertha* his wife, the first Christian of our English Princes.

Unto all which felicity, if the Lord in mercy should have added also some issue of their royall bodies (as was not impossible, when first this noble match was moved,) we then (doubtlesse) had been the most fortunate people under heaven, and might have been (perhaps) the meane to have restored the Gospell throughout all Europe besides, as our Brethren of France well considered and hoped.

Of all which singular benefits both present and to come, both in *Re* and *Spe*, this tyrant for his own private lucre (fearing lest hereby his ambition might be restrained, and his treachery revealed) hath bereaved the Realme, and done what in him lyeth besides, to alienate for ever and make our mortall enemy this great Prince, who sought the love of her Majesty with so much honour & confidence as never Prince the like, putting twice his owne person in jeopardy of the Sea, and to the perill of his malicious enviors here in England, for her Majesties sake.

When you speak of *Monsieur* (said the Lawyer) I cannot but greatly be moved, both for these considerations well touched by you, as also for some other; especially one wherein (perhaps) you will thinke me partiall, but truly I am not; for that I speake it onely in respect of the quiet and good of my Countrey, and that is, that by *Monsieurs* match with our noble Princesse, besides the hope of issue (which was the principall) there wanted not also probability, that some union or little toleration

in

(marginal note, left:) Ethelbert King of Kent, converted An. Dom. 603

(marginal note, left:) Lawyer.

in religion, between you and us, might have been procured in this state, as we see that in some other Countries is admitted to their great good. Which thing (no doubt) would have cut off quite all dangers and dealings from forraine Princes, & would have stopped mane devises and plots within the Realme: wheras now by this breach with France, we stand alone as me seemeth without any great unition or friendship abroad, and our differences at home grow more vehement and sharp then ever before. Upon which two heads, as also upon infinit other causes, purposes, drifts and pretences, there doe ensue daily more deepe, dangerous and desperate practises, every man using either the commodity or necessity of the time and state for his owne purpose, especially now when all men presume that her Majesty (by the continuall thwartings which have been used against all her marriage) is not like to leave unto the Realme, that precious jewell so much and long desired of all English hearts, I meane the Royall heires of her owne body.

Thwartings call you the defeating of all her Majesties most honourable offers of marriage? (said the other) truly in my opinion, you should have used another word to expresse the nature of so wicked a fact: wherby alone, if there were no other, this unfortunate man, hath done more hurt to this Common wealth, then if he had murdered many thousands of her subjects, or betrayd whole armies to the professed enemy. I can remember well my selfe, foure treatises to this purpose, undermined by his meanes: the first with the Swethen King, the second with the Archduke of Austria, the third with *Henry* King of France that now reigneth, and the fourth with the brother and heire of the said Kingdome. For I let passe many other

Tolleration in Religion, with union in defence of our Countrey.

Gentleman.

Divers marriages of her Majestie treated.

other fecret motions made by great Potentates
to her Majefty for the fame purpofe, but thefe
foure are openly known, and therefore I name
them. Which foure are as well knowne to have
been all difturbed by this *Dawer*, as they were
earneftly purfued by the other.

And for the firft three Suters,he drove them a-
way,by protefting and fwearing that himfelfe was
contracted unto herMajefty,wherof her highneffe
was fufficiently advertifed by Cardinall *Chatilian*
in the firft treaty for France, and the Cardinall
foone after punifhed (as is thought) by this man
with poyfon. But yet this fpeech he gave out then,
every where among his friends both ftrangers
and others,that he, forfooth, was affured to her
Majefty, and confequently that all other Princes
muft give over their faits, for him. Whereunto
notwithftanding, when the Sweden would hardly give eare,this man conferred with his Privado
to make a moft unfeemly and difloyal proof therof, for the others fatisfaction, which thing I
am enforced by duty to paffe over with filence,
for honour to the parties who are touched therein : as alfo I am to conceale his faid filthy Privado, though worthy otherwife for his difhone-
fty to be difplayed to the world: but my Lord
himfelfe, I am fure, doth well remember both
the man and the matter. And albeit there was
no wife man at that time who knowing my Lord
fufpected not the falf-hood, and his arrogant af-
firmation touching this contract with her Majefty, yet fome both abroad and at home might

doubt thereof perhaps : but now of late, by his
knowne marriage with his Minion Dame *Lettice*
of *Effex*, he hath declared manifeftly his owne
moft impudent and difloyall dealing with his foveraigne in this report.

For

For that report (quoth the Lawyer) I know that it was common, and maintained by many for divers yeeres; yet did the wiser fort make no account thereof, seeing it came onely from himself, and in his own behalfe. Neither was it credible, that her Majesty who refused so noble Knights and Princes, as Europe hath not the like, would make choice of so meane a peere as *Robin Dudley* is, noble onely in two descents, and both of them stained with the block, from which also himselfe was pardoned but the other day, being codemned therunto by law for his deserts, as appeareth yet in publick records. And for the widow of Essex, I marvaile sir (quoth he) how you call her his wife, seeing the Canon-law standeth yet in force touching matters of marriage within the Realme.

Lawyer.

The basenesse of Leicesters ancestors.

Anno 1.R.Mary.

Oh (said the Gentleman laughing) you meane for that he procured the poisoning of her husband in his journey from Ireland. You must think that Doctor *Dale* will dispence in that matter, as he did (at his Lordships appointment) with his Italian physitian Doctor *Iulio*, to have two wives at once; at the leastwise the matter was permitted, and born out by them both publiquely (as all the world knoweth) and that against no lesse persons then the Archbishop of Canterbury himselfe, whose overthrew was principally wrought by this tyrant for contrarying his will, in so beastly a demand. But for this controversie whether the marriage be good or so, I leave it to be tried hereafter, between my yong Lord of Denbighe, and Master *philip Sidney*, whom the same most concerneth: for that it is like to deprive him of a goodly inheritance, if it take place (as some will say that in no reason it can) not only in respect of the precedent adultery and murder betweene the parties; but also for that my Lord was contracted

Gentleman.

Doctor Dale.

Doctor Iulio.

The Archbishops overthrow for not allowing two wives to Leicester his Physitian

at

The Lady Shef-
field now Em-
baffadreffe in
France.

at leaft, to another Lady before, that yet liveth,
whereof Mafter *Edward Diar* and Mafter *Edmond
Tilney*, both Courtiers, can be witneffes, and con-
fumated the fame contract by generation of children. But this (as I faid) muft be left to be tried
hereafter by them who fhall have moft intereft in
the cafe. Onely for the prefent I muft advertife
you, that you may not take hold fo exactly of all
my L. doings in womens affaires, neither touching their marriages, neither yet their husbands.

For firft his Lordfhip hath a fpeciall fortune,
that when he defireth any womans favour, then
what perfon fo ever ftandeth in his way, hath the
luck to dye quickly for the finifhing of his defire.

The death of
Leicefters firft
Lady and wife.

As for example, when his Lordfhip was in full
hope to marry her Majefty, and his owne wife
ftood in his light, as he fuppofed; he did but fend
her afide to the houfe of his fervant *Forfter* of
Cumner by Oxford, where fhortly after fhe had
the chance to fall from a paire of ftaires, and fo
to breake her neck, but yet without hurting of her
hood that ftood upon her head. But Sir *Richard*

Sir Richard Var-
ney.

Varney, who by commandement remained with
her that day alone, with one man onely, and had
fent away perforce all her Servants from her, to a
Market two miles of, he (I fay) with his man can
tell how fhe died, which man being taken afterward for a fellony in the marches of Wales, and
offering to publifh the manner of the faid murder,
was made away privily in the prifon: and Sir
Richard himfelf dying about the fame time in London, cried pitioufly and blafphemed God, and faid
to a Gentleman of worfhip of mine acquaintance, not long before his death, that all the divels
in hell did teare him in pieces. The wife alfo of

Bald Buttler.

Bald Buttler kinfman to my Lord, gave out the
whole fact a little before her death. But to return
unto

unto my purpofe, this was my Lords good fortun
to have his wife dye, at that time when it was like
to turne moft to his profit.

Long after this he fell in love with the Lady
Sheffield, whom I fignified before, and then alfo
had he the fame fortune to have her husband dye
quickly, with an extreame rheume in his head (as
it was given out) but as others fay, of an artificiall catarre that ftopped his breath. The like good
chance had he in the death of my Lord of Essex
(as I have faid before) and that at a time moft
fortunate for his purpose ; for when he was coming home from Ireland, with intent to revenge
himfelfe upon my Lord of Leycefter, for begetting
his wife with childe in his abfence (the childe was
a daughter, and brought up by the Lady Shandoies,
W.Knooles his wife:) my Lord of Ley. hearing therof, wanted not a friend or two to accompany the
Deputy, as among other, a couple of the Earles
owne fervants, Crompton (if I mifle not his name)
yeoman of his bottles, and Lloid his Secretary, entertained afterward by my Lord of Leicefter: and
fo he dyed in the way of an extreame flux, caufed
by an Italian Recipe, as all his friends are well affured ; the maker whereof was a Chyrurgeon (as
is beleeved) that then was newly come to my
Lord from Italy: a cunning man, and fure in operation, with whom if the good Lady had beene
fooner acquainted and ufed his helpe, fhe fhould
not have needed to fitten fo penfive at home and
fearefull of her husbands former returne out of
the fame Countrey, but might have fpared the
yong childe in her belly, which fhe was enforced
to make away (cruelly and unnaturally) for clea-
ring the houfe againft the good mans arrivall.

Neither muft you marvaile though all thefe died in divers manners of outward difeafes, for this

The fufpitious death of the Lord Sheffield.

The poifoning of the Earle of Essex.

The fhifting of a childe in dame Lettice belly.

is

is the excellency of the Italian art, for which this Chyrurgian and Doctor *Iulio* were entertained so carefully, who can make a man dye, in what manner or shew of sicknesse you will: by whose instructions no doubt but his Lordship is now cunning, especially adding also to these the counsell of his Doctor *Bayly*, a man also not a little studied (as he seemeth) in his art: for I heard him once my selfe in publique Act in Oxford, and that in presence of my Lord of *Leicester*, (if I be not deceived) maintain, that poyson might so be tempered and given as it should not appeare presently, and yet should kill the party afterward at what time should be appointed. Which argument belike pleased well his Lordship, and therefore was chosen to be discussed in his audience, if I be not deceived of his being that day present. So, though one dye of a flux, and another of a catarre, yet this importeth little to the matter, but sheweth rather the great cunning and skill of the Artificer.

So Cardinall *Chatilian* (as I have said before) having accused my Lord of *Leicester* to the Queens Majesty, and after that, passing from London towards France about the marriage, died by the way at Canterbury of a burning fever: and so proved Doctor *Baylies* assertion true, that poyson may be given to kill at a day.

At this the Lawyer cast up his eyes to heaven, and I stood somewhat musing and thinking of that which had beene spoken of the Earle of *Essex*, whose case indeed moved me more then all the rest, for that he was a very noble Gentleman, a great advancer of true Religion, a Patron to many Preachers and Students, and towards me and some of my friends in particular, he had beene in some things very beneficiall: and there-

The divers operation of Roylor

Doctor Bayly the yonger.

ridiculous

Death of Cardinall Chatilian.

Scholar.

therefore I said that it grieved me extreamly to
heare or thinke of so unworthy a death contrived
by such meanes to so worthy a Peere. And so
much the more, for that it was my chance, to come
to the underſtanding of divers particulars concerning that thing, both from one *Lea* an Iriſh-man,   Lea.
Robin Honnies, and others, that were preſent at   Honnies.
Penteneis the Merchants houſe in *Dublin* upon the
Key, where the murder was committed. The
matter was wrought eſpecially by *Crompton* yeoman of the bottels, by the procurement of *Lloyd*
as you haue noted before, and there was poyſo-
ned at the ſame time, and with the ſame cup (as
given of curteſie by the Earle) one Miſtreſſe *Alis*
Draykot, a goodly Gentlewoman, whom the Earle   Miſtris Draykot
affectioned much, who departing thence towards   poiſoned with
her owne houſe, (which was 18. miles off, the   the Earl of Eſſex
foreſaid *Lea* accompanying her, and waiting upon
her) ſhe began to fall ſick very grievouſly upon
the way, and continued with increaſe of paines
and exceſſive torments, by vomiting, untill ſhe
died, which was the Sunday before the Earles
death, enſuing the Friday after; and when ſhe
was dead, her body was ſwolne unto a mon-
ſtrous bigneſſe and deformity, whereof the good
Earle hearing the day following, lamented the
caſe greatly, and ſaid in the preſence of his Servants, Ah poore *Alice*, the cup was not prepared
for thee, albeit it were thy hard deſtiny to taſte
thereof.

Yong *Honnies* alſo, whoſe father is Maſter of
the children of her Majeſties chappell, being at
that time Page to the ſaid Earle, and accuſtomed
to take the taſte of his drinke (though ſince entertained alſo among other by my Lord of *Leiceſter*,
for better covering of matter) by his taſte that he
then tooke of the compound cup, (though in very

C

ſmall

small quantity, as you know the fashion is :) yet was he like to have lost his life, but escaped in the end (being yong) with the losse onely of his haire; which the Earle perceiving, and taking compassion of the youth, called for a cup of drinke a little before his death, and drunke to *Honnies*, saying, I drinke to thee my *Robin*, and be not afraid, for this is a better cup of drinke then that whereof thou tookest the taste when we were both poysoned, and whereby thou hast lost thy haire and I must lose my life. This hath yong *Honnies* reported openly in divers places, and before divers Gentlemen of worship sithence his coming into England; and the foresaid *Lea* Irishman, at his passage this way towards France, after he had been present at the forenamed Mistris *Draykots* death, with some other of the Earles servants, have and doe most constantly report the same, where they may do it without the terrour of my Lord of *Leicesters* revenge. Wherefore in this matter there is no doubt at all, though most extreame vile and intollerable indignity, that such a man should be so openly murdered without punishment. What Noble-man within the Realme may be safe, if this be suffered? or what worthy personage will adventure his life in her Majesties service, if this shall be his reward? But, Sir, I pray you pardon me, for I am somewhat perhaps too vehement in the case of this my Patron and noble Peere of our Realme. And therefore I beseech you to goe forward in your talke whereas you left.

I was recounting unto you others (said the Gentleman) made away by my Lord of *Leicester* with like art, and the next in order I think was Sir *Nicolas Throgmarton*, who was a man whom my Lord of *Leicester* used a great while (as all the World know-

The Earle of Essex speech to his Page Robin Honnies.

Gentleman.

Death of Sir Nicholas Throgmarton.

knoweth) to overthwart and croſſe the doings of
my Lord Treaſurer then Sir *William Cicill*, a man
ſpecially miſliked alwayes of *Leiceſter*, both in reſpect of his old Maſter the Duke of *Somerſet*, as alſo for that his great wiſdome, zeale and ſingular
fidelity to the Realme, was like to hinder much
this mans deſignments; wherefore underſtanding
after a certaine time that theſe two Knights were
ſecretly made friends, and that Sir *Nicholas* was
like to detect his doings (as he imagined) which
might turne to ſome prejudice of his purpoſes:
(having conceived alſo a ſecret grudge and griefe
againſt him, for that he had written to her Majeſty at his being Embaſſadour in France, that he
heard reported at Duke *Memorances* table, that
the Queene of England had a meaning to marry
her Horſekeeper) he invited the ſaid Sir *Nicho-*
las to a ſupper at his houſe in London, and at
ſupper time departed to the Court, being called
for, as he ſaid, upon the ſudden by her Majeſty,
and ſo perforce would needs have Sir *Nicholas* to
ſit and occupie his Lordſhips place, and therein to be ſerved as he was: and ſoone after by
a ſurfeit there taken, he died of a ſtrange and
incurable vomit. But the day before his death,
he declared to a deare friend of his, all the cir-
cumſtance and cauſe of his diſeaſe, which he
affirmed plainly to be of poiſon, given him in
a Salet at ſupper, inveying moſt earneſtly a-
gainſt the Earles cruelty and bloody diſpoſition, affirming him to be the wickedeſt, moſt
perilous, and perfidious man under heaven. But
what availed this, when he had now received the
bait?

This then is to ſhew the mans good fortune, in
ſeeing them dead, whom for cauſes he would not
have to live. And for his art of poiſoning, it is ſuch

Sir William Ci-
cill now Lord
Treaſurer.

The poiſoning of
Sir Nicholas in a
ſalet.

C 2   now

now, and reacheth so far, as he holdeth all his foes in England and elsewhere, as also a good many of his friends in fear therof, and if it were knowne how many he hath dispatched or assaulted that way, it would be marvailous to the posterity. The late Eale of *Suſſex* wanted not a scruple for many yeers before his death, of some dram received, that made him incurable. And unto that noble Gentleman Monſieur *Simiers*, it was discovered bygreat providence of God, that his life was to be attempted by that art, and that not taking place (as it did not through his owne good circumspection,) it was concluded that the same should be assaulted by violence, whereof I shall have occasion to say more hereafter.

The Lord Chamberlin.

Monſieur Simiers

It hath beene told me also by some of the servants of the late Lady *Lenox*, who was also of the blood Royall by Scotland, as all men know, and consequently little liked by *Leiceſter*; that a little before her death or sickneſſe, my Lord tooke the paines to come and viſit her with extraordinary kindneſſe, at her house at Hackney, beſtowing long discourſes with her in private: but as soone as he was departed, the good Lady fell into such a flux, as by no meanes could be ſtayed so long as ſhe had life in her body; whereupon both ſhe her selfe, and all such as were neere about her, saw her diſeaſe and ending day, were fully of opinion, that my Lord had procured her diſpatch at his being there. Whereof let the women that served her be examined, as also *Fowler* that then had the chiefe doings in her affaires, and ſince hath beene entertained by my Lord of *Leiceſter*. *Mallet* also, a ſtranger borne, that then was about her, a ſober and zealous man in religion, and otherwise well qualified, can say somewhat in this point (as I thinke) if he were deman-

The poisoning of the Lady Lenox.

demanded. So that this art and exercife of poifoning, is much more perfect with my Lord then
praying, and he feemeth to take more pleasure
therein.

Now for the fecond point, which I named,
touching marriages and contracts with Women:
you muft not marvaile though his Lordfhip be
fomewhat divers, variable and inconftant with
himfelfe, for that according to his profit or pleafure, and as his luft and liking fhall vary (wherein by the judgement of all men, he furpaffeth,
not onely *Sardanapalus* and *Nero*, but even *Heliogabalus* himfelfe :) fo his Lordfhip alfo changeth
Wives and Minions, by killing the one, deny-
ing the other, ufing the third for a time, and he
fawning upon the fourth. And for this caufe he
hath his tearmes and pretences (I warrant you)
of Contracts, Precontracts, Poftcontracts, Pro-
tracts and Retracts ; as for example : after he
had killed his firft wife, and fo broken that contract, then forfooth would he needs make himfelfe Husband to the Queenes Majefty, and fo
defeat all other Princes by vertue of his precontract. But after this, his luft compelling to another place, he would needs make a poftcontract
with the Lady *Sheffield*, and fo he did, begetting
two children upon her, the one a boy called *Robin Sheffield* now living, fome time brought up at
Newington ; and the other a daughter, borne
(as is knowne) at *Dudley* Caftle. But yet after,
his concupifcence changed againe (as it never
ftayeth) he refolved to make a retract of this
poftcontract, (though it were as furely done (as I
have faid) as bed and Bible could make the fame)
and to make a certaine new protract, (which is
a continuation of ufing her for a time) with the
widow of *Effex* : but yet to ftop the mouthes of

C 3   out-

Leicefters moft
variable dealing
with women in
contracts and
marriages.

Contracts.

Precontracts.

Poftcontracts.

Retract.

Protract.

Leicesters two testaments.

out-criars, and to bury the Synagogue with some honour, (for these two wives of *Leicester* were merrily and wittily called his old and new Testaments, by a person of great excellency within the Realme) he was content to assigne to the former a thousand pounds in money with other petty considerations, (the pittifullest abused that ever was poore Lady) and so betake his lims to the latter, which latter notwithstanding, he so useth (as we see) now confessing, now forswearing, now dissembling the marriage ; as he will alwayes yet keepe a void place for a new surcontract with any other, when occasion shall require.

Scholar.

Now by my truth sir (quoth I) I never heard nor read the like to this in my life;yet have I read much in my time,of the carnality and licenciousnesse of divers outragious persons, in this kinde of sin, as namely these whom you have mentioned before ; especially the Emperour *Heliogabalus* who passed all other, and was called *Varius*, of the varity of filth which he used in this kinde of carnality or carnall beastlinesse : whose death was, that being at length odious to all men, and so slain by his own Souldiers,was drawn through the City upon the ground like a dog, and cast into the common privy,with this Epitaph ; *Hic projectus est indomitæ & rabidæ libidinis catulus*. Here is thrown in the Whelpe of unruly and raging lust : which Epitaph may also one day chance to serve my Lord of *Leicester* (whom you call the Bearewhelp) if he go forward as he hath begun, and dye as he deserveth.

Varius Heliogabalus, and his most infamous death.

An Epitaph.

But,good sir,what a compassion is this,that among us Christians,& namely in so wel governed and religious a Common-wealth as ours is, such a riot should be permitted upon mens wives, in a subject ?

U. A pittifull permission. Preface p. 2. v. 4

subject? whereas we read that among the very
Heathens, lesse offences then these, in the same
kinde, were extreamly punished in Princes themselves, and that not onely in the person delinquent alone, but also by extirpation of the whole
family for his sake, as appeareth in the example
of the *Tarquinians* among the Romans. And
here also in our owne Realme, we have registred in Chronicle, how that one King *Edwin*
above six hundred yeeres past, was deprived of
his Kingdome, for much lesse scandalous facts
then these.

The exterpation of the Tarquinians. Anno Dom. 959.

I remember well the story (quoth the Gentleman) & thereby doe easily make conjecture, what
difference there is betwixt those times of old, and
our dayes now: seeing then, a crowned Prince
could not passe unpunished with one or two outragious acts, whereas now a subject raised up but
yesterday from the meaner sort, rangeth at his
pleasure in all licenciousnesse, and that with security, void of fear both of God and man. No mans
wife can be free from him, whom his fiery lust
liketh to abuse, nor their husbands able to resist
nor save from his violence, if they shew dislike, or
will not yeeld their consent to his doings. And if
I should discover in particular how many good
husbands he had plagued in this nature, and for
such delights, it were intolerable; for his concu-
piscence and violence do run joyntly together, as
in furious beasts we see they are accustomed. Neither holdeth he any rule in his lust besides onely
the motion and suggestion of his own sensuality;
kindred, affinity or any other bond of consangui-
nity; religion, honour or honesty taketh no place
in his outragious appetite: what he best liketh,
that he taketh as lawfull for the time. So that
kinswoman, allie, friends wife or daughter,

Gentleman.

The intollerable licenciousnes of Leicesters carnality.

C 4　　　　or

or whatsoever female sort besides doth please his eye: (I leave out of purpose, and for honour sake, tearmes of kinred more neere) that must yeeld to his desire.

The keeping of the Mother with two or three of her daughters at once or succeſſively, is no more with him, then the eating of an Hen & her chicken together. There are not (by report) two noble women about her Majeſty (I speake upon some accompt of them that know much) whom he hath not solicited by potent wayes: neither contented with this place of honour, he hath descended to seeke paſture among the waiting Gentlewomen of her Majeſties great chamber, offering more for their allurement, then I thinke *Lais* did commonly take in Corinth, if three hundreth pounds for a night, will make up the sum; or if not, yet will he make it up otherwiſe: having reported himselfe (so little ſhame he hath) that he offered to another of higher place, an 100. pound lands by the yeere, with as many jewels as moſt women under her Majeſty uſed in England; which was no mean bait to one that uſed traffick in ſuch merchandize; ſhe being but the leavings of another man before him, wherof my Lord is nothing ſquemiſh, for ſatisfying of his luſt, but can be content (as they ſay) to gather up crums when he is hungry, even in the very Landry it ſelfe, or other place of baſer quality.

Mony well ſpent

Anne Vauiſour.

The puniſhments of God upon Leiceſter to do him good.

And albeit the Lord of his great mercy, to doe him good, no doubt, if he were revokeable, hath laid his hand upon him, in some chaſtiſement in this world, by giving him a broken belly on both ſides of his bowels, whereby miſery and putrifaction is threatned to him daily: and to his yong Sonne, by the widow of *Eſſex* (being *Filius peccati*) ſuch a ſtrange calamity of the falling

ing sicknesse in his infancy, * as well may be a vitnesse of the Parents sinne and wickednesse, nd of both their wasted natures in iniquity : yet s this man nothing amended thereby, but according to the custome of all old adulterers, is more ibidinous at this day then ever before, more given to procure love in others by conjuring, sorcey, and other such meanes. And albeit for himelfe, both age, and nature spent, doe somewhat :ame him from the act, yet wanteth he not will, as appeareth by the Italian ointment, procured nor many yeers past by his Chyrurgion or Mountibanke of that Countrey, whereby (as they say) he is able to move his flesh at all times, for keeking of his credit, howsoever his inability be otherwise for performance : as also one of his Physitians reported to an Earle of this Land, that his Lordship had a bottle for his bed-head, of ten pounds the Pint to the same effect. But my Masters whether are we fallen, unadvisedly ? I am ashamed to have made mention of so base filthinesse.

*The children of adulterers shall be consumed, and the seed of a wicked bed shall be rooted out, saith God, Sap. 3.

Leicesters oyntment.

Leicesters bottle

Not without good cause (quoth I) but that we are here alone, and no man heareth us. Wherefore I pray you let us returne whereas we left : and when you named my Lord of *Leicesters* Daughter borne of the Lady *Sheffield* in *Dudley* Castle, there came into my head a prety story concerning that affaire : which now I will recount (though somewhat out of order) thereby to draw you from the further stirring of this unsavory puddle and foule dunghill, whereunto we are slipped, by following my Lord somewhat too far in his paths and actions.

Scholar.

Wherefore to tell you the tale as it fell out : I grew acquainted three months past with a certain Minister, that now is dead, and was the same man
that

that was used in *Dudley* Castle, for complement
of some sacred ceremonies at the birth of my
Lord of *Leicesters* daughter in that place : and the
A pretty device. matter was so ordained, by the wily wit of him
that had sowed the seed, that for the better co-
vering of the harvest and secret delivery of the
Lady *Sheffield*, the good wife of the Castle also
(whereby *Leicesters* appointed gossips might without other suspition have accesse to the place)
should faine her selfe to be with childe, and after long and sore travell, God wot, to be delivered of a cushion (as she was indeed) and a little
after a faire coffin was buried with a bundell of
clouts, in shew of a childe ; and the Minister
caused to use all accustomed prayers and ce-
An act of atheism remonies for the solemne interring thereof : for which thing afterward, before his
death, he had great griefe and remorse of conscience, with no small detestation of the most
irreligious device of my Lord of *Leicester* in such
a case.

Lawyer. Here the Lawyer began to laugh a pace both
at the device and at the Minister ; and said, now
truly if my Lords contracts hold no better, but
hath so many infirmities, with subtilties, and by-
places besides : I would be loth that he were married to my daughter, as mean as she is.

Gentleman. But yet (quoth the Gentleman) I had rather of
the two be his wife, for the time, then his guest :
especially if the Italian Chyrurgian or Physitian
be at hand.

Lawyer. True it is (said the Lawyer) for he doth not
poison his wives, whereof I somewhat mervaile,
especially his first wife ; I muse why he chose ra -
ther to make her away by open violence, then by
some Italian confortive. *v. 96. 6.*

Gentleman. Hereof (said the Gentleman) may be divers
reasons

reasons alleaged. First, that he was not at that
time so skilfull in those Italian wares, nor had
about him so fit Physitians and Chyrurgions for
the purpose: nor yet in truth doe I thinke that
his minde was so setled then in mischiefe, as it
hath beene sithence. For you know, that men are
not desperate the first day, but doe enter into
wickednesse by degrees, and with some doubt or
staggering of conscience at the beginning. And so
he at that time might be desirous to have his wife
made away, for that she letted him in his designements, but yet not so stony harted as to
appoint out the particular manner of her death,
but rather to leave that to the discretion of the
murderer. The first reason why Leicester slew his wife by violence, rather then by poyson.

Secondly, it is not also unlike that he prescribed
unto Sir *Richard Varney* at his going thither, that
he should first attempt to kill her by poyson, and
if that tooke not place, then by any other way to
dispatch her howsoever. This I prove by the report of old Doctor *Bayly*, who then lived in Oxford (another manner of man then he who now
liveth about my Lord of the same name) and
was Professour of the Physicke Lecture in the
same University. This learned grave man reported for most certaine, that there was a practice in Cumner among the conspiratours, to
have poysoned the poore Lady a little before
she was killed, which was attempted in this
oder. The second reason. Doctor Bayly the elder.

They seeing the good Lady sad and heavy (as
one that wel knew by her other handling that her
death was not far off) began to perswade her, that
her disease was abundance of melancholly and o-
ther humors, and therefore would needs counsaile
her to take some potion, which she absolutely refusing to do, as suspecting still the worst; they sent
one

A practice for poifoning the Lady Dudley.

day, (unwares to her) for Doctor *Bayly*, and defired him to perfwade her to take fome little potion at his hands, and they would fend to fetch the fame at Oxford upon his prefcription, meaning to have added alfo fomewhat of their owne for her comfort, as the Doctor upon juft caufes fufpected, feeing their great importunity, and rhe fmall need which the good Lady had of Phyfick; and therefore he flatly denied their requeft, mifdoubting (as he after reported) left if they had poifoned her under the name of his Potion, he might after have beene hanged for a colour of their finne. Marry the faid Doctor remained well affured that this way taking no place, fhe fhould not long efcape violence, as after enfued. And the thing was fo beaten into the heads of the principall men of the Univerfity of Oxford, by thefe and other meanes: as for that fhe was found murdered (as all men faid) by the Crowners inqueft, and for that fhe being haftily and obfcurely buried at Cumner (which was condemned above, as not advifedly done) my good Lord, to make plain to the world the great loue he bare to her in her life, and what a griefe the loffe of fo vertuous a Lady was to his tender heart, would needs have her taken up againe and reburied in the Univerfity Church at Oxford, with great pomp and folemnity: that Doctor *Babington* my Lords. Chaplain, making the publike funerall Sermon at her fecond buriall, tript once or twice in hisfpeech by recommending to their memories that vertuous Lady fo pitifully murdered, inftead of fo pitifully flaine.

Doct. Babington

A third reafon.

A third caufe of this manner of the Ladies death, may be the difpofition of my Lords nature; which is bold and violent where it feareth no refiftance (as all cowardly natures are by kinde)

kinde) and where any difficulty or danger appeareth, there, more ready to attempt all by art, sub-
tilty, treason and treachery. And so for that he
doubted no great resistance in the poore Lady to
withstand the hands of them which should offer
to break her neck: he durst the bolder attempt the
same openly.

But in the men whom he poisoned, for that they
were such valiant Knights, the most part of them,
as he durst as soon have eaten his scabard, as draw
his sword in publike against them: he was inforced (as all wretched irefull and dastardly creatures
are) to supplant them by fraud, and by other mens
hands. As also at other times, he hath sought to
doe unto divers other noble and valiant personz-
ges, when he was afraid to meet them in the field,
as a Knight should have done.

His treacheries towards the noble late Earl of
Sussex in their many breaches, is notorious to all
England. As also the bloody practises against di-
vers others.

But as among many, none were more odious and
misliked of all men, then those against Monsieur
Simiers, a stranger and Embassadour; whom first
he practised to have poisoned (as hath bin touched
before) and when that device tooke not place, The intended
then he appointed that Robin Tider his man (as af- murder of Mon-
ter upon his Ale-bench he confessed) should have sieur Simiers by
slaine him at the Blackfriars at Greenwich as he sundry meanes.
went forth at the garden gate; but missing also
that purpose, for that he found the Gentleman
better provided and guarded then he expected, he
dealt with certaine Flushiners and other Pirates
to sinke him at Sea, with the English Gentlemen his favourers, that accompanied him at
his returne into France. And though they mis-
sed of this practice also, (as not daring to set upon
                                                    him

him for feare of some of her Majesties ships, who to breake off this designment attended by speciall commandement, to waft him over in safety) yet the foresaid English Gentlemen were holden foure houres in chace at their coming backe, as Master *Rawley* well knoweth, being then present, and two of the chasers, named *Clark* and *Harris*, confessed afterward the whole designment.

The intended murder of the Earle of Ormond

The Earl of *Ormond* in likewise hath often declared, and will avouch it to my Lord of *Leicesters* face, whensoever he shall be called to the same, that at such time as this man had a quarell with him, and thereby was likely to be enforced to the field (which he trembled to thinke of) he first sought by all meanes to get him made away by secret murder, offering five hundred pounds for the doing thereof. And secondly, when that device tooke no place, he appointed with him the field, but secretly suborning his servant *William*

William Killegre

Killigre to lye in the way where *Ormond* should passe, and so to massacre him with a caliver, before he came to the place appointed. Which murder, though it tooke no effect, for that the matter was taken up, before the day of meeting: yet was *Killigre* placed afterward in her Majesties privy Chamber by *Leicester*, for shewing his ready minde to doe for his Master so faithfull a service.

Scholar.

So faithfull a service (quoth I) truly, in my opinion, it was but an unfit preferment; for so facinorous a fact. And as I would be loth that many of his Italians, or other of that art, should come nigh about her Majesties kitchen; so, much lesse would I, that many such his bloody Champions, should be placed by him in her Highnesse chamber. Albeit for this Gentleman in particular, it may be, that with change of his

place

place in service, he hath changed also his minde and affection, and received better instruction in the feare of the Lord.

But yet in general, I must needs say, that it cannot be but prejudiciall and exceeding dangerous unto our noble Prince and Realme, that any one man whatsoever (especially such a one as the world taketh this man to be) should grow to so absolute authority and commandry in the Court, as to place about the Princes person (the head, the heart, the life of the land) whatsoever people liketh him best, and that now upon their deserts towards the Prince, but towards himselfe; whose fidelity being more obliged to their advancer, then to their soveraigne, doe serve for watchmen about the same, for the profit of him, by whose appointment they were placed. Who by their meanes casting indeed but nets and chaines, and invisible bands about that person, whom most of all he pretendeth to serve, he shutteth up his Prince in a prison most sure, though sweet and senselesse.

Preoccupation of her Maiesties person. f not

Neither is this art of aspiring new or strange unto any man that is experienced in affaires of former time; for that it hath been from the beginning of all government a troden path of all aspirers. In the stories both sacred and prophane, foraine and domesticall of all Nations, Kingdomes, Countries and States, you shall read, that such as ment to mount above others, and to governe all at their owne discretion; did lay this for the first ground and principle of their purpose; to possesse themselves of all such as were in place about the principall; even as he who intending to hold a great City at his owne disposition, dareth not mak open war against the same; getteth secretly into his hands or at his devotion, al the Towns,

An ordinary way of aspiring by preoccupation of the Princes person.

A comparison.

Vil-

Villages, Castles, Fortresses, bulwarks, Rampires, Waters, Wayes, Ports and Passages, about the same, and so without drawing any sword against the said City, he bringeth the same into bondage to abide his will and pleasure.

This did all these in the Roman Empire, who rose from subjects to be great Princes, and to put downe Emperours. This did all those in France and other Kingdomes, who at sundry times have tyrannized their Princes. And in our owne Countrey the examples are manifest of *Vortiger*, *Harold*, *Henry* of Lancaster, *Richard* of Warwicke, *Richard* of Glocester, *Iohn* of Northumberland, and divers others, who by this meane specially, have pulled downe their lawfull Soveraignes.

And to speake onely a word or two of the last, for that he was this mans Father; doth not all England know, that he first overthrew the good Duke of *Somerset*, by drawing to his devotion the very servants and friends of the said Duke? And afterward did not he possesse himselfe of the Kings owne person, and brought him to the end which is knowne, and before that, to the most shamefull disheriting of his owne royall Sisters: and all this, by possessing first the principall men, that were in authority about him?

The way of aspiring in Duke Dudley.

Wherefore sir, if my Lord of *Leicester* have the same plot in his head (as most men thinke) and that he meaneth one day to give the same push at the Crowne by the House of *Huntington*, against all the race and line of King *Henry* the seventh in generall, which his Father gave before him, by pretence of the House of *Suffolke*, against the Children of King *Henry* the eight in particular; he wanteth not reason to follow the same

meanes

meanes and platform of planting speciall persons for his purpose about the Prince, for surely his fathers plot lacked no witty device or preparation, but onely that God overthrew it at the instant: (as happely he may doe this mans) also notwithstanding any diligence that humane wisedome can use to the contrary.

To this said the Gentleman: that my Lord of Leycester hath a purpose to shoot one day at the Diadem by the title of Huntington, is not a thing obscure in it selfe, and it shall bee more plainly proved hereafter. But now will I shew unto you for your instruction, how well this man hath followed his fathers platforme (or rather passed the same) in possessing himselfe of all her Majesties servants, friends, and forces, to serve his turne at that time for execution, and in the meane space for preparation. Gentleman.

First, in the privy Chamber, next unto her Majesties person, the most part are his own creatures (as he calleth them) that is, such as acknowledge their being in that place, from him: and the rest he so over-ruleth, either by flattery or feare, as none may dare but to serve his turne. As his reign is so absolute in this place, (as also in all other parts of the Court) as nothing can passe but by his admission, nothing can be said, done, or signified, whereof hee is not particularly advertised: no bill, no supplication, no complaint, no sute, no speech, can passe from any man to the Princesse (except it be from one of the Councell) but by his good liking: or if there doe, he being admonished thereof (as presently he shall,) the party delinquent is sure after to abide the smart thereof. Whereby he holdeth as it were a locke upon the eares of his Prince, and the tongues of all her Majesties servants, so surely chained to his girdle, Leycesters power in the privy Chamber.

D   as

as no man dareth to speak any one thing that may offend him, though it be never so true or behovefull for her Majesty to know.

As well appeared in the late marriage with Dame *Essex*, which albeit it was celebrated twise: first at Killingworth, and secondly at Waenstead (in the presence of the Earle of Warwick, Lord *North*, Sir *Francis Knovies*, and others) and this exactly known to the whole Court, with the very day, the place, the witnesses, and the Minister that married them together: yet no man durst open his mouth to make her Majesty privy therunto, untill Monsieur *Simiers* disclosed the same, (and therby incurred his high displeasure) nor yet in many dayes after for feare of *Lycester*. Which is a subjection most dishonorable and dangerous to any Prince living, to stand at the devotion of his subject, what to heare or not to heare of things that passe within his own Realme.

And herof it followeth that no sute can prevaile in Court, be it never so meane, except he first be made acquainted there with, and receive not only the thankes, but also be admitted unto a great part of the gaine and commodity therof. Which, as it is a great injury to the suter: so is it a far more greater to the bounty, honour and security of the Prince, by whose liberality this man feedeth only, and fortifieth himselfe, depriving his soveraigne of all grace, thanks and good will for the same. For which cause also he giveth out ordinarily, to every suter, that her Majesty is nigh and persimonious of her selfe, and very difficile to grant any sute, were it not only upon his incessant solicitation. Whereby he filleth his own purse the more, and emptieth the hearts of such as receive benefit, from due thankes to their Princes for the sute obtained.

Hereof

Marginal notes:

Leycester married at Waenstead: when her Majesty was at M. Stoneis Houf Doctor Culpeper Physition Minister.

No sute can passe but by Leycester.

Read Polidore in the 7. yeare of King Richard 1. and you shall find this proceeding of certaine about that K. to be put as a great cause of his overthrow.

Hereof also ensueth, that no man may be preferred in Court (be he otherwise never so well a deserving servant to her Majesty) except he be one of *Leycesters* faction or followers: none can be advanced, except he be liked and preferred by him: none receive grace, except he stand in his good favour, no one may live in countenance, or quiet of life, except he take it, use it, acknowledge it from him, so as all the favours, graces, dignities, riches, and rewards, which her Majesty bestoweth, or the Realme can yeeld, must serve to purchase this man private friends, and favourers, onely to advance his party, and to fortifie his faction. Which faction if by these meanes it be great, (so as indeed it is:) you may not marvile, seeing the riches and wealth, of so worthy a Common weale, doe serve him but for a price to buy the same.

Which thing himselfe well knowing, frameth his spirit of proceeding accordingly. And first, upon confidence thereof, is become so insolent and impotent of his Ire that no man may beare the same, how justly or injustly soever it bee conceived: for albeit he begin to hate a man upon bare surmises onely (as commonly it falleth out, ambition being alwayes the mother of suspicion) yet he prosecuteth the same with such implacable cruelty, as there is no long abiding for the party in that place. As might bee shewed by the examples of many whom hee hath chased from the Court, upon his only displeasure, without other cause, being known to be otherwise, zealous Protestant. As Sir *Ierome Bowes*, Mr. *George Scot*, and others that we could name.

To this insolency is also joyned (as by nature it followeth) most absolute and peremptory dealing in all things whereof it pleaseth him to dispose,

No preferments but by Leycester to Leycestrians.

Leycesters anger and insolency.

Leycesters peremptory dealing.

D 2   pose,

pose, without respect either of reason, order, due, right, subordination, custome, conveniency, or the like: whereof notwithstanding Princes themselves are wont to have regard in disposition of their matters: as for example, among the servants of the Queenes Majesties houshold, it is an ancient and most commendable order and custome, that when a place of higher roome falleth voyd, he that by succession is next, and hath made proof of his worthinesse in an inferiour place, should rise and possesse the same, (except it be for some extraordinary cause) to the end that no man unexperienced or untryed, should be placed in the higher roomes the first day, to the prejudice of others, and disservice of the Prince.

Breaking of order in her Majesties houshold.

Which most reasonable custome this man condemning and breaking at his pleasure, thrusteth into higher roomes any person whatsoever, so he like his inclination, or feele his reward: albeit he neither be fit for the purpose, nor have beene so much as Clarke in any inferiour office before.

Leycesters violating of all order in the Country abroad.

The like hee useth out of the Court, in all other places where matters should passe by order, election, or degree: as in the Vniversities, in election of Scholars, and Heads of houses, in Ecclesiasticall persons, for dignities in Church, in Officers, Magistrates, Stewards of lands, Sheriffes and knights of Shires, in Burgesses of the Parliament, in Commissioners, Judges, Justices of the peace, (whereof many in every shire must weare his livery) and all other the like: where this mans will must stand for reason, and his letters for absolute lawes, neither is there any man, magistrate, or communer in the Realme, who dareth not sooner deny their petition of her Majesties letters, upon just causes (for that her highnesse is content after to be satisfied with reason) then to resist the commandement

mandement of this mans letters, who will admit no excuse or satisfaction, but onely the execution of his said commandement, be it right or wrong.

To this answered the Lawyer, Now verily, sir, *Lawyer.* you paint unto me a strange patterne of a perfect Potentate in the Court: belike that stranger, who calleth our State in his printed booke *Leycestren* A Leycestrian *sem Rempublicam,* a Leycestrian Commonwealth, Commonwealth or the Commonwealth of my Lord of Leycester, knoweth much of these matters. But to hold, sir, still within the Court: I assure you that by considerations, which you have laid downe, I doe begin now to perceive that his party must needs be very great and strong within the said Court, seeing that hee hath so many wayes and meanes to encrease, enrich, and encourage the same, and so strong abilities to tread downe his enemies. The common speech of many wanteth not reason, I perceive, which calleth him the heart and life of the Court.

They which cal him the heart (said the Gentle- *Gentleman.* man) upon a little occasion more, would call Leycester called him also the head: and then I marvell what the heart and life should bee left for her Majesty, when they take of the Court. from her both life, heart, and headship in her own Realme? But the truth is, that he hath the Court at this day in almost the same case as his father had it in King *Edwards* dayes, by the same device, (the Lord forbid that ever it come fully to the same state, for then we know what ensued to the principall:) and if you will have an evident demonstration of this mans power and favour in that place, call you but to minde the times when her Majesty upon most just and urgent occasions, did withdraw but a little her wonted favour and countenance towards him: did not all

D 3 the

A demonstration
of Leycesters
tyranny in the
Court.

the Court as it were, mutiny presently? did not e-
very man hang the lippe? except a few, who afterward paid sweetly for their mirth; were there
not every day new devices sought out, that some
should be on their knees to her Majesty, some
should weepe and put finger in their eyes: other
should find out certaine covert manner of threatning: other reasons and perswasions of love: o-
ther of profit: other of honour: other of
necessity: and all to get him recalled back to favour againe? And had her Majesty any rest permitted unto her, untill she had yeelded and granted to the same?

Consider then (I pray you) that if at that time,
in his disgrace, he had his faction so fast assured
to himself: what hath he now in his prosperity
after so many yeares of fortification? wherin by all
reason he hath not been negligent, seeing that in
policy the first point of good fortification is, to
make that fort impregnable, which once hath been
in danger to be lost. Wherof you have an example
in *Richard* Duke of York, in the time of K. *Henry*
the sixt, who being once in the Kings hands by his
own submission, and dismissed againe (when for
his deserts, he should have suffered) provided after, the King should never be able to over-reach
him the second time, or have him in his power to
do him hurt, but made himselfe strong enough to
pull downe the other with extirpation of his
family.

Leycester provi-
deth never to
come in the
Queenes danger
againe.

Anno Regni 31.

And this of the Court, houshold and Chamber
of her Majesty. But now if we shall passe from
Court to Councell, we shall find him no lesse fortified but rather more: for albeit the providence
of God hath bin such, that in this most honourable assemblie, there hath not wanted some two or
three of the wisest, gravest, and most experienced
in

Leycesters puis-
sance in the privy
Councell.

in our ſtate, that have ſeen and marked this mans perillous proceedings from the beginning, (wherof notwithſtanding two are now deceaſed, and their places ſupplied to *Leyceſters* good liking:) yet (alas) the wiſdom of theſe worthy men, hath diſcovered alwayes more, then their authorities were able to redreſſe: (the others great power and violence conſidered) and for the reſidue of that bench and table, though I doubt not but there be divers, who do in heart deteſt his doings (as there were alſo, no doubt among the Councellours of King *Edward*, who miſliketh this mans fathers attempts, though not ſo hardy as to contrary the ſame:) yet for moſt part of the Councell preſent, they are known to be ſo affected in particular, the one for that he is to him a Brother, the other a Father, the other a Kinſman, the other an allie, the other a faſt obliged friend, the other a fellow or follower in faction, as none will ſtand in the breach againſt him : none dare reſiſt or encounter his deſignemeat : but every man yeelding rather to the force of his flow, permitteth him to pierce, and paſſe at his pleaſure in whatſoever his will is once ſetled to obtaine.

And hereof (were I not ſtaied for reſpect of ſome whom I may not name) I could alledge ſtrang examples, not ſo much in affaires belonging to ſubjects and to privat men, as (were the cauſe of *Snowden* forreſt, *Denbigh* of *Killingworth*, of his faire Paſtures fouly procured by *Southam*, of the Archbiſh. of *Canterbury*, of the L. *Barkley*, of Sir *Iohn Throgmarton*, of M. *Robinſon* and the like;) wherin thoſe of the Councell that diſliked his doings, leaſt dared to oppoſe themſelves to the ſame, but alſo in things that appertaine directly to the Crown and dignity, to the State and Common weal, and to the ſafety and continuance therof. It is not ſecure for any

L. Keeper.

L. Chamberlain.

Matters wherin the Councell are inforced to wink at Leyceſter.

any one Councellor, or other of authority, to take notice of my Lords errours or misdeeds, but with extreame perill of their owne ruine.

Leycesters intelligence with the rebellion in Ireland.

As for example: in the beginning of the rebellion in Ireland, when my Lord of Leycester was in some disgrace, and consequently, as hee imagined, but in fraile state at home, he thought it not unexpedient, for his better assurance, to hold some intelligence also that way, for all events, and so he did: whereof there was so good evidence and testimony found, upon one of the first of accompt, that was there slaine, (as honourable personages of their knowledge have assured me) as would have beene sufficient, to touch the life of any subject in the land, or in any state Christian, but onely my Lord of Leycester, who is a subject without subjection.

For what thinke you? durst any man take notice hereof, or avouch that he had seen thus much? durst he that tooke it in Ireland, deliver the same where especially hee should have done? or they who received it in England, for it came to great hands, use it to the benefit of their Princesse and Countrey? No surely: for if it had beene but onely suspected that they had seene such a thing, it would have beene as dangerous unto them as it

Acteons case now come in England.

was to *Acteon* to have seene *Diana* and her maidens naked: whose case is so common now in England as nothing more, and so doe the examples of divers well declare: whose unfortunate knowledge of too many secrets brought them quickly to unfortunate ends.

Salvatour slaine in his bed.

For we heare of one *Salvatour* a stranger, long used in great mysteries of base affaires and dishonest actions, who afterward (upon what demerit I know not) sustained a hard fortune, for being late with my Lord in his study, well neare untill

mid-

midnight, (if I be rightly informed) went home
to his chamber, and the next morning was found
slaine in his bed. Wee heare also of one *Doughty*, Doughty hanged
hanged in haste by Captaine *Drake* upon the Sea, by Drake.
and that by order, as is thought, before his departure out of England, for that he was over privy to the secrets of this good Earle.

There was also this last Summer past, one The story of
Gates hanged at Tiborne, among others, for rob- Gates hanged
bing of Carriers, which *Gates* had beene lately at Tiborne.
Clarke of my Lords kitching, and had layd out
much money of his owne, as he said, for my Lords
provision, being also otherwise in so great favour
and grace with my Lord, as no man living was
thought to bee more privy of his secrets then this
man, whereupon also it is to be thought, that hee
presumed the rather to commit this robbery, (for
to such things doth my Lords good favour most
extend,) and being apprehended, and in danger
for the same, he made his recourse to his Honour
for protection, as the fashion is, and that hee
might hee borne out, as divers of lesse merit had
beene by his Lordship, in more haynous causes
before him.

The good Earle answered his servant and
deare Privado courteously, and assured him for
his life, howsoever for outer shew and complement the forme of Law might passe against him.
But *Gates* seeing himselfe condemned, and nothing now betweene his head and the halter, but
the word of the Magistrate which might come in
an instant, when it would bee too late to send to
his Lord: remembring also the small assurance
of his said Lords word by his former dealings
towards other men, whereof this man was too
much privy, he thought good to sollicite his case
also by some other of his friends, though not so
puissant

puiſſant as his Lord and Maſter, who dealing indeed, both diligently and effectually in his affaire,
found the matter more difficult a great deale then
either he or they had imagined: for that my Lord
of Leyceſter was not onely not his favourer, but
a great haſtener of his death under hand; and that
with ſuch care, diligence, vehemency, and irreſiſtable méanes, (having the Law alſo on his ſide)
that there was no hope at all of eſcaping: which
thing when *Gates* heard of, he eaſily beleeved for
the experience he had of his maſters good nature,
and ſaid, that he alwayes miſtruſted the ſame, con-
ſidering how much his Lordſhip was in debt to
him, and hee made privy to his Lordſhips foule
ſecrets, which ſecrets hee would there preſently
have uttered in the face of all the world, but that
he feared torments or ſpeedy death, with ſome extraordinary cruelty, if hee ſhould ſo have done,
and therefore hee diſcloſed the ſame onely to a
Gentleman of worſhip, whom hee truſted ſpecially, whoſe name I may not utter for ſome cauſes,
(but it beginneth with H.) and I am in hope ere
it be long, by meanes of a friend of mine, to have
a ſight of that diſcourſe and report of *Gates*,
which hitherto I have not ſeene nor ever ſpake
I with the Gentleman that keepeth it, though I
be well aſſured that the whole matter paſſed in
ſubſtance as I have here recounted it.

Scholar.
This relation of
Gates may ſerve
hereafter for an
addition in the
ſecond edition
of this booke.

Whereunto I anſwered, that in good faith it
were pitty that this relation ſhould be loſt, for
that it is very like, that many rare things bee declared therein, ſeeing it is done by a man ſo privie to the affaires themſelves, wherein alſo hee
had beene uſed an inſtrument. I will have it
(quoth the Gentleman) or elſe my friends ſhall
faile me, howbeit not ſo ſoone as I would, for
that he is in the Weſt Countrey that ſhould procure

ure it for me, and will not returne for certaine
months, but after I shall see him againe, I will
not leave him untill he procure it for me, as hee
hath promised: well (quoth I) but what is become of that evidence found in Ireland under my
Lords hand, which no man dare pursue, avouch, or
behold.

Truly (said the Gentleman) I am informed
that it lyeth safely reserved in good custody, to be
brought forth and avouched whensoever it shall
please God so to dispose of her Majesties heart, as
to lend an indifferent eare, as well to his accusers,
as to himselfe, in judgement.

Gentleman.

Neither must you thinke that this is strange,
nor that the things are few which are in such sort
reserved in decke for the time to come, even a-
mong great personages, and of high calling,
for seeing the present state of his power to bee
such, and the tempest of his tyranny to be so
strong and boysterous, as no man may stand in
the rage thereof, without perill, for that even
from her Majesty her selfe, in the lenity of her
Princely nature, hee extorteth what hee designe-
eth, either by fraud, flattery, false information,
request, pretence, or violent importunity, to
the over-bearing of all, whom hee meaneth
to oppresse: No marvaile then though many,
even of the best and faithfullest Subjects
of the Land, doe yeeld to the present time,
and doe keepe silence in some matters,
that otherwise they would take it for dutie
to utter.

The deck reser-
ved for Leyce-
ster.

Leycesters puis-
sant violence
with the Prince
her selfe.

And in this kind it is not long sithence a worshipfull and wise friend of mine told mee a testimony in secret, from the mouth of as noble
and grave a Councellour as England hath enjoyed these many hundred yeares: I meane the
late

The Earle of Suffex his fpeech of the Earle of Leyceſter.

late Lord Chamberlaine, with whom my ſaid friend being alone at his houſe in London, not twenty dayes before his death, conferred ſomewhat familiarly about theſe and like matters, as with a true father of his Countrey and Commonwealth: and after many complaints in the behalf of divers, who had opened their griefs unto Councellours, and ſaw that no notice would be taken thereof, the ſaid Nobleman, turning himſelfe ſomewhat about from the water, (for hee ſate neare his pond ſide, where hee beheld the taking of a Pike or Carpe) ſaid to my friend, It is no marvell, ſir, for who dareth intermeddle himſelfe in my Lords affaires? I will tell you (quoth he) in confidence betweene you and me, there is as wiſe a man and as grave, and as faithfull a Coun-

The Lord Burghley.

cellour as England breedeth, (meaning thereby the Lord Treaſurer) who hath as much of his keeping of Leyceſters owne hand writing, as is ſufficient to hang him, if either he durſt preſent the ſame to her Majeſty, or her Majeſty doe juſtice when it ſhould be preſented. But indeed (quoth he) the time permitteth neither of them both, and therefore it is in vaine for any man to ſtruggle with him.

These were that Noblemans words, whereby you may conſider whether my Lord of Leyceſter be ſtrong this day in Councell or no: and whether his fortification be ſufficient in that place.

Leyceſters power in the countrey abroad.

But now if out of the Councell, we will turne but our eye in the Countrey abroad, we ſhall finde as good fortification alſo there, as we have peruſed already in Court and Councell: and ſhall well perceive that this mans plot is no fond or indiſcreet plot, but excellent well grounded, and ſuch as in all proportions hath his due correſpondence.

Conſi-

Confider then the chiefe and principall parts of this land for martiall affaires, for ufe and commodity of armour, for ftrength, for opportunity, for liberty of the people, as dwelling fartheft off from the prefence and afpect of their Prince, fuch parts (I fay) as are fitteft for fudden enterprifes, without danger of interception: as are the North, the Weft, the Countries of Wales, the Iflands round about the land, and fundry other places within the fame: are they not all at this day at his difpofition? are they not all (by his procurement) in the onely hands of his friends and allyes? or of fuch, as by other matches have the fame complot and purpofe with him?

In Yorke is prefident the man that of all other **Yorke Earle of** is fitteft for that place, that is, his neareft in affi- **Huntington.** nity, his deareft in friendfhip, the head of his faction, and open competitor of the Scepter. In Bar- **Barwick.** wicke is a Captaine, his wives uncle, moft affured **The Lord Hunf-** to himfelfe and Huntington, as one who at con- **den.** venient time may as much advance their defignements, as any one man in England.

In Wales the chiefe authority from the Prince **Wales.** is in his owne brother in law: but among the **Sir Henry Sidney** people, of naturall affection, is in the Earle of **The Earle of** Pembrooke, who both by marriage of his fifters **Pembrooke.** daughter is made his ally, and by dependance is knowne to be wholly at his difpofition.

The Weft part of England is under Bedford, **The Weft.** a man wholly devoted to his and the Puritans fa- **Earle of Bed-** ction. **ford.**

In Ireland was governour of late the principal **The Lord Grey.** inftrument appointed for their purpofes: both in refpect of his heat and affection toward their defignements, as alfo of fome fecret difcontentment which he hath towards her Majefty and the ftate prefent, present for certaine hard † speeches and ingrate recompences, as he pretendeth: but indeed for that he is knowne to bee of nature fyrie, and impatient of stay, from seeing that Commonwealth on foot, which the next competitours for their gaine have painted out to him and such others, more pleasant then the Terrestriall Paradise it selfe.

This then is the *Hectar*, this is the *Ajax* appointed for the enterprise, when the time shall come. This must be (forsooth) another *Richard* of Warwicke, to gaine the Crowne for *Henry* the ninth of the House of Yorke: as the other *Richard* did put downe *Henry* the sixt of the House of Lancaster, and placed *Edward* the fourth, from whom Huntington deriveth his title therefore this man is necessarily to be entertained from time to time (as we see now he is) in some charge and martiall action, to the end his experience, power, and credit may grow the more, and he be able at the time to have souldiers at his commandment. And for the former charge which held of late in Ireland, as this man had not beene called away, but for execution of some other secret purpose, * for advancement of their designements: so bee well assured that for the time to come, it is to bee furnished againe with a sure and fast friend to Leycester and to that faction.

In the Ile of Wight I grant that Leycester hath lost a great friend and a trusty servant by the death of Captaine *Horsey*, but yet the matter is supplied by the succession of another, no lesse assured unto him then the former, or rather more, through the band of affinity by his wife. The two Ilands of Gersey and Gernsey are in the possession of two friends and most obliged dependents. The one, by reason he is exceedingly addicted to

the

the Puritan proceedings : the other, as now being joyned unto him by the marriage of miſtris *Boſſe*, his wives ſiſter, both daughters to Sir *Francis*, or (at leaſt) to my Lady *Knooles*, and ſo become a rivall, companion and brother, who was before (though truſty) yet but his ſervant.

And theſe are the chiefe Keyes, Fortreſſes, and Bulwarkes, within, without and about the Realm, which my Lord of Leyceſter poſſeſſing, (as hee doth) hee may be aſſured of the body within : where notwithſtanding (as hath beene ſhewed) he wanteth no due preparation for ſtrength : having at his diſpoſition (beſides all aydes and other helpes ſpecified before) her Majeſties horſe, **Her Maieſties** and ſtables, by intereſt of his owne office : her **ſtable, her armour, munition,** Armour, Artillery, and Munition, by the office of **and artillery.** his brother the Earle of Warwicke. The Tower **The Tower.** of London and treaſure therein, by the dependence of Sir *Owin Hopton* his ſworne ſervant, as ready to reſcue and furniſh him with the whole, if occaſion ſerved, as one of his predeceſſours was, to receive his Father in King *Edwards* dayes, for the like effect, againſt her Majeſty and her Siſter.

And in the City of London it ſelfe, what this **London.** man at a pinch could doe, by the helpe of ſome of **Sir Rowland** the principall men, and chiefe Leaders, and (as it **Heyward, &c.** were) Commanders of the Commons there, and **Mad Fleetwood.** by the beſtirring of *Fleetwood* his madde Recorder, and other ſuch his inſtruments : as alſo in **Gentleman.** all other Townes, Ports, and Cities of importance, by ſuch of his owne ſetting up, as hee hath placed there to ſerve his deſignements, and Juſtices of peace, with other, that in moſt Shires doe weare his livery, and are at his appointmente the ſimpleſt man within the Realme, doth conſider.

Where-

Whereunto if you adde now his owne forces
and furniture which hee hath in Killingworth
Castle, and other places, as also the forces of Huntington in particular, with their friends, followers,
allies and compartenors, you shall finde that they
are not behinde in their preparations.

Scholar.
**My Lord of
Huntingtons
preparation at
Ashby.**

For my Lord of Huntingtons forwardnesse in
the cause (said I) there is no man, I thinke, which
maketh doubt : marry for his private forces, albeit
they may be very good, for any thing I doe know
to the contrary, (especially at his house within
five and twenty miles of Killingworth, where one
told mee some yeares past, that he had furniture
ready for five thousand men :) yet do I not think
but they are farre inferiour to my Lord of Leycester, who is taken to have excessive store, and that

**Killingworth
Castle.**

in divers places. And as for the Castle last mentioned by you, there are men of good intelligence,
and of no small judgement, who report that in the
same he hath to furnish ten thousand good souldiers, of all things necessary both for horse and
man, besides all other munition, armour, and artillery, (whereof great store was brought thither
under pretence of triumph, when her Majesty was
there, and never as yet carried backe againe) and
besides the great abundance of ready coyne there
(as is said) sufficient for any great exploit to bee
done within the Realme.

And I know that the estimation of this place
was such, among divers, many yeares agoe : as
when at a time her Majesty lay dangerously sick,
and like to dye, at Hampton Court, a certaine

Ralph Lane.

Gentleman of the Court came unto my Lord of
Huntington, and told him, that for so much as he
tooke his Lord to be next in succession after her
Majesty, hee would offer him a meane of great
helpe for compassing of his purpose, after the
disease

decease of her Majesty which was, the possession
of Killingworth Castle (for at that time these
two Earles were not yet very friends, nor confe-
derate together) and that being had, he shewed to
the Earle the great furniture, and wealth which
thereby he should possesse for pursuit of his purpose.

The proposition was well liked, and the matter esteemed of great importance, and consequently received with many thankes. But yet afterward
her Majesty by the good providence of God, reco-
vering againe, letted the execution of the bargain:
and my Lord of Huntington having occasion to
joyne amity with Leycester, had more respect to
his owne commodity, then to his friends security,
(as commonly in such persons and cases it falleth
out) and so discovered the whole device unto him,
who forgat not after, from time to time, to plague
the deviser by secret means, untill he had brought
him to that poore estate, as all the world seeth:
though many men be not acquainted with the true
cause of this his disgrace and bad fortune.

To this answered the Lawyer: In good faith
(Gentlemen) you open great mysteries unto me,
which either I knew not, or considered not so particularly before; and no marvell, for that my profession and exercise of Law, restraineth me from
much company keeping: and when I happen to
be among some that could tell mee much herein,
I dare not either aske, or heare if any of himselfe
beginne to talke, lest afterward the speech comming to light, I be fetched over the coales (as the
proverb is) for the same, under pretence of another thing. But you (who are not suspected for
religion) have much greater priviledge in such
matters, both to heare and speake againe, which
men of mine estate dare not doe: Onely this I

The offer and acceptation of Killingworth Castle.

Lawyer.

E   knew

The prerogative
of my Lord of
Leyceſter.

knew before, that throughout all England my
Lord of Leyceſter is taken for *Dominus fac totum* :
whoſe excellency above others is infinite, whoſe
authority is abſolute, whoſe commandment is dread-
full, whoſe diſlike is dangerous, and whoſe favour
is omnipotent.

And for his will, though it be ſeldome Law,
yet alwayes is his power above law : and therefore wee Lawyers in all caſes brought unto us,
have as great regard to his inclination, as Aſtronomers have to the Planet dominant, or as Sea-
men have to the North Pole.

Leyceſter the
Star directory to
Lawyers in their
clients affaires.

For as they that ſaile, doe direct their courſe
according to the ſituation and direction of that
ſtarre which guideth them at the Pole : and as
Aſtronomers who make Prognoſtications, doe
foretell things to come, according to the aſpect
of the Planet dominant, or bearing rule for the
time : ſo we doe guide our Clients barke, and do
prognoſticate what is like to enſue of his cauſe, by
the aſpect and inclination of my Lord of Leyceſter. And for that reaſon, as ſoone as ever wee
heare a caſe propoſed, our cuſtome is to ask, what
part my Lord of Leyceſter is like to favour in the
matter; (for in all matters lightly of any importance he hath a part) or what may be gathered of
his inclination therein : and according to that
we give a gueſſe, more or leſſe, what end will enſue. But this (my Maſters) is from the purpoſe :
and therefore returning to your former ſpeech a-
gaine, I do ſay, that albeit I was not privy before
to the particular proviſions of my Lord and his
friends, in ſuch and ſuch places : yet ſeeing him
accompted Lord Generall over all the whole
Realme, and to have at his commandement all
theſe ſeverall commodities and forces pertaining
to her Majeſty which you have mentioned before,

fore, and so many more as be in the Realme, and not mentioned by you (for in fine he hath al:) I could not but account him (as hee is) a potent Prince of our State, for all furniture needfull to defence or offence, or rather the onely Monarch of our Nobility, who hath sufficient needfull to plunge his Prince, if he should bee discontented, especially for his abundance of money, (which, by the wise, is tearmed the Sinewes of Martiall actions) wherein by all mens judgements, hee is better furnished at this day, then ever any subject of our land, either hath beene heretofore, or lightly may be hereafter, both for bankes without the Realme, and stuffed coffers within. Insomuch that being my selfe in the last Parliament, when the matter was moved for the grant of a Subsidie, after that, one for her Majesty had given very good reasons, why her Highnesse was in want of money, and consequently needed the assistance of her faithfull subjects therein, another that sate next me, of good account, said in mine eare secretly, these reasons I doe well allow, and am contented to give my part in money: but yet for her Majesties need, I could make answer as one answered once the Emperour *Tiberius* in the like case and cause; *Abundè ei pecuniam fore, si à liberto suo in societatem recipietur*; that her Majesty should have Money enough, if one of her servants would vouchsafe to make her Highnesse partaker with him; meaning thereby my Lord of Leycester, whose treasure must needs in one respect be greater then that of her Majesty; for that he layeth up whatsoever he getteth, and his expences he casteth upon the purse of his Princesse.

Leycesters furniture in money.

The saying of a Knight of the Shire touching Leycesters mony

For that (said the Gentleman) whether he doe *Gentleman* or no, it importeth little to the matter: seeing both that which hee spendeth, and that he hord-

E 2   eth,

eth, is truly and properly his Princes Treasure:
and seeing hee hath so many and divers wayes of
The infinit waies of gaining that Leycester hath.
gaining, what should he make account of his own
private expences? if hee lay out one for a thousand, what can that make him the poorer? hee
that hath so goodly lands, possessions, Seignio-
ries, and rich offices of his owne, as he is knowne
to have: hee that hath so speciall favour and authority with the Prince, as he can obtaine whatsoever he listeth to demand: he that hath his part
Sutes.
and portion in all sutes besides, that passe by grace,
or else (for the most part) are ended by Law: he
Lands.
that may chop and change what lands hee listeth
with her Majesty, dispoile them of al their woods
and other commodities, and rack them afterward
to the uttermost penny, and then returne the same
so tenter-stretched, and bare-shorne, into her Majesties hands againe, by fresh exchange, rent for
rent, for other lands never enhansed before: hee
Licences.
that possesseth so many gainfull Licences to himselfe alone, of Wine, Oyles, Currants, Cloath,
Velvets, with his new office for Licence of alienation, most pernicious unto the Commonwealth
as hee useth the same, with many other the like,
which were sufficient to enrich whole Townes,
Corporations, Countries and Commonwealths:
he that hath the art, to make gainfull to himselfe
Falling out with her Maiesty. Offices.
every offence, displeasure, and falling out of her
Majesty with him, and every angry countenance
cast upon him: he that hath his share in all offices of great profit, and holdeth an absolute Mono-
poly of the same: he that disposeth at his will the
Ecclesiasticall livings of the Realme, maketh Bishops, none, but such as will doe reason, or of his
Clergy.
Chaplains whom he listeth, and retaineth to himselfe so much of the living as liketh him best: hee
that sweepeth away the glebe from so many Benefices

nefices throughout the Land, and compoundeth Benefices.
with the perfon for the reft. He that fo fcoureth
the Univerfity and Colledges where he is Chan- Vniverfity.
cellour, and felleth both Headfhips and Scholars
places, and all other offices, roomes and dignities, that by art or violence may yeeld money : he
that maketh title to what land or other thing he
pleafe, and driveth the parties to compound for Oppreffions.
the fame fame : he that taketh in whole Forefts,
Commons, Woods, and Paftures to himfelfe,
compelling the Tenants to make him pay new
rent, and what he cefleth : he that vexeth and op-
prefleth whomfoever hee lift, taketh from any Rapines.
what hee lift, and maketh his owne claime, fuit,
and end as he lift : he that felleth his favour with Princes favour.
the Prince, both abroad in forraine countries, and
at home, and fetteth the price thereof what himfelfe will demand : he that hath and doth all this, Prefents.
and befides this, hath infinite prefents daily
brought unto him of great value, both in Jewels,
Plate, all kinde of Furniture, and ready Coine :
this man (I fay) may eafily beare his owne expences, and yet lay up fufficiently alfo to weary
his Prince when need fhall require.

You have faid much, fir, (quoth the Lawyer) Lawyer.
and fuch matter as toucheth nearly both her Majefty and the Commonwealth : and yet in my
confcience if I were to plead at the barre for my
Lord, I could not tell which of all thefe members
to deny. But for that which you mention in the
laft part, of his gaining by her Majefties favour,
both at home and abroad : Touching his home- Leycefters home
gaine, it is evident, feeing all that he hath it got- gaine by her Ma-
ten onely by the opinion of her Majefties favour jefties favour.
towards him, and many men doe repaire unto
him with fat prefents, rather for that they fuppofe
he may by his favour do them hurt, if he feele not
their

their reward, then for that they hope he will labour any thing in their affaires.

A pretty ſtory.

You remember (I doubt not) the ſtory of him that offered his Prince a great yearly rent, to have but this favour onely, that hee might come every day in open audience, and ſay in his eare, God ſave your Majeſty, aſſuring himſelfe, that by the opinion of confidence and ſecret favour, which hereby the people would conceive to be in the Prince towards him, he ſhould eaſily get up his rent againe double told. Wherefore my Lord of Leyceſter receiving daily from her Majeſty greater tokens of grace and favour then this, and himſelfe being no evill Merchant, to make his owne bargaine for the beſt of his commodities, cannot but gaine exceedingly at home by his favour.

Leyceſters forraine gaine by her Maieſties favour.

And for his lucre abroad upon the ſame cauſe, I leave to other men to conceive what it may be, ſithence the beginning of her Majeſties reigne, the times whereof and condition of all Chriſtendome hath beene ſuch, as all the Princes and Potentates round about us, have beene conſtrained at one time or other, to ſue to h r Highneſſe for aid, grace, or favour : in all which ſutes, men uſe not to forget (as you know) the parties moſt able by their credit, to further or let the ſame.

In particular onely this I can ſay, that I have heard of ſundry Frenchmen, that at ſuch time as the treaty was betweene France and England, for the re-delivery of Callis unto us againe, in the firſt yeare of her Majeſties reigne that now is, when the Frenchmen were in great diſtreſſe and miſery, and King *Philip* refuſed abſolutely to make peace with them, except Callis were reſtored to England (whither for that purpoſe he had now delivered the French hoſtages :) the Frenchmen doe

doe report (I say) that my Lord of Leycester stood them in great stead at that necessity, for his reward, (which you may well imagine was not small, for a thing of such importance) and became a suiter, that peace might be concluded, with the release of Callis to the French: which was one of the most impious facts (to say the truth,) that ever could be devised against his Commonwealth.

Leycesters bribe for betraying of Callis.

A small matter in him (said the Gentleman) for in this he did no more, but as Christ said of the Jewes: that they filled up the measure of their Fathers sinnes. And so if you reade the story of King *Edwards* time, you shall finde it most evident, that this mans father before him, sold Bulloigne to the French by like treachery. For it was delivered up upon composition, without necessity or reason, the five and twentieth of April, in the fourth year of King *Edward* the sixt, when he (I meane Duke *Dudley*) had now put in the Tower the Lord Protector, and thrust out of the Councell whom he listed, as namely, the Earles of Arundel and Southampton, and so invaded the whole government himselfe, to sell, spoile, or dispose at his pleasure. Wherefore this is but naturall to my Lord of Leycester by discent, to make merchandise of the State, for his Grandfather *Edmund* also was such a kinde of Copesman.

Gentleman.

Leycesters father sold Bulloigne.

Earles of Arundel and Southampton put out of the Councell by D. Dudley.

An evill race of Merchants for the Commonwealth (quoth the Lawyer), but yet, Sir, I pray you (said he) expound unto me somewhat more at large, the nature of these licences which you named, as also the changing of lands with her Majesty, if you can set it downe any plainer: for they seeme to be things of excessive gaine: especially his way of gaining by offending her Majesty, or

Lawyer.

E 4   by

by her Highnesse offence towards him, for it seemeth to be a device above all skill or reason.

Leycesters gaine by falling out with her Maiesty

Not so (quoth the Gentleman) for you know that every falling out must have an attonement againe, whereof hee being sure by the many and puissant meanes of his friends in Court, as I have shewed before, who shall not give her Majesty rest untill it be done: then for this attonement, and in perfect reconciliation on her Majesties part she must grant my Lord some sute or other, which he will have alwayes ready provided for that purpose, and this sute shall bee well able to reward his friends, that laboured for his reconcilement, and leave also a good remainder for himselfe. And this is now so ordinary a practice with him, as all the Realme observeth the same, and disdaineth that her Majesty should bee so unworthily abused. For if her Highnesse fall not out with him as often as he desireth to gaine this way, then he picketh some quarrell or other, to shew himselfe discontented with her, so that one way or other, this gainfull reconciliation must be made, and that often for his commodity. The like art he exerciseth in inviting her Majesty to his banquets, and to his houses, where if shee come, she must grant him in sutes, tenne times so much as the charges of all amount unto: so that *Robin* playeth the Broker in all his affaires, and maketh the uttermost penny of her Majesty every way.

Gentleman.

Now for his change of lands, I thinke I have beene reasonable plaine before: yet for your fuller satisfaction, you shall understand his further dealing therein, to be in this sort. Besides the good lands, and of ancient possession to the Crowne, procured at her Majesties hand, and used as before was declared: hee useth the same tricke for his worst lands, that he possesseth

sesseth any way, whether they come to him, by extort meanes and plaine oppression, or through maintenance and broken titles, or by cousenage of simple Gentlemen, to make him their heire, or by what hard title or unhonest meanes so ever, (for hee practizeth store of such and thinketh little of the reckoning:) after he had tried them likewise to the uttermost touch, and letten them out to such as shall gaine but little by the bargaine: then goeth he and changeth the same with her Majesty for the best lands he can pick out of the Crowne, to the end that hereby he may both enforce her Majesty to the defence of his bad titles, and himselfe fill his coffers with the fines and uttermost commodity of both the lands. Leycesters fraudulent change of lands with her Maiesty whereby he hath notably endammaged the Crowne.

His licences do stand thus: first he got licence for certaine great numbers of cloaths, to be transported out of this land, which might have beene an undoing to the Marchant subject, if they had not redeemed the same with great summes of mony: so that it redounded to great dammage of all occupied about that kind of commodity. After that he had the grant for carrying over of barrell staves and of some other such like wares. Then procured hee a Monopolie, for bringing in of sweet wines, oyles, currants and the like: the gaine wherof is inestimable. He had also the forfeit of all wine that was to be drawn above the old ordinary price, with licence to give authority to sell above that price: wherin Captaine *Horsey* was his instrument, by which meanes it is incredible what treasure and yearely rent was gathered of the Vintners throughout the land. Leycesters licences.

To this adde now his licence of silkes and velvets, which only were enough to enrich the Major and Aldermen of London, if they were all decaied Silkes and Velvets.

(2

(as often I have heard divers Marchants affirme.) And his licence of alienation of lands, which (as in part I have opened before) serveth him not onely to exceſſive gaine, but alſo for an extreame ſcourge, wherewith to plague whom he pleaſeth in the Realm. For ſeeing that without this licence, no man can buy, ſell, paſſe, or alienate, any land that any waies may be drawne to that tenure, as holden in chiefe of the Prince: (as commonly now moſt land may) he calleth into queſtion whatſoever liketh him beſt, be it never ſo cleare: and under this colour, not only enricheth himſelfe without all meaſure, but revengeth himſelfe alſo, where he will, without all order.

The Tyrannicall licence of alienation.

Gentleman.

Here the Lawyer ſtood ſtill a pretty while, biting his lip, as he were aſtoniſhed, and then ſaid; Verily I have not heard ſo many and ſo apparant things, or ſo odious, of any man that ever lived in our Common wealth. And I marvaile much of my Lord of Leyceſter, that his Grandfathers fortune doth not move him much, who loſt his head in the beginning of King Henry the eights dayes, for much leſſe and fewer offences, in the ſame kind, committed in the time of King Henry the ſeventh: for he was thought to be the inventour of theſe poolings and moleſtations, wherewith the people were burthened, in the latter days of the ſaid King. And yet had he great pretence of reaſon to alledged for himſelfe: in that theſe exactions were made to the Kings uſe, and not to his, (albeit no doubt) but his own gaine was alſo there. Maſter Stow writeth in his Cronicle, that in the time of his impriſonment in the Tower, he wrote a notable book, intituled The tree of Common wealth, which book the ſaid Stow ſaith, that hee hath delivered to my Lord of Leyceſter many

Edmund Dudley.

Edmund Dudleis booke written in the Tower.

many years agone. And if the said book be so notable as Maister *Stow* affirmeth : I marvile that
his Lord in so many yeares, doth not publish the
same, for the glory of his ancestors ?

It may be (said the Gentleman) that the secrets *Gentleman.*
therein contained, be such, as it seemeth good to
my Lord, to use them onely himselfe , and to gather the fruit of the tree into his owne house
alone. For if the tree of the Common-wealth in
Edmund Dudlis book, be the Prince and his race :
and the fruits to be gathered from that tree , bee
riches, honours, dignities, and preferments : then
no doubt, but as the writer *Edmund* was cunning
therein : so have his two followers, *Iohn* and *Ro-*
bert , well studied and practized the same, or rather have , exceeded and farre passed the authour
himselfe. The one of them gathering so eagerly,
and with such vehemency, as he was like to have
broken down the maine boughes for greedinesse:
the other yet plucking and heaping so fast to himselfe and his friends , as it is and may be , most
justly doubted , that when they have cropped all
they can , from the tree left them by their father The supplanting
Eamund (I meane the race of King *Henry* the se- of the race of
venth) then will they pluck up the Stemme it self Henry the 7.
by the rootes, as unprofitable : and pitch in his The inserting of
place another Trunke that is the line of *Huntin-* Huntington.
gton) that may begin to feed a new , with fresh
fruits againe , and so for a time content their ap-
petites, untill of gatherers, they may become trees,
(which is their finall purpose) to feed themselves
at their own discretion.

And howsoever this be, it cannot be denied, but Edmund Dud-
that *Edm. Dudlis* brood, have learned by this book, lies brood more
and by other meanes to be more cunning gathe- cunning then
rers, then ever their first progenitor was, that made himselfe.
the book. First for that he made profession to gather

ther to his Prince (though wickedly) and these
men make demonstration, that they have gathered for themselves : and that with much
more iniquity. Secondly, for that *Edmund Dudley*, though hee got himselfe neare about the
tree , yet was he content to stand on the ground,
and to serve himselfe from the tree , as commodity was offered : but his children not esteeming that safe gathering, will needs mount aloft
upon the tree, to pull, croppe, and rifle at
their pleasure. And as in the second point the
Sonne *Iohn Dudley* was more subtile , then *Edmund* the Father : so in a third point, the Ne-
phey *Robert Dudley* is more crafty then they both.
For that, hee seeing the evill successe of those
two that went before him , hee hath provided
together so much in convenient time , and to
make himselfe therewith so fat and strong ,
(wherein the other two failed) as he will never
be in danger more , to be called to any accompt
for the same.

In the margin: Northumberland and Leycester with their Prince will not be ruled.

In good faith Sir (quoth the Lawyer) I thanke
you heartily, for this pleasant discourse upon *Edmund Dudleis* tree of Common-wealth. And by
your opinion , my Lord of Leycester is the most
learned of all his kindred , and a very cunning
Logitioner indeed, that can draw for himselfe so
commodious conclusions, out of the perillous premisses of his progenitors.

In the margin: Lawyer.

No marvail (quoth the Gentleman) for that his
L. is Master of Art in Oxford, and Chancelour
besides of the same Vniversity, where he hath store
(as you know) of many fine wits and good Logi-
tioners at his commandement: and where he lear-
neth not only the rules and art of cunning gathering : but for the very practize (as I have touched
before) seeing there is no one Colledge, or other
thing

In the margin: Gentleman.

In the margin: Leycester Master of Art, and a cunning Logitioner.

thing of commodity within that place, where hence he hath not pulled, whatsoever was possibly to be gathered, either by art or violence.

Touching Oxford (said I) for that I am an University man my selfe, and have both experience of Cambridge, and good acquaintance with divers students of the other university: I can tell you enough, but in fine all tendeth to this conclusion, that by his Chancellorship, is cancelled almost all hope of good in that University: and by his protection, it is very like soone to come to destruction. And surely if there were no other thing, to declare the oddes and difference betwixt him and our Chancellour, (whom he cannot beare: for that every way he seeth him, to passe him in all honour and vertue) it were sufficient to behold the present state of the two Universities, whereof they are heads and governours.

For our own, I will not say much, lest I might perhaps seeme partiall: but let the thing speak for it selfe. Consider the fruit of the Garden, and therby you may judge of the Gardiners diligence. Looke upon the Bishopricks, Pastorships, and Pulpits of England, and see whence principally they have received their furniture for advancement of the Gospell. And on the contrary side, looke upon the Seminaries of Papistry at Rome and Rhems, upon the Colledges of Jesuists, and other companies of Papists beyond the seas, and see where-hence they are, especially, fraught.

The Priests and Jesuists here executed within the land, and other that remaine either in prison, or abroad in corners: are they not all (in a manner) of that University? I speak not to the disgrace of any good that remaine there, or that have issued out thence into the Lords Vineyard: but for

the

[marginal notes:] Scholar. — Leycesters abusing and spoiling of Oxford. — The Lord Treasurer. — Cambridge.

the moſt part there, of this our time, have they not either gone beyond the ſeas, or left their places for diſcontentment in Religion, or elſe become Servingmen, or followed the bare name of Law or Phyſick, without greatly profiting therein, or furthering the ſervice of Gods Church, or their Commonwealth?

And wherehence (I pray you) enſueth all this, but by reaſon that the chiefe Governour thereof is an Atheiſt himſelfe, and uſeth the place onely for gaine and ſpoile? for herehence it commeth, that all good order and diſcipline is diſſolved in that place, the fervour of ſtudy extinguiſhed: the publique Lectures abandoned (I meane of the more part:) the Tavernes and Ordinary tables frequented; the apparell of Students growne monſtruous: and the ſtatutes and good ordinance both of the Univerſity and of every Colledge and Hall in private, broken and infringed at my Lords good pleaſure, without reſpect either of oath, cuſtome, or reaſon to the contrary. The heads and Officers are put in and out at his onely diſcretion: and the Scholars places either ſold, or diſpoſed by his letters, or by theſe of his ſervants and followers: nothing can be had there, now, without preſent money: it is as common buying and ſelling of places in that Univerſity, as of horſes in Smithfield: whereby the good and vertuous are kept out, and companions thruſt in, fit to ſerve his Lord afterward, in all affaires that ſhall occurre.

And as for leaſes of Farmes, Woods, Paſtures, Perſonages, Benefices, or the like, which belong any way to any part of the Univerſity, to let or beſtow, theſe, his Lord and his Servants have ſo fleeced, ſhorne, and ſcraped already, that there remaineth little to feed upon hereafter: albeit hee

want

The diſorders of Oxford by the wickedneſſe of their Chancellor

Leaſes.

want not ſtill his ſpies and intelligences in the place, to advertiſe him from time to time, when any new little morſell is offered. And the princi- Leyceſters in-ſtruments. pall inſtruments which for this purpoſe he hath had there before this, have been two Phyſitians, *Bayly* and *Culpiper*, both knowne Papiſts a little while agoe, but now juſt of *Galens* religion, and ſo much the fitter for my Lords humour: for his Lordſhip doth alwaies covet, to be furniſhed with certaine choſen men about him, for divers affairs: as theſe two Galeniſts in the Univerſity: *Dee* and *Allen* (two Atheiſts) for figuring and conjuring: *Iulio* the Italian, and *Lopes* the Jew, for poiſoning, and for the art of deſtroying children in womens bellies: *Verneis* for murdering: *Digbies* for * Bauds: and the like in occupations which his * At Digbies houſe in War-wickſhire dame Lettice lay, and ſome other ſuch pieces of plea-ſure. Lordſhip exerciſeth.

Wherefore to returne to the ſpeech where we began: moſt cleare it is, that my Lord of Leyce-ſter hath meanes to gaine and gather alſo by the Univerſity, as wel as by the country abroad. Wher-in (as I am told) he beareth himſelfe ſo abſolute a Lord, as if he were their King, and not their Chan-cellour. Nay far more then if he were the gene-rall and particular founder of all the Colledges and other houſes of the Univerſity; no man daring to contrary or interrupt the leaſt word or ſignifi-cation of his will, but with his extreame danger: which is a proceeding more fit for *Phalaris* the ty-rant, or ſome Governour in Tartary, then for a Chancellour of a learned Univerſity.

To this anſwered the Lawyer, for my Lords Lawyer. wrath towards ſuch as will not ſtand to his judg-ment and opinion, I can my ſelfe be a ſufficient witneſſe, who having had often occaſion to deale for compoſition of matters betwixt his Lordſhip and others, have ſeene by experience, that al-wayes

wayes they have fped beſt, who ſtood leaſt in contention with him, whatſoever their cauſe were. For as a great and violent river, the more it is ſtopped or contraried, the more it riſeth and ſwelleth bigge, and in the end, dejecteth with more force the thing that made reſiſtance : ſo his Lordſhip being the great and mighty Potentate of this Realme, and accuſtomed now to have his will in all things, cannot beare to bee croſſed or reſiſted by any man, though it were in his owne neceſſary defence.

The perill of ſtanding with Leyceſter in any thing.

Hereof I have ſeene examples in the cauſes of Snowden foreſt in Wales, of Denbighe, of Killingworth, of Drayton, and others : where the parties that had intereſt, or thought themſelves wronged, had beene happy if they had yeelded at the firſt to his Lordſhips pleaſure, without further queſtion: for then had they eſcaped much trouble, charges, diſpleaſure, and vexation, when by reſiſtance they incurred, to their great ruine, (and * loſſe of life to ſome) and in the end were faine to ſubmit themſelves unto his will, with far worſe conditions then in the beginning were offered unto them : which thing was pittifull indeed to behold, but yet ſuch is my Lords diſpoſition.

* Poore men reſiſting Warwicks incloſure at North hall were hanged for his pleaſure by Leyceſters authority Gentleman. Great Tyranny.

A noble diſpoſition (quoth the Gentleman,) that I muſt give him my coat, if hee demand the ſame, and that quickly alſo, for feare leſt if I ſtagger or make doubt thereof, hee compell me to yeeld both coat and doublet, in penance of my ſtay. I have read of ſome ſuch Tyrants abroad in the world: marry their end was alwayes according to their life, as it is very like that it will be alſo in this man, for that there is ſmal hope of his amendment, and God paſſeth not over commonly ſuch matters unpuniſhed in this life, as well as in the life to come.

But

But I pray you sir, seeing mention is now made of the former oppressions, so much talked of throughout the realm, that you will take the pains to explain the substance therof unto me; for albeit in generall, every man doth know the same, and in heart doe detest the tyranny therof; yet we abroad in the Countrey, doe not understand it so well and distinctly as you that be Lawyers, who have seene and understood the whole processe of the same.

The case of Killingworth and Denbigh (said the Lawyer) are much alike, in matter and manner of proceeding, though different in time, place and importance. For that the Lordship in Denbigh in Northwales, being given unto him by her Majesty a great while agoe, at the beginning of his rising; (which is a Lordship of singular great importance in that Countrey, having (as I have heard) well neere 200. worshipfull Gentlemen freeholders to the same;) the tenants of the place, considering the present state of things, and having learned the hungry disposition of their new Lord, made a common purse of a thousand pounds, to present him withall, at his first entrance: which though he received (as he refuseth nothing;) yet accounted he the sum of small effect for satisfaction of his appetite; and therefore applied himselfe, not onely to make the uttermost that he could by Leases, and such like wayes of commoditie; but also he would needs enforce the Freeholders to raise their old rent of the Lordship, from two hundreth and fifty pounds a yeere, or thereabouts (at which rate he had received the same in gift from her Majesty,) unto eight or nine hundreth pounds by the yeere. For that he had found out (forsooth) an old record, (as he said) whereby he could prove, that in ancient time

Lawyer.

The Lordship of Denbigh and Leicesters oppression used therein.

E   long

long paft, that Lordfhip had yeelded fo much old rent: and therefore he would now enforce the prefent tenants, to make up fo much againe upon their lands, which they thought was againft all reafon for them to doe: but my Lord perforce, would have it fo, and in the end compelled them to yeeld to his will, to the impoverifhing of all the whole Countrey about.

The Manor of Killingworth, and Leycefters op-preffion there.

The like proceeding he ufed with the tenants about Killingworth, where he received the faid Lordfhip and Caftle from the Prince, in gift of twenty foure pounds yeerely rent or thereabout, hath made it now better then five hundreth by yeere: by an old record alfo, found by great fortune in the hole of a wall, as is given out (for he hath fingular good luck alwayes in finding out records for his purpofe) by vertue whereof, he hath taken from the tenants round about, their Lands, Woods, Paftures and Commons, to make himfelfe Parkes, Chaces, and other commodities therwith, to the fubverfion of many a good family, which was maintained there, before this devourer fet foot in that Countrey.

The caufe of Snowden foreft moft pitifull.

But the matter of Snowden Foreft, doth paffe all the reft, both for cunning and cruelty: the tragedy whereof was this, he had learned by his intelligencers abroad (whereof he had great ftore in every part of the Realme) that there was a goodly ancient Foreft in North wales, which hath almoft infinite borderers about the fame: for it lyeth in the middeft of the Countrey, beginning at the hils of Snowden (whereof it hath his name) in Carnarvanfhire, and reacheth every way towards divers other fhires. When my Lord heard of this, he entered prefently into the conceit of a fingular great prey: going to her Majefty, fignified that her highneffe was often times abufed,

abused, by the incroaching of such as dwelt upon
her Forests, which was necessary to be restrained;
and therefore beseeched her Majesty to bestow
upon him the incrochments only, which he should
be able to finde out upon the Forest of Snowden,
which was granted.

And thereupon he chose out Commissioners fit
for the purpose, and sent them into Wales, with
the like Commission as a certaine Emperour was
wont to give his Majestrates, when they departed
from him to governe, as *Suetonius* writeth, *Scitis* An old tyranni-
quid velim, & quibus opus habeo. You know what I call Commission
would have; and what I have need of. Which re-
commendation, these Commissioners taking to
heart, omitted no diligence in execution of the
same; and so going into Wales, by such meanes as
they used, of setting one man to accuse another;
brought quickly all the Countrey round about in
three or foure shires, within the compasse of Forest ground; and so entred upon the same, for my
Lord of *Leicesters.* Whereupon, when the people
were amazed, and expected what order my Lord
himselfe would take therein: his Lord was so far
off from refusing any part of that, which his Commissioners had presented and offered him: as he
would yet further stretch the Forest beyond the
Sea, into the Isle of Anglesey, and make that also A rediculous de-
within his compasse and bounder.   monstration of
                                                    excessive avarice
Which when the Commonalty saw, and that
they profited nothing by their complaining and
crying out of this tyranny: they appointed to
send some certaine number of themselves, to
London, to make supplication to the Prince:
and so they did; choosing out for that purpose a
dozen Gentlemen, and many more of the Commons of the Countrey of Llin, to deale for the
whole. Who coming to London, and exhibiting

a moſt humble ſupplication to her Majeſty for redreſſe of their oppreſſion : received an anſwer, by the procurement of my Lord of *Leiceſter*, that they ſhould have juſtice, if the commonalty would returne home to their houſes, and the Gentlemen remaine there, to ſolicite the cauſe. Which as ſoone as they had yeelded unto, the Gentlemen were all taken and caſt into priſon, and there kept for a great ſpace, and afterward were ſent downe to Ludlow, (as the place moſt eminent of all theſe Countries) there to weare papers of perjury, and receive other puniſhments of infamy, for their complaining : which puniſhments notwithſtanding, afterward upon great ſuit of the parties and their friends, were turned into great fines of money, which they were conſtrained to pay, and yet beſides to agree alſo with my Lord of *Leiceſter* for their owne lands, acknowledging the ſame to be his, and ſo to buy it of him againe.

A ſingular oppreſſion.

Wherby not onely theſe private Gentlemen, but all the whole Countrey thereabout, was and is (in a manner) utterly undone. And the participation of this injury, reacheth ſo far and wide, and is ſo generall in theſe parts, as you ſhall ſcarce finde a man that cometh from that coaſt, who feeleth not the ſmart thereof; being either impoveriſhed, beggered or ruinated thereby.

Leyceſter extreamly hated in Wales.

Whereby I aſſure you that the hatred of all that Countrey, is ſo univerſall and vehement againſt my Lord ; as I think never thing created by God, was ſo odious to that Nation, as the very name of my Lord of *Leiceſter* is. Which his Lordſhip well knowing, I doubt not, but that he will take heed how he go thither to dwell, or ſend thither his poſterity.

Gentleman.

For his poſterity (quoth the Gentleman) I ſuppoſe

pose he hath little cause to be solicitour; for that God himselfe taketh care commonly, that goods and honours so gotten and maintained, as his be, shall never trouble the third heire. Marry for himselfe, I confesse (the matter standing as you say) that he hath reason to forbeare that Country, and to leave off his building begun at Denbigh, as I heare say he hath done: for that the universall hatred of a people, is a perilous matter; and if I were in his Lordships case, I should often thinke of the end of *Nero*; who after all his glory, upon fury of the people was adjudged to have his head thrust into a Pilory, and so to be beaten to death with rods and thongs.

Or rather I should feare the successe of *Vitellius* the third Emperor after *Nero*, who for his wickednesse and oppression of the people, was taken by them at length, when fortune began to faile him, and led out of his Palace naked, with hooks of Iron fastned in his flesh, and so drawn through the City with infamy, where, loden in the streets with filth and ordure cast upon him, and a prick put under his chin, to the end he should not looke downe or hide his face, was brought to the banke of Tyber, and there, after many hundred wounds received, was cast into the river. So implacable a thing is the furour of a multitude, when it is once stirred, and hath place of revenge. And so heavy is the hand of God upon tyrants in this world, when it pleaseth his divine Majesty to take revenge of the same.

I have read in *Leander*, in his description of Italy, how that in Spoleto (if I be not deceived) the chiefe City of the Country of Umbria, there was a strange tyrant; who in the time of his prosperity, contemned all men, and forbare to injury no man that came within his claws; esteeming himself sure

The end of tyrants.

Nero.

Vitellius.

A most terrible revenge taken upon a tyrant.

F 3   enough

enough for ever being called to render account in this life, and for the next he cared little. But God upon the sudden turned upside-downe the wheele of his felicity, and cast him into the peoples hands; who tooke him, and bound his naked body upon a planke, in the Market-place, with a fire and iron-tongues by him: and then made proclamation, that seeing this man was not otherwise able to make satisfaction, for the publique injuries that he had done; every private person annoyed by him, should come in order, and with the hot-burning tongues there ready, should take of his flesh so much, as was correspondent to the injury received, as indeed they did untill the miserable man gave up the ghost, and after too: as this author writeth.

But to the purpose: seeing my Lord careth little for such examples, and is become so hardy now, as he maketh no account to injury and op-

Leyeesters op-presse whole Countries and Commonalties toge-
preffion of parti ther; it shall be bootlesse to speake of his pro-
cular men. ceedings towards particular men, who have not so great strength to resist, as a multitude hath. And yet I can assure you, that there are so many and so pitifull things published daily of his tyranny in this kinde; as doe move great compassion towards the party that doe suffer, and horrour against him who shameth not daily to offer such injury.

As for example: whose heart would not bleed to heare the case before mentioned of Master
Master Robinson *Robinson* of Staffordshire; a proper yong Gentle-man, and well given both in religion and other vertues; whose Father died at Newhaven, in her Majesties service, under this mans brother the Earle of Warwick; and recommended at his death this his eldest Son, to the special protection of *Leicester*

cester and his Brother, whose servant also this *Robinson* hath bin, from his youth upward, and spent the most of his living in his service. Yet notwithstanding all this, when *Robinsons* Lands were intangled with a certaine Londoner, upon interest for his former maintenance in their service, whose title my Lord of *Leicester* (though craftily, yet not covertly) under *Ferris* his cloak, had gotten to himselfe : he ceased not to pursue the poore Gentleman even to imprisonment, arraignment, and sentence of death, for greedinesse of the said living ; together with the vexation of his brother in law Master *Harcourt*, and all other his friends, upon pretence, forsooth, that there was a man slaine by *Robinsons* party, in defence of his owne possession against *Leicesters* intruders, that would by violence breake into the same.

Master Harcourt.

What shall I speake of others, whereof there would be no end ? as of his dealing with Master *Richard Lee*, for his Manor of Hooknorton (if I faile not in the name :) with Master *Ludowick Grivell*, by seeking to bereaue him of all his living at once, if the drift had taken place ? with *George Witney*, in the behalfe of Sir *Henry Leigh*, for inforcing him to forgoe the Controlership at Woodstock, which he holdeth by Patent from King *Henry* the seventh ? with my Lord *Barkley*, whom he enforced to yeeld up his lands to his brother *Warwick*, which his ancestors had held quietly for almost two hundreth yeeres together ?

M. Richard Lee.
Ludowick Grivel
George Witney.
Lord Barkley.

What shall I say of his intollerable tyranny upon the last Archbishop of Canterbury, for Doctor *Iulio* his sake, and that in so foule a matter ? Vpon Sir *Iohn Throgmarton*, whom he brought pitifully to his grave before his time, by continuall vexations, for a peece of faithfull service done by him to his Countrey, and to all the line

Archbishop of Canterbury.
Sir Iohn Throgmarton.

F 4   of

of King *Henry*, againſt this mans Father; in King *Edward* and Queen *Maries* dayes ? Upon divers of the *Lanes*; for one mans ſake of that name before mentioned, that offered to take Killingworth-Caſtle ? upon ſome of the *Giffords*, and other for *Thregmartons* ſake ? (for that is alſo his Lords diſpoſition, for one mans cauſe whom he brooketh not, to plague a whole generation, that any way pertaineth, or is allied to the ſame :) his endleſſe perſecuting of Sir *Drew Drewry*, and many other Courtiers, both men and women ? All theſe (I ſay) and many others, who daily ſuffer injuries, rapines and oppreſſions at his hands, throughout the Realme, what ſhould it availe to name them in this place ? ſeeing neither his Lord careth any thing for the ſame, neither the parties agrieved are like to attain any leaſt releaſe of affliction thereby, but rather double oppreſſion, for their complaining.

Wherefore to return again wheras we began ; you ſee by this little, who, and how great, & what manner of man, my Lord of *Leyceſter* is this day, in the ſtate of England. You ſee, and may gather, in ſome part, by that which hath bin ſpoken, his wealth, his ſtrength, his cunning, his diſpoſition. His wealth is exceſſive in all kinde of riches for a private man, and muſt needs be much more, then any body lightly can imagine, for the infinite wayes he hath had of gaine, ſo many yeeres together. His ſtrength and power is abſolute and irreſiſtable, as hath beene ſhewed both in Chamber, Court, Councell and Country. His cunning in plotting and fortifying the ſame, both by force and fraud, by Mines and countermines, by trenches, bulwarkes, flankers and rampiers : by friends, enemies, allies, ſervants, creatures, and dependents, or any other that may ſerve his turne; is very rare and

Lane.

Gifford.

Sir Drew Drewry

The preſent ſtate of my Lord of Leyceſter.

Leiceſters wealth

Leyceſt. ſtrength

Leyceſt. cunning

and singular: His difpofition to cruelty, murder, Leycefters dif-
treafon and tyranny : and by all thefe to fupream pofition.
Soveraignty over other, is moft evident and
cleare. And then judge you whether her Majefty that now raigneth (whofe life and profperity,
the Lord in mercy long preferve,) have not juft
caufe to feare, in refpect of thefe things onely ; if
there were no other particulars to prove his afpi-
ring intent befides ?

No doubt (quoth the Lawyer) but thefe are Lawyer.
great matters, in the queftion of fuch a caufe as is
a Crown And we have feen by example, that the
leaft of thefe four, which you have here named, or Caufes of iuft
rather fome little branch contained in any of feare for her
them, hath bin fufficient to found juft fufpicion, Maiefty.
diftruft or jealoufie, in the heads of moft wife
Princes, towards the proceedings of more affured
fubjects, then my Lord of Leycefter, in reafon may
be prefumed to be. For that the fafety of a ftate
and Prince, ftandeth not onely in the readineffe
and habilityof refifting open attempts, when they
fhall fall out ; but alfo (and that much more as
Statifts write) in a certaine provident watchful-
neffe, of preventing all poffibilities and likeli-
hoods of danger of fuppreffion, for that no Prince
commonly, will put himfelfe to the curtefie of
another man) be he never fo obliged) whether
he fhall retaine his Crowne or no : feeing
the caufe of a Kingdome, acknowledgeth neither kindred, duty, faith, friendfhip, nor fo-
ciety.

I know not whether I doe expound or declare
my felf well or no; but my meaning is, that wheras every Prince hath two points of affurance from
his fubject ; the one, in that he is faithfull, and
lacketh will to annoy his Soveraigne ; the other,
for

for that he is weake and wanteth ability to do the same: the first is alwayes of more importance then the second, and consequently more to be eyed and observed in policy: for that our will may be changed at our pleasure, but not our ability.

Considering then upon that which hath beene said and specified before, how that my Lord of *Leicester* hath possessed himself of all the strength, powers and sinewes of the Realme, hath drawne all to his own direction, and hath made his party so strong, as it seemeth not resistable: you have great reason to say, that her Majesty may justly conceive some doubt, for that if his will were according to his power, most assured it is, that her Majesty were not in safety.

Say not so, good sir, (quoth I) for in such a case truly, I would repose little upon his will, which is so many wayes apparant, to be most insatiable of ambition. Rather would I thinke that as yet his ability serveth not, either for time, place, force, or some other circumstance: then that any part of good will should want in him; seeing that not onely his desire of soveraignty, but also his intent and attempt to aspire to the same, is sufficiently declared (in my conceit) by the very particulars of his power and plots already set downe. Which if you please to have the patience, to heare a Scholars argument, I will prove by a principle of our Philosophy.

For if it be true which *Aristotle* saith, there is no agent so simple in the world, which worketh not for some finall end, (as the bird buildeth not her nest but to dwell and hatch her yong ones therein:) and not onely this, but also that the same agent, doth alwayes frame his worke according to the proportion of his intended end: (as when the Fox or Badger maketh a wide earth

or

Marginal notes:

A point of necessary policy for a Prince.

Scholar.

A philosophicall argument to prove Leycesters intent of soveraignty.

or den, it is a signe that he meaneth to draw thither great store of prey:) then must we also in reason thinke, that so wise and politick an agent, as is my Lord of *Leicester* for himselfe, wanteth not his end in these plottings and preparations of his; I meane an end proportionable in greatnesse to his preparations. Which end can be no lesse nor meaner then supreame Soveraignty, seeing his provision and furniture doe tend that way, and are in every point fully correspondent to the same.

What meaneth his so diligent besieging of the Princes person? his taking up the wayes and passages about her? his insolency in Court? his singularity in the Councell? his violent preparation of strength abroad? his enriching of his complices? the banding of his faction, with the abundance of friends every where? what doe these things signifie (I say) and so many other, as you have well noted and mentioned before; but onely his intent and purpose of Supremacy? What did the same things portend in times past in his Father, but even that which now they portend in the Sonne? Or how should we thinke, that the Son hath another meaning in the very same actions, then had his Father before him, whose steps he followeth. *The preparations of Leycester declare his intended end.*

I remember I have heard oftentimes of divers ancient and grave men in Cambridge, how that in King *Edwards* dayes the Duke of Northumberland this mans Father, was generally suspected of all men, to mean indeed as afterward he shewed, especially when he had once joyned with the house of *Suffolk*, and made himselfe a principall of that faction by marriage. But yet for that he was potent, and protested every where, and by all occasions his great love, duty, and speciall care, above all others, *How the Duke of Northumberland dissembled his end.*

others, that he bare towards his Prince & Country; no man durst accuse him openly, untill it was too late to withstand his power, (as commonly it falleth out in such affaires) and the like is evident in my Lord of *Leycesters* actions now (albeit to her Majesty, I doubt not, but that he will pretend and protest, as his Father did to her Brother) especially now after his open association with the faction of *Huntington*; which no lesse impugneth under this mans protection, the whole line of *Henry* the seventh for right of the Crowne, then the house of *Suffolke* did under his Father the particular progeny of King *Henry* the eight.

Nay rather much more (quoth the Gentleman) for that I doe not read in King *Edwards* raigne, (when the matter was in plotting notwithstanding) that the house of *Suffolke* durst ever make open claime to the next succession. But now the house of *Hastings* is become so confident, upon the strength & favor of their fautors, as they dare both plot, practice & pretend, all at once, and fear not to set out their title, in every place where they come.

And do they not fear the statute (said the Lawyer) so rigorous in this point, as it maketh the matter treason to determine of titles?

No: they need not (quoth the Gentleman) seeing their party is so strong and terrible, as no man dare accuse them: seeing also they well know, that the procurement of that Statute, was onely to endanger or stop the mouthes of the true Successors, whiles themselves in the meanespace went about under hand, to establish their owne ambushment.

Well: (quoth the Lawyer) for the pretence of my Lord of *Huntington* to the Crowne, I will not stand with you, for that it is a matter sufficiently known and seen throughout the Realme. As also that

---

Gentleman.

The boldnesse of the titlers of Clarence.

Lawyer.

Gentleman.
The abuse of the Statute for silence in the true succession.

Lawyer.

that my Lord of *Leyceste.* is at this day a principall favourer and patron of that cause, albeit some yeers past, he were an earnest adversary and enemy to the same. But yet I have heard some friends of his, in reasoning of these matters, deny stoutly a point or two, which you have touched here, and doe seeme to beleeve the same.

And that is, first, that howsoever my Lord of *Leicester* do meane to helpe his friend, when time shall serve, yet pretendeth he nothing to the Crowne himselfe. The second is that whatsoever may be meant for the title, or compassing the Crowne after her Majesties death, yet nothing is intended during her raigne. And of both these points they alledge reasons.

Two excuses alledged by Leycesters friends.

As for the first, that my Lord of *Leycester* is very well knowne to have no title to the Crowne himselfe, either by discent in blood, alliance or otherwayes. For the second, that his Lord. hath no cause to be a Malecontent in the present government, nor hope for more preferment, if my Lord of *Huntington* were King to morrow next, then he receiveth now at her Majesties hands; having all the Realme (as hath bin shewed) at his owne disposition.

For the first (quoth the Gentleman) whether he meane the Crowne for himself, or for his friend, it importeth not much; seeing both wayes it is evident, that he meaneth to have all at his owne disposition. And albeit now for the avoyding of envy, he give it out, as a crafty Fox, that he meaneth not but to run with other men, and to hunt with *Huntington* and other hounds in the same chase; yet is it not unlike, but that he will play the Beare, when he cometh to dividing of the pray, and will snatch the best part to himselfe. Yea, and these self same persons

Gentleman.

Whether Leycester meane the Crown sincerely for Huntington or for himselfe.

fons

sons of his traine and faction, whom you call his friend, though in publique, to excuse his doings, and to cover the whole plot, they will and must deny the matters to be so meant : yet otherwise they both thinke, hope and know the contrary, and will not stick in secret to speak it, and among themselves, it is their talke of consolation.

The words of the Lord North, to Master Pooly.

The words of his speciall Councellour the Lord *North*, are known, which he uttered to his trusty *Pooly*, upon the receit of a letter from Court, of her Majesties displeasure towards him, for his being a witnesse at *Leycesters* second marriage with Dame *Lettice* (although I know he was not ignorant of the first) at Wanstead : of which displeasure, this Lord making far lesse ac-compt then, in reason he should, of the just of-

Pooly told this to Sir Robert Iermine.

fence of his soveraigne, said : that for his owne part he was resolved to sinke or swimme with my Lord of *Leycester*, who (said he) if once the Cards may come to shuffling (I will use but his very own words) I make no doubt but he alone shall beare away the Bucklers,

The words of Sir Thomas Layton brother in law to my Lord.

The words also of Sir *Thomas Layton*, to Sir *Henry Nevile*, walking upon the Tarresse at Windsor are known, who told him, after long discourse of their happy conceived Kingdome, that hee doubted not, but to see him one day, hold the same office in Windsor, of my Lord of *Leycester*, which now my Lord did hold of the Queene. Meaning thereby the goodly office of Constable-ship, with all Royalties and honours belong-ing to the same, which now the said Sir *Henry* exerciseth onely as Deputy to the Earle. Which was plainely to signifie, that, he doubted not but to see my Lord of *Leycester* one day King, or els his other hope could never possibly take effect or come to passe.

To

To the same point tended the words of Mistresse *Anne West*, Dame *Lettice* sister, unto the Lady *Anne Askew*, in the great Chamber, upon a day when her brother *Robert Knowles* had danced disgratiously and scornfully before the Queen in presence of the French. Which thing for that her Majesty tooke to proceed of will in him, as for dislike of the strangers in presence, and for the quarrell of his sister *Essex*; it pleased her Majesty to check him for the same, with addition of a reproachfull word or two (full well deserved) as though done for despite of the forced absence from that place of honour, of the good old Gentlewoman (I mitigate the words) his sister. Which words, the other young twig receiving in deepe dudgen, brake forth in great choler to her forenamed companion, and said, That she nothing doubted, but that one day shee should see her sister, upon whom the Queene railed now so much (for so it pleased her to tearme her Majesties sharpe speech) to sit in her place and throne, being much worthier of the same, for her qualities and rare vertues, then was the other. Which undutifull speech, albeit it were over-heard and condemned of divers that sate about them; yet none durst ever report the same to her Majesty, as I have heard sundry Courtiers affirme, in respect of the revenge which the reporters should abide at my Lord of Leycesters hands, whensoever the matter should come to light.

And this is now concerning the opinion and secret speeches of my Lords owne friends, who cannot but utter their conceit and judgement in time and place convenient, whatsoever they are willed to give out publikely to the contrary, for deceiving of such as will beleeve faire painted words,

The words of Mistris Anne West sister unto this holy Countesse.

words, againſt evident and manifeſt demonſtrati-
on of reaſon.

Three arguments
of Leyceſters
meaning for
himſelfe before
Huntington.

I ſay reaſon, for that if none of theſe ſignes and
tokens were, none of theſe preparations nor any
of theſe ſpeeches and detections, by his friends
that know his heart ; yet in force of plain reaſon, I
could alleadge unto you three arguments onely,
which to any man of intelligence, would eaſily
perſwade and give ſatisfaction, that my Lord of
Leyceſter meaneth beſt and firſt for himſelfe in this
ſuit. Which three arguments, for that you ſeeme
to be attent ; I will not ſtick to run over in all
brevity.

The firſt argu-
ment, the Nature
of ambition.

And the firſt, is the very nature and quality of
ambition it ſelf, which is ſuch, (as you know) that
it never ſtayeth, but paſſeth from degree to degree
and the more it obtaineth, the more it covereth;
and the more eſteemeth it ſelfe, both worthy and
able to obtaine. And in our matter that now we
handle; even as in wooing, he that ſueth to a Lady for another, and obtaineth her good will, en-
tereth eaſily into conceit of his owne worthineſſe
thereby, and ſo commonly into hope of ſpeeding
himſelfe, while he ſpeaketh for his friend : ſo
much more in Kingdomes : he that ſeeth himſelf
of power to put the Crowne of another mans
head, will quickly ſtep to the next degree, which
is, to ſet it of his owne, ſeeing that alwayes the
charity of ſuch good men, is wont to be ſo orderly, as (according to the precept) it beginneth with
it ſelfe firſt.

Adde to this, that ambition is jealous, ſuſpitious
and fearfull of it ſelfe, eſpecially when it is joyned
with a conſcience loden with the guilt of many
crimes, whereof he would be loth to be called to
account, or be ſubject to any man that might by
authority take review of his life & actions, when it
ſhould

fhould pleafe him. In which kinde, feeing my Lord
of *Leycefter* hath fo much to encreafe his feare, as before hath beene fhewed by his wicked dealings: it is
not like, that ever hee will put himfelfe to another
mans courtefie, for paffing his audiĉt in particular
reckonings, which he can no way anfwer or fatisfie:
but rather will ftand upon the groffe Sum, and generall *Quietus eft*, by making himfelfe chiefe Au-
ditour, and Mafter of all accompts for his owne
part in this life, howfoever he do in the next: whereof fuch humours have little regard. And this is for
the nature of ambition in it felfe.

The fecond argument may bee taken from my
Lords particular difpofition : which is fuch, as may
give much light alfo to the matter in queftion: being a difpofition fo well liking and inclined to a
Kingdome, as it hath beene tampering about the
fame, from the firft day that hee came in favour.
Firft, by feeking openly to marry with the Queenes
Majeftie her felfe, and fo to draw the Crowne upon
his owne head, and to his pofterity. Secondly, when
that attempt tooke not place, then hee gave it out,
as hath beene fhewed before, how that he was privily contraĉted to her Majefty, (wherein as I told
you his dealing before for fatisfaction of a ftranger,
fo let him with fhame and difhonour remember now
alfo, the fpeĉtacle hee fecretly made for the per-
fwading of a fubjeĉt, and Counfellour of great honour in the fame caufe) to the end that if her Highneffe fhould by any way have mifcarried, then he
might have entituled any one of his owne brood,
(whereof he hath ftore in many places as is knowne)
to the lawfull fucceffion of the Crowne, under colour of that privy and fecret marriage, pretending
the fame to bee by her Majeftie : wherein hee
will want no witneffes to depofe what hee will.

G   Thirdly,

Marginal notes:

The fecond argument.
Leycefters particular difpofition.

Leycefters difpofition to tamper for a Kingdome.

I meane the noble old Earle of *Pembrooke.*

The unduti-
full devise
of Naturall
issue, in the
Statute of
succession.

Thirdly, when he saw also that this devise was subject to danger, for that his privy contract might
be denied more easily, then he able justly to prove
the same, after her Majesties decease: he had a new
fetch to strengthen the matter, and that was to
cause these words of (*Naturall issue*) to be put into the Statute of succession for the Crowne, against
all order and custome of our Realme, and against
the knowne common stile of Law, accustomed
to bee used in Statutes of such matter: whereby
hee might be able after the death of her Majesty,
to make ligitimate to the Crowne any one bastard
of his owne, by any of so many hacknies as he keepeth, affirming it to bee the *Naturall issue* of her
Majesty by himselfe. For no other reason can bee
imagined why the ancient usuall words of *Lawfull issue* should so cunningly bee changed into
Naturall issue; thereby not onely to indanger our
whole Realme with new quarrels of succession, but
also to touch (as farre as in him lyeth) the Royall
honour of his Soveraigne, who hath beene to him
but too bountifull a Princesse.

Fourthly, when after a time these fetches and devices began to be discovered, he changed straight
his course, and turned to the Papists and Scottish
faction, pretending the marriage of the Queene in
prison. But yet after this againe, finding therein
not such successe as contented him throughly, and
having in the meane space a new occasion offered
of baite; he betooke himselfe fitly to the party of
Huntington: having therein (no doubt) as good
meaning to himselfe, as his Father had by joyning
with *Suffolke.* Marry yet of late, he hath cast anew
about, once againe, for himselfe in secret, by trea-
The marriage ting the marriage of young *Arbella* with his Son,
of *Arbella.* intitled the Lord *Denbigh.*

So

So that by this we see the difposition of this man bent wholly to a fcepter. And albeit in right title, and difcent of bloud (as you fay) hee can juftly claime neither Kingdome nor Cottage (confidering either the bafeneffe or difloyalty of his Anceftours:) if in refpect of his prefent ftate and power, and of his naturall pride, ambition, and crafty conveyance, received from his Father, hee hath learned how to put himfelfe firft in poffeffion of chiefe rule, under other pretences, and after to devife upon the title at his leafure.

But now to come to the third argument: I fay more, and above all this, that the nature and ftate of the matter it felfe, permitteth not, that my Lord of *Leycefter* fhould meane fincerely the Crowne for *Huntington*; efpecially feeing there hath paffed betweene them fo many yeares of diflike and enmity: which albeit, for the time and prefent commodity, bee covered and preffed downe: yet by reafon and experience we know, that afterward when they fhall deale together againe in matters of importance, and when jealoufie fhall bee joyned to other circumftances of their actions, it is impoffible that the former miflike fhould not breake out in farre higher degree, then ever before.

The third argument.

The nature of the caufe it felfe.

As wee faw in the examples of the reconciliation, made betwixt this mans Father, and *Edward*, Duke of *Somerfet*, bearing rule under King *Edward* the fixt: and betweene *Richard* of *Torke*, and *Edmund* Duke of *Somerfet*, bearing rule in the time of King *Henry* the fixt. Both which Dukes of *Somerfet*, after reconciliation with their old, crafty, and ambitious enemies, were brought by the fame to their deftruction foone after. Whereof I doubt not, but my Lord of *Leycefter* will take good heed, in joyning

The nature of old reconciled enmity.

G 7   ning

ning by reconciliation with *Huntington* ; after so
long a breach : and will not be so improvident, as
to make him his soveraigne, who now is but his de-
pendent. He remembreth too well the successe of
the Lord *Stanley* , who helped King *Henry* the sea-
venth to the Crowne : of the Duke of *Buckingham*,
who did the same for *Richard* the third: of the Earle
of *warwicke*, who set up King *Edward* the fourth:
and of the three *Percies*, who advanced to the Scepter King *Henry* the fourth. All which Noblemen
upon occasions that after fell out , were rewarded
with death by the selfe same Princes, whom they
had preferred.

The reason
of *Machavell.*

And that not without reason, as Seignior *Machavell*, my Lords Counsellour affirmeth. For that
such Princes, afterward can never give sufficient
satisfaction to such friends, for so great a benefit
received. And consequently, least upon discontentment, they may chance to doe as much for others
against them, as they have done for them against
others: the surest way is, to recompence them with
such a reward, as they shall never after be able to
complaine of.

The meaning
of the Duke
of Northum-
berland with
Suffolke.

Wherefore I can never thinke that my Lord of
Leycester will put himselfe in danger of the like successe at *Huntingtons* hands : but rather will follow
the plot of his owne Father, with the Duke of *Suffolke*, whom no doubt, but hee meant onely to use
for a pretext and helpe, whereby to place himselfe
in supreame dignity, and afterward whatsoever had
befallen of the state, the others head could never
have come to other end, then it enjoyed. For if
Queene *Mary* had not cut it off, King *John* of *Northumberland* would have done the same in time,
and so all men doe well know, that were privy to
any of his cunning dealings.

And

And what *Huntingtons* secret opinion of *Leycester* is, (notwithstanding this outward shew of dependance) it was my chance to learne, from the mouth of a speciall man of that hasty King, who was his Ledger or Agent in *London*; and at a time falling in talke of his Masters title, declared that he had heard him divers times in secret, complaine to his Lady, (*Leycesters* sister) as greatly fearing that in the end, he would offer him wrong, and pretend some title for himselfe. *South-house.*

Well (quoth the Lawyer) it seemeth by this last point, that these two Lords are cunning practitioners in the art of dissimulation: but for the former whereof you speake, in truth, I have heard men of good discourse affirme, that the Duke of *Northumberland* had strange devises in his head, for deceiving of *Suffolke*, (who was nothing so fine as himselfe,) and for bringing the Crowne to his owne Family. And among other devises it is thought, that hee had most certaine intention to marry the Lady *Mary* himselfe, after once hee had brought her into his owne hands) and to have bestowed her Majestie that now is, upon some one of his children (if it should have beene thought best to give her life, (and so consequently to have shaken off *Suffolke* and his pedegree, with condigne punishment, for his bold behaviour in that behalfe. *Lawyer. The meaning of the D. of Northumberland towards the D. of Suffolke.*

Verily (quoth I) this had beene an excellent Stratageme, if it had taken place. But I pray you (Sir) how could himselfe have taken the Lady *Mary* to wife, seeing hee was at that time married to another? *Scholar.*

O (quoth the Gentleman) you question like a Schollar. As though my Lord of *Leycester* had not a wife alive, when hee first began to pretend marriage *Gentleman.*

riage

riage to the Queenes Majesty. Do not you remember the story of King *Richard* the third, who at such time as he thought best for the establishing of his title; to marry his owne Neece, that afterward was married to King *Henry* the seventh; how he caused secretly to be given abroad that his owne wife was dead, whom all the World knew to bee then alive, and in good health, but yet soone afterward she was seene dead indeed. These great personages in matters of such weight, as is a Kingdome, have priviledges to dispose of Womens bodies, marriages, lives and deaths; as shall be thought for the time most convenient.

The practise of King Richard for dispatching his Wife.

And what doe you thinke (I pray you) of this new *Triumvirat* so lately concluded about *Arbella*? (for so I must call the same, though one of the three persons bee no *Vir*, but *Virago*;) I meane of the marriage betweene young *Denbigh* and the little Daughter of *Lenox*, whereby the Father-in-law, the Grand-mother, and the Uncle of the new designed Queene, have conceived to themselves a singular triumphant raigne. But what doe you think may ensue hereof? is there nothing of the old plot of Duke *John* of *Northumberland* in this?

A new Triumvirat betweene Leycester, Talbot, and the Countesse of Shrewesbury.

Marry Sir, (quoth the Lawyer) if this be so, I dare assure you there is sequell enough pretended hereby. And first, no doubt but there goeth a deep drift, by the wife and sonne, against old *Abraham* (the Husband and Father) with the well-lined large pouch. And secondly, a farre deeper, by trusty *Robert* against his best Mistresse: but deepest of all by the whole Crew, against the designements of the hasty Earle; who thirsteth a Kingdome with great intemperance, and seemeth (if there were plaine dealing) to hope by these good people to quench shortly his drought.

Lawyer.

Huntington.

But

But either part, in truth, seeketh to deceive other: and therefore it is hard to say where the game in fine will rest.

Well, howsoever that be (quoth the Gentleman) *Gentleman.* I am of opinion, that my Lord of *Leycester* will use both this practise and many more, for bringing the Scepter finally to his owne head : and that he will **The sleights** not onely imploy *Huntington* to defeate *Scotland,* **of *Leycester*** and *Arbella* to defeate *Huntington* : but also would **for bringing** use the marriage of the Queene imprisoned, to de- **all to him-** feat them both, if she were in his hand : and any one **selfe.** of all three to dispossesse her Majesty that now is: as also the authority of all foure to bring it to him-selfe : with many other fetches, flings and friscoes besides, which simple men as yet doe not conceive.

And howsoever these two conjoyned Earles, doe **Scambling** seeme for the time to draw together, and to play **between *Ley-*** booty : yet am I of opinion, that the one will be- ***cester* & *Hun-*** guile the other at the upshot. And *Hastings*, for ***tington* at the** ought I see, when hee commeth to the scambling, **upshot.** is like to have no better luck by the Beare, then his Ancestour had once by the Boare. Who using his helpe first in murdering the Sonne and Heire of King *Henry* the sixt, and after in destroying the ***Richard* of** faithfull Friends and Kinsmen of King *Edward* ***Glocester, An.*** the fift, for his easier way to usurpation : made an **1. *Edw.* 5.** end of him also in the Tower, at the the very same day and houre, that the other were by his coun-sell destroyed in *Pontfret Castle.* So that where the Goale and price of the game is a Kingdome, there is neither faith, neither good fellowship, nor faire play among the *Gamesters.* And this shall be enough for the first point : (*viz.*) what good my Lord of *Leycester* meaneth to himselfe in respect of *Huntington.*

Touching the second, whether the attempt be

G 4 purpo-

purposed in her Majesties dayes or no, the matter is much lesse doubtfull, to him that knoweth or can imagine what a torment the delay of a Kingdome is, to such a one as suffereth hunger thereof, and feareth that every houre may breed some alteration, to the prejudice of his conceived hope. Wee see oftentimes that the childe is impatient in this matter, to expect the naturall end of his parents life. Whom, notwithstanding, by nature he is enforced to love: and who also by nature, is like long to leave this World before him: and after whose decease, hee is assured to obtaine his desire: but most certaine of dangerous event, if he attempt to get it, while yet his parent liveth. Which foure considerations are (no doubt) of great force to containe a child in duty, and bridle his desire: albeit sometimes not sufficient to withstand the greedy appetite of raigning.

Foure considerations. But what shall wee thinke, where none of these foure considerations do restraine? where the present Possessor is no parent? where she is like by nature, to out-live the expector? whose death must needs bring infinite difficulties to the enterprise? and in whose life-time the matter is most easie to be atchieved, under colour and authority of the present Possessor? shall we thinke that in such a case the ambitious man will over-rule his owne passion, and leese his commodity.

A thing worthy to be noted in ambitious men. As for that which is alleadged before, for my Lord in the reason of his Defenders: that his present state is so prosperous, as hee cannot expect better in the next change whatsoever should be: is of small moment, in the conceipt of an ambitious head, whose eye and heart is alwayes upon that, which he hopeth for, and enjoyeth not: and not upon that which already hee possesseth, be it never so good.

Especially

Especially in matters of honour and authority, it is an infallible rule, that one degree desired and not obtained, afflicteth more then five degrees already possessed, can give consolation : the story of Duke *Haman* confirmeth this evidently, who being the greatest subject in the World under King *Assuerus*, Histor. 5. after he had reckoned up all his pompe, riches, glory, and felicity to his friends, yet hee said, that all this was nothing unto him, untill he could obtaine the revenge which hee desired, upon *Mardichæus* his enemy : and hereby it commeth ordinarily to passe, that among highest in authority are found the greatest store of Male-contents, that most doe endanger their Prince and Countrey.

When the *Percies* took part with *Henry* of *Boling-* The *Percies.* *brooke*, against King *Richard* the second their lawfull Soveraigne : it was not for lack of preferment, for they were exceedingly advanced by the said King, and possessed the three Earledomes of *Northumberland, worcester,* and *Stafford* together, besides many other offices and dignities of honour.

In like sort, when the two *Neviles* tooke upon The two them to joyne with *Richard* of *Yorke*, to put downe *Neviles.* their most benigne Prince, King *Henry* the sixt : and after again in the other side, to put downe King *Edward* the fourth; it was not upon want of advancement: they being Earles both of *Salusbury* and *warwick*, and Lords of many notable places besides. But it was upon a vaine imagination of future fortune, whereby such men are commonly led : and yet had not they any smell in their nostrils of getting the Kingdome for themselves, as this man hath to prick him forward.

If you say that these men hated their Soveraigne, *Leycesters* haand that thereby they were led to procure his de-tred to her struction: the same I may answer of my Lord living, Majest-
though

though of all men he hath leaft caufe fo to do. But yet fuch is the nature of wicked ingratitude, that where it oweth moft, and difdaineth to be bound, there upon every little difcontentment, it turneth double obligation into triple hatred.

This he fhewed evidently in the time of his little difgrace, wherein hee not onely did diminifh, vilipend, and debafe among his friends, the ineftimable benefits hee hath received from her Majeftie, but alfo ufed to exprobrate his owne good fervices and merits, and to touch her highneffe with ingrate confideration and recompence of the fame; which behaviour, together with his hafty preparation to rebellion, and affault of her Majefties Royall perfon and dignity, upon fo fmall a caufe given, did well fhew what minde inwardly he beareth to his Soveraigne, and what her Majefty may expect, if by offending him, fhee fhould once fall within the compaffe of his furious pawes: feeing fuch a fmoke of difdaine could not proceed, but from a fierie fornace of hatred within.

And furely it is a wonderfull matter to confider what a little check, or rather the bare imagination of a fmall overthwart, may worke in a proud and difdainfull ftomacke. The remembrance of his marriage mifled, that hee fo much pretended and defired with her Majeftie, doth fticke deeply in his breaft, and ftirreth him daily to revenge. As alfo doth the difdaine of certaine checks and difgraces received at fometimes, efpecially that of his laft marriage: which irketh him fo much the more, by how much greater feare and danger it brought him into at that time; and did put his Widow in fuch open phrenfie, as fhee raged many moneths after againft her Majeftie, and is not cold yet, but remaineth as it were a fworne enemy for that injury,

injury, and ſtandeth like a fiend or fury at the elbow of her *Amadis* , to ſtirre him forward when occaſion ſhall ſerve. And what effect ſuch female ſuggeſtions may worke , when they finde an humour proud and pliable to their purpoſe , you may remember by the example of the Ducheſſe of *Somerſet* , who inforced her Husband to cut off the head of his onely deare Brother , to his owne evident deſtruction, for her contentation. The force of female ſuggeſtions.

Wherefore , to conclude this matter without further diſpute or reaſon : ſaying, there is ſo much diſcovered in the caſe as there is : ſo great deſire of raigne, ſo great impatience of delay, ſo great hope and hability of ſucceſſe , if it be attempted under the good fortune and preſent authority of the competitours : ſeeing the plots be ſo well laid , the preparation ſo forward, the favourers ſo furniſhed, the time ſo propitious, and ſo many other cauſes conviting together : ſeeing that by differing , all may be hazarded, and by haſtening, little can be indangered; the ſtate and condition of things well weyed : finding alſo the bands of duty ſo broken already in the conſpiratours, the cauſes of miſlike and hatred ſo manifeſt , and the ſolicitours to execution , ſo potent and diligent, as women, malice, and ambition, are wont to bee : it is more then probable, that they will not leeſe their preſent commodity, eſpecially ſeeing they have learned by their Archi-tipe or Proto-plot which they follow, (I meane the conſpiracy of *Northumberland* and *Suffolke* in King *Edwards* dayes) that herein there was ſome errour committed at that time , which overthrew the whole ; and that was, the deferring of ſome things untill after the Kings death , which ſhould have beene put in execution before. An evident concluſion that the execution is meant in time of her Maieſty.

An errour of the Father now to bee corrected by the Sonne.

For if in the time of their plotting; when as yet their

their defignements were not publifhed to the world, they had under the countenance of the King (as well they might have done) gotten into their hands the two Sifters, and difpatched fome other few affaires, before they had caufed the young Prince to die : no dobut, but in mans reafon the whole defignement had taken place : and confequently it is to be prefuppofed, that thefe men (being no fooles in their owne affaires) will take heed of falling into the like errour by delay : but rather will make all fure, by ftriking while the iron is hot, as our proverbe warneth them.

Lawyer. It cannot bee denied in reafon (quoth the Lawyer) but that they have many helpes of doing what they lift now, under the prefent a favour, countenance, and authority of her Majefty, which they fhould not have after her Highneffe deceafe : when each man fhali remaine more at liberty for his fupreame obedie   e, by reafon of the ftatute provided for the uncert.   ty of the next fucceffor: and therefore I for my part, would rather counfell them to make much of her Maje   life; for after that, they little know what may enfue, or befall their defignements.

Gentleman. They will make the moft thereof (quoth the Gentleman) for their owne advantage, but after that, what is like to follow, the examples of *Edward* and *Richard* the fecond, as alfo of *Henry* and *Edward* the fixt, doe fufficiently fore-warne us : whofe lives were prolonged, untill their deaths were thought more profitable to the confpiratours, and not longer. And for the ftatute you fpeak of, procured by themfelves, for eftablifhing the incertainty of the next true fucceffour, (whereas all our former ftatutes were wont to be made for the declaration and certainty of the fame) it is with *Provifo*, (as you know)

Her Majefties life and death, to ferve the confpiratours turne.

know) that it shall not endure longer then the life
of her Majesty, that now raigneth: that is, indeed,
no longer then untill themselves be ready to place
another. For then, no doubt, but wee shall see a *A Proclama-*
faire Proclamation, that my Lord of *Huntington* is *tion with*
the onely next-heire: with a bundle of halters to *halters.*
hang all such, as shall dare once open their mouth
for deniall of the same.

At these words the old Lawyer stepped back, as *Lawyer.*
somewhat astonied, and began to make Crosses in *Papisticall*
the ayre after their fashion, whereat we laughed; *blessing.*
and then he said, truly my Masters I had thought
that no man had conceived so evill imagination of
this statute as my selfe: but now I perceive that I
alone am not malitious. For my owne part, I must *The statute*
confesse unto you, that as often as I reade over this *of concea-*
statute, or thinke of the same (as by divers occasi- *ling the heire*
ons many times I doe) I feele my selfe much gree- *apparant.*
ved and afflicted in minde, upon feares which I
conceive what may be the end of this statute to our
Countrey, and what privy meaning the chiefe pro-
curers thereof might have for their owne drifts, a-
gainst the Realme and life of her Majestie that
now raigneth.

And so much more it maketh mee to doubt, for *Richard go-*
that in all our records of law, you shall not find (to *ing towards*
my remembrance) any one example of such a devise *Hierusalem,*
for concealing of the true inheritour: but rather in *began the*
all ages, states, and times, (especially from *Richard* *custome by*
the first downeward) you shall finde statutes, ordi- *as Polidore*
nances, and provisions, for declaration and mani- *noteth, Anno*
festation of the same, as you have well observed and *10. of Richard*
touched before. And therefore, this strange and new *the second, to*
devise must needs have some strange and unaccu- *declare the*
stomed meaning: and God of his mercy grant, that *next heire.*
it have not some strange and unexpected event.

In

The danger of our Countrey by concealing the next heire.

In sight of all men, this is already evident, that never Countrey in the world was brought into more apparent danger of utter ruine, then ours is at this day, by pretence of this Statute. For whereas there is no Gentleman so meane in the Realme, that cannot give a guesse more or lesse, who shall bee his next heire, and his Tenants soone conjecture, what manner of person shall be their next Lord: in the title of our noble Crown, whereof all the rest dependeth; neither is her Majesty permitted to know or say, who shall be her next successor, nor her subjects allowed to understand or imagine, who in right may be their future Soveraigne: An intollerable injury in a matter of so singular importance.

Great inconveniences.

For (alas) what should become of this our native Countrey, if God should take from us her most excellent Majesty (as once he will) and so leave us destitute upon the sudden, what should become of our lives, of our states, and of our whole Realme or governement? can any man promise himselfe one day longer, of rest, peace, possession, life or liberty within the land, then God shall lend us her Majesty to raigne over us? Which albeit, wee doe and are bound to wish that it may bee long: yet reason telleth us, that by course of nature, it cannot bee of any great continuance, and by a thousand accidents it may be much shorter. And shall then our most noble Common-wealth and Kingdome, which is of perpetuity, and must continue to our selves and our posterity, hang onely upon the life of her Highnesse alone, well strucken in yeares, and of no great good health, or robustious and strong complexion?

Sir Christopher Hattons Oration.

I was within hearing some six or seaven yeares agoe, when Sir Christopher Hatton, in a very great assembly, made an eloquent oration (which after I

wene

wene was put in print) at the pardoning and delivery of him from the gallowes, that by errour (as
was thought) had difcharged his peece upon her
Majefties Barge, and hurt certaine perfons in her
Highneffe prefence. And in that Oration he declared and defcribed very effectually, what ineftimable dammage had enfued to the Realme, if her Majefty by that or any other means fhould have beene
taken from us. He fet forth moft lively before the
eyes of all men, what divifion, what diffenfion, what
bloudfhed had enfued, & what fatall dangers were
moft certaine to fall upon us, whenfoever that dolefull day fhould happen: wherein no man fhould be
fure of his life, of his goods, of his wife, of his children: no man certain whether to flie, whom to follow, or where to feeke repofe or protection.

And as all the hearers there prefent did eafily grant
that he therein faid truth, and farre leffe then might
have beene faid in that behalfe, things ftanding as
they doe: fo many one (I trow) hath heard thefe
words proceed from a Councellour, that had good
caufe to know the ftate of his own Countrey, entred
into this cogitation, what punifhment they might
deferve then, at the whole State and Common- **Intollerable**
wealths hands, who firft by letting her Majefty from **Treafons.**
marriage, and then by procuring this Statute of
diffembling the next inheritour, had brought their
Realme into fo evident and inevitable dangers? for
every one well confidered and weighed with himfelfe, that the thing which yet only letted thefe dangers and miferies fet downe by Sir *Chriftopher*, muft
neceffarily one day faile us all, that is, the life of her
Majefty now prefent: and then (fay we) how falleth it out, that fo generall a calamity as muft needs
overtake us ere it be long (and may, for any thing
we know to morrow next) is not provided for, afwell
as fore-feene.   Is

Is there no remedy, but that wee must willingly and wittingly runne into our owne ruine ? and for the favour or feare of some few afpirours, betray our Countrey, and the bloud of so many thousand innocents as live within the land ?

The miseries to follow upon her Majesties death. For tell mee (good Sirs) I pray you, if her Majestie should die to morrow next (whose life God long preserve and blesse,) but if she should be taken from us, (as by condition of nature and humane frailty she may) what would you doe ? which way would you looke ? or what head or part knew any good subject in the Realme to follow? I speake not of the conspiratours, for I know they will bee ready and resolved whom to follow : but I speake of the plaine, simple, and well-meaning subject, who following now the utter letter of this fraudulent statute, (fraudulent I meane in the secret conceipt of the cunning afpirours:) shall bee taken at that day upon the sudden, and being put in a maze by the unexpected contention about the Crowne, shall be brought into a thousand dangers, both of body and goods, which now are not thought upon by them who are most in danger of the same. And this is for the Common-wealth and Countrey.

The danger to her Majesty by this statute. But unto her Majesty, for whose good and safety the statute is onely pretended to be made, no doubt but that it bringeth farre greater dangers then any devise that they have used besides. For hereby under colour of restraining the claimes and titles of true successours, (whose endeavours notwithstanding, are commonly more calme and moderate then of usurpers,) they make unto themselves, a meane to forster and set forward their owne conspiracy without controlement : seeing no man of might may oppose himselfe against them, but with suspiti-

on;

on, that he meaneth to claime for himselfe. And so
they being armed on the one side, with their authority and force of present fortune, and defended on
the other side, by the pretence of the statute : they
may securely worke and plot at their pleasure, as
you have well proved before that they doe. And
whensoever their grounds and foundations shall be
ready, it cannot be denied, but that her Majesties
life lyeth much at their discretion, to take it, or use
it, to their best commodity : (and there is no doubt
but they will,) as such men are wont to doe in such
affaires. Marry one thing standeth not in their
powers so absolutely, and that is, to prolong her
Majesties dayes, or favour towards themselves, at
their pleasures : whereof it is not unlike but they
will have due consideration, least perhaps upon any
sudden accident, they might be found unready.

They have good care thereof I can assure you, *Gentleman.*
(quoth the Gentleman) and meane not to bee
prevented by any accident, or other mishap whatsoever : they will bee ready for all events : and
for that cause, they hasten so much their prepa- The hast-
rations at this day, more then ever before : by ning of the
sending out their spies and sollicitours every- Conspira-
where, to prove and confirme their friends, by tours.
delivering their common watch-word : by complaining on all hands of our Protestants Bishops
and Clergy, and of all the present state of our ir-
reformed Religion, (as they call it:) by amplifying
onely the danger of Papists and Scottish faction :
by giving out openly that now her Majesty is past
hope of Child-birth, and consequently, seeing God
hath given no better successe that way in two Women one after the other : it were not convenient(say
they) that another of that sexe should ensue, with
high commendation of the Law *Salick* in *France,*

where-

whereby women are forbidden to fucceed. Which fpeech, though in fhew it be delivered againft the Queen of *Scots*, and other of King *Henry* the feventh his line, that difcend of Sifters : yet all men fee that it toucheth as well the difabling of her Majefty, that is prefent, as others to come : and fo tendeth directly to Maturation of the principall purpofe, which I have declared before.

Schollar.

Here faid I, for the reft which you fpeake of, befides the Watch-word, it is common and every where treated in talke among them : but yet for the Watch-word it felfe (for that you name it) I thinke (Sir) many know it not, if I were the firft that told you the ftory, as perchance I was. For in truth I came to it by a rare hap (as then I told you) the thing being uttered and expounded by a Baron of their owne faction, to another Noble man of the fame degree and religion, though not of the fame opinion in thefe affaires. And for that I am requefted not to utter the fecond, who told it me in fecret, I muft alfo fpare the name of the firft, which otherwife I would not; nor the time and place where he uttered the fame.

The Watch-word of the Confpiratours.

Lawyer.

To this (faid the Lawyer) you doe well in that : but yet I befeech you, let me know this Watch-word (if there bee any fuch) for mine inftruction and helpe when need fhall require. For I affure you that this Gentlemans former fpeech of halters hath fo terrified mee, as if any fhould come and aske, or feele my inclination in thefe matters, I would anfwer them fully to their good contentment, if I knew the Watch-word whereby to know them. For of all things, I love not to bee hanged for quarrels of Kingdomes.

Schollar.
Are you fetled,

This Watch-word is, (faid I) *whether you be fetled or no ?* and if you anfwer yea, and feeme to underftand

derftand

derstand the meaning thereof: then are you knowne to be of their faction, and so to bee accompted and dealt withall for things to come. But if you stagger or doubt in answering, as if you knew not perfectly the mistery, (as the Nobleman iny good Lord did, imagining that it had beene meant of his religion, which was very well knowne to be good, and setled in the Gospell) then are you discried thereby, either not to be of their side, or else to be but a Punie not well instructed; and consequently, he that moveth you the question, will presently break off that speech, and turne to some other talke, untill afterward occasion be given to perswade you, or else instruct you better in that affaire. A great mistery.

Marry the Noble man, whereof I spake before, perceiving by the demanding, that there was some mistery in covert, under the question: tooke hold of the words, and would not suffer the propounder to slip away (as he endeavoured) but with much intreaty brought him at length to expound the full meaning and purpose of the riddle. And this was the first occasion (as I thinke) whereby this secret came abroad. Albeit afterwards at the publique Communions, which were made throughout so many Shires, the matter became more common: especially among the strangers that inhabite (as you know) in great numbers with us at this day. All which (as they say) are made most assured to this faction, and ready to assist the same with great forces at all occasions.

Good Lord (quoth the Lawyer) how many misteries and secrets be there abroad in the world, whereof we simple men know nothing, and suspect lesse. This Watch-word should I never have imagined: and for the great & often assemblies, under pretence of Communions, though of themselves, and of their Lawyer, Assemblies at Communions.

H 2 owne

owne nature, they were unaccuftomed, and confequently fubject to fufpition, yet I did never conceive fo farre forth as now I doe : as neither of the
lodging and entertaining of fo many ftrangers in
the Realme, whereof our Artizans doe complaine
every-where. But now I fee the reafon thereof,
which (no doubt) is founded upon great policy for
the purpofe. And by this alfo I fee that the houfe of
Huntington prefleth farre forward for the game,
and fhouldreth neare the goale to lay hands upon
the fame. Which to tell you plainly, liketh me but
a little : both in refpect of the good will I beare to
the whole Line of King *Henry*, which hereby is like
to be difpofleffed ; as alfo for the mifery which I doe
fore-fee, muft necefsarily enfue upon our Countrey,
if once the challenge of *Huntington* take place in
our Realme. Which challenge being derived from
the title of *Clarence* onely in the Houfe of *Yorke*, before the union of the two great Houfes : raifeth up
againe the old contention betweene the Families of
Yorke and *Lancafter*, wherein fo much *Englifh* bloud
was fpilt in times paft, and much more like to bee
powred out now, if the fame contention fhould bee
fet on foot againe. Seeing that to the controverfie
of Titles, would bee added alfo the controverfie of
Religion, which of all other differences is moft
dangerous.

Sir (quoth the Gentleman) now you touch a
matter of confequence indeed, and fuch as the very
naming thereof maketh my heart to fhake and tremble. I remember well what *Philip Cominus* fetteth
downe in his Hiftory of our Countries calamity, by
that contention of thofe two Houfes, diftinguifhed
by the Red Rofe and the White : but yet both in
their Armes might juftly have borne the colour of
Red, with a fierie fword in a black field ; to fignifie
the

Strangers within the Land.

The perill of our Counrrey if *Huntingtons* claime take place.

Gentleman.

le Red Rofe & the White.

the abundance of bloud and mortality which enſued in our Countrey, by that moſt wofull and cruell contention.

I will not ſtand here to ſet downe the particulars, obſerved & gathered by the foreſaid author, though a ſtranger, which for the moſt part he ſaw himſelfe, while hee lived about the Duke of *Burgundy*, and King *Lewes* of *France*, of that time: namely the pittifull deſcription of divers right Noble men of our Realme, who beſides all other miſeries, were driven to begge openly in forraine Countries, and the like. Mine owne obſervation in reading over our Country affaires, is ſufficient to make me abhorre the memory of that time, and to dread all occaſion that may lead us to the like in time to come: ſeeing that in my judgement, neither the Civill warres of *Marius* and *Silla*, or of *Pompey* and *Cæſar* among the *Romanes*, nor yet the *Guelphians* and *Gibilines* among the *Italians*, did ever worke ſo much woe, as this did to our poore Countrey. Wherein by reaſon of the contention of *Yorke* and *Lancaſter*, were foughten ſixteene or ſeventeen pitched fields, in leſſe then an hundred yeares. That is, from the eleventh or twelfth yeare of King *Richard* the ſecond his raigne, (when this controverſie firſt began to bud up) unto the thirteenth yeare of K. *Henry* the ſeventh. At what time by cutting off the chiefe titler of *Huntingtons* houſe, to wit, yong *Edward Plantaginet* Earle of *warwick*, Son and Heire to *George*, Duke of *Clarence*, the contention moſt happily was quenched and ended, wherein ſo many fields (as I have ſaid) were foughten between Brethren and Inhabitants of our owne Nation. And therein, and otherwiſe onely about the ſame quarrel, were ſlain, murdered, and made away, about nine or ten Kings, and Kings Sonnes; beſides above forty Earles, Marqueſſes, and Dukes of name:

but

The miſery of England by the contention betweene Yorke and Lancaſter.

Guelphians and Gibilines

Edward Plantaginet Earle of Warwick.

H 3

but many more Lords, Knights, and great Gentlemen and Captaines: and of the Common people without number, and by particular conjecture very neare two hundred thousand. For that in one Battell, fought by King *Edward* the fourth, there are recorded to be slaine on both parts, five and thirty thousand seven hundred and eleven persons, besides others wounded and taken prisoners, to be put to death afterward, at the pleasure of the Conquerour: at divers Battels after, ten thousand slaine at a Battell. And in those of *Barnet* and *Tukesbury,* fought both in one yeare.

This suffered our afflicted Country in those dayes, by this unfortunate and deadly contention, which could never be ended, but by the happy conjunction of those two Houses together, in *Henry* the seventh: neither yet so (as appeareth by Chronicle) untill (as I have said) the state had cut off the issue male of the Duke of *Clarence,* who was cause of divers perils to King *Henry* the seventh, though he were in prison. By whose Sister the faction of *Huntington* at this day, doth seeke to raise up the same contention againe, with farre greater danger both to the Realme and to her Majesty that now raigneth, then ever before.

And for the Realme it is evident, by that it giveth roome to strangers, Competitours of the House of *Lancaster:* better able to maintaine their owne title by sword, then ever was any of that linage before them. And for her Majesties perill present, it is nothing hard to conjecture: seeing the same title in the fore-said Earle of *warwick,* was so dangerous and troublesome to her Grandfather (by whom she holdeth) as hee was faine twice to take armes in defence of his right, against the said title, which was in those dayes preferred and advanced by the friends

of

The Battell by Tadcaster on Palme Sunday, An. 1460.

The danger of Huntingtons claime, to the Realme, and to her Majesty.

of *Clarence*, before that of *Henry*: as also this of *Huntington* is at this day, by his faction, before that of her Majesty though never so unjustly.

Touching *Huntingtons* title, before her Majesty, *Lawyer.* (quoth the Lawyer) I will say nothing : because in reason, I see not by what pretence in the World, he may thrust himselfe so farre forth : seeing her Majesty is descended, not onely of the House of *Lancaster*, but also before him most apparently from *How Huntington maketh his title before her Majesty.* the House of *Yorke* it selfe, as from the eldest Daughter of King *Edward* the fourth, being the eldest Brother of that House. Whereas *Huntington* claimeth onely by the Daughter of *George* Duke of *Clarence*, the younger Brother. Marry yet I must confesse, that if the Earle of *warwicks* title were better then that of King *Henry* the seventh, (which is most false, though many attempted to defend the same by sword;) then hath *Huntington* ** The most of Huntingtons Ancestors by whom hee maketh title, attainted of Treason.* some wrong at this day by her Majesty. Albeit in very truth, the * attaints of so many of his Ancestours by whom he claimeth, would answer him also sufficiently in that behalfe, if his title were otherwise allowable.

But I know besides this, they have another fetch *The infamous device of king Richard the third, allowed by Huntington.* of King *Richard* the third, whereby he would needs prove his elder Brother King *Edward* to bee a Bastard : and consequently his whole line, aswell male as female to be void. Which devise though it be ridiculous, and was at that time when it was first invented : yet, as *Richard* found at that time a Doctor *Shaw*, that shamed not to publish and defend the same, at *Pauls* Crosse in a Sermon : and *John* of Northumberland my Lord of *Leycesters* Father found out *Anno 1. Mariæ.* divers Preachers in his time, to set up the title of *Suffolke*, & to debase the right of K. *Henries* daughter, both in *London*, *Cambridge*, *Oxford*, and other places,

H 4 most

most apparently against all Law and reason: so I doubt not but these men would finde out also both *Shawes*, *Sands*, and others, to set out the title of *Clarence*, before the whole interest of King *Henry* the seventh and his posterity, if occasion served. Which is a point of importance to bee considered by her Majesty; albeit for my part, I meane not not now to stand thereupon, but onely upon that other of the House of *Lancaster*, as I have said.

A point to be noted by her Majesty.

For as that most honourable, lawfull, and happy conjunction of the two adversary Houses, in King *Henry* the seventh and his Wife, made an end of the shedding of *English* bloud within it selfe, and brought us that most desired peace, which ever since wee have enjoyed, by the raigne of their two most noble issue: so the plot that now is in hand, for the cutting off the residue of that issue, and for recalling backe of the whole Title to the House of *Yorke* againe; is like to plung us deeper then ever in civile discord, and to make us the bait of all forraine Princes: seeing there be among them at this day, some of no small power (as I have said) who pretend to bee the next heires by the House of *Lancaster*: and consequently, are not like to give over or abandon their owne right, if once the doore bee opened to contention for the same, by disanulling the Line of King *Henry* the seventh: wherein onely the keyes of all concord remaine knit together.

The joyning of both houses.

The Line of Portugall.

And albeit I know well that such as be of my Lord of *Huntingtons* party, will make small accompt of the Title of *Lancaster*, as lesse rightfull a great deale then that of *Yorke*, (and I for my part meane not greatly to avow the same, as now it is placed, being my selfe no favourer of forraine Titles:) yet indifferent men have to consider how it was taken in

H

times

times paſt, and how it may againe in time to come,
if contention ſhould ariſe : how many Noble perſo- The old eſti-
nages of our Realme did offer themſelves to die in mation of the
defence thereof : how many Oaths and Lawes were Houſe of Lan-
given and received throughout the Realme for caſter.
maintenance of the ſame, againſt the other Houſe of
Yorke for ever : how many worthy Kings were crowned, and raigned of that Houſe and Race; to wit, the
foure moſt Noble Henries, one after another ; the
fourth, the fitt, the ſixt, and the ſeventh : who both
in number, government, ſanctity, courage, and feats
of armes, were nothing inferiour (if not ſuperiour)
to thoſe of the other Houſe and Line of Yorke, after
the diviſion betweene the Families.

It is to bee conſidered alſo as a ſpeciall ſigne of
the favour and affection of our whole Nation unto
that Family : that Henry Earle of Richmond, though Henry Earle
diſcending but of the laſt Sonne, and third Wife of of Richmond.
John of Gaunt, Duke of Lancaſter, was ſo reſpe-
cted for that onely by the univerſall Realme : as
they inclined wholly to call him from baniſhment,
and to make him King with the depoſition of Richard, which then ruled of the Houſe of Yorke, upon
condition onely, that the ſaid Henry ſhould take to
Wife a Daughter of the contrary Family : ſo great
was in thoſe dayes the affection of Engliſh hearts towards the Line of Lancaſter, for the great worthineſſe of ſuch Kings as had raigned of that Race,
how good or bad ſoever their Title were : which I
ſtand not here at this time to diſcuſſe, but onely to
inſinuate what party the ſame found in our Realme
in times paſt; and conſequently, how extreame dangerous the contention for the ſame may be hereaf- The Line of
ter : eſpecially, ſeeing that at this day the remainder Portugall.
of that Title is pretended to reſt wholly in a ſtranger, whoſe power is very great. Which we Lawyers

are wont to esteeme as a point of no small importance, for justifying of any mans title to a Kingdome.

You Lawyers want not reason in that Sir (quoth I) howsoever you want right: for if you will examine the succession of governements, from the beginning of the World untill this day, either among Gentile, Jew, or Christian people, you shall finde that the sword hath beene alwayes better then halfe the title, to get, establish, or maintaine a Kingdome: which maketh me the more apalled to heare you discourse in such sort of new contentions, and forraine titles, accompanied with such power and strength of the titlers, which cannot bee but infinitely dangerous and fatall to our Realme, if once it come to action; both for the division that is like to be at home, and the variety of parties from abroad. For as the Prince whom you signifie, will not faile (by all likelyhood) to pursue his title with all forces that hee can make, if occasion were offered: so reason of state and policy will enforce other Princes adjoyning, to let and hinder him therein what they can: and so by this meanes shall we become *Juda* and *Israel* among our selves, one killing and vexing the other with the sword: and to forraine Princes we shall be, as the Iland of *Salamina* was in old time to the *Athenians* and *Megatians*: and as the Iland of *Cicilia* was afterward to the *Grecians*, *Carthaginians*, and *Romans*: and as in our dayes, the Kingdome of *Naples* hath beene to the *Spaniards*, *French-men*, *Germans*, and *Venetians*; That is, a bait to feed upon, and a game to fight for.

Wherefore, I beseech the Lord, to avert from us all occasions of such miseries. And I pray you Sir, for that wee are fallen into the mention of these matters,

matters, to take so much paines as to open unto me the ground of these controversies, so long now quiet betweene *Yorke* and *Lancaster*: seeing they are now like to bee raised againe. For albeit in generall I have heard much thereof, yet in particular, I either conceive not, or remember not the foundation of the same : and much lesse the state of their severall titles at this day, for that it is a study not properly pertaining unto my profession.

The controversie betweene the Houses of *Yorke* **Lawyer.** and *Lancaster* (quoth the Lawyer) took his actuall beginning in the issue of King *Edward* the third, **The begin-** who died somewhat more then two hundred yeares **ning of the** agone : but the occasion, pretence, or cause of that **controversie** quarrell, began in the children of King *Henry* **and** *Lancaster.* the third, who died an hundred yeares before that, and left two Sonnes ; *Edward*, who was King after him, by the name of *Edward* the first, and was Grandfather to *Edward* the third : and *Edmond* (for his deformity called Crookebacke) Earle of *Lancaster*, and beginner of that House, whose inheritance afterward in the fourth discent, fell upon a Daughter named *Blanch*, who was married to the fourth Son of King *Edward* the third, named *John* of *Gaunt*, for that he was borne in the City of *Gaunt* in *Flanders*, and so by this his first wife, hee became Duke of *Lancaster*, and heire of that House. And for *Edmond Crook-* that his Son *Henry* of *Bolingbrooke* (afterward cal- *back* beginner led King *Henry* the fourth) pretended among other of the House things, that *Edmond Crookeback*, great Grandfather of *Lancaster.* to *Blanch* his mother, was the elder Sonne of King *Blanch.* *Henry* the third, and unjustly put by the inheritance of the Crowne, for that he was Crook-backed *John of Gaunt.* and deformed : hee tooke by force the Kingdome from *Richard* the second, Nephew to King *Edward* the third, by his first Sonne ; and placed the same

in

How the King in the House of *Lancaster*, where it remained for dome was three whole difcents, untill afterward, *Edward* firſt brought Duke of *Yorke* defcended of *Iohn* of *Gaunts* yonger to the Houfe brother, making claime to the Crowne by title of of *Lancaster*. his Grandmother, that was heire to *Lionel*, Duke of *Clarence*, *Iohn* of *Gaunts* elder Brother, tooke the fame by force from *Henry* the fixt, of the Houfe of *Lancaster*, and brought it backe againe to the Houfe of *Yorke*: where it continued with much trouble in two Kings onely, untill both Houfes were joyned together in King *Henry* the feventh, and his noble iffue.

Hereby wee fee how the iffue of *Iohn* of *Gaunt*, Duke of *Lancaster*, fourth Son to King *Edward* the third, pretended right to the Crowne by *Edmond* *Crookebacke*, before the iffue of all the other three Sonnes of *Edward* the third, albeit they were the elder Brothers, whereof wee will fpeake more hereThe iffue of after. Now *Iohn* of *Gaunt* though hee had many *Iohn* of *Gaunt*. children, yet had he foure onely, of whom iffue remaine, two Sonnes and two Daughters. The firſt Son was *Henry* of *Bolingbrooke*, Duke of *Lancaster*, who tooke the Crowne from King *Richard* the fecond, his Unkles Sonne, as hath beene faid; and firſt of all planted the fame in the Houfe of *Lancaster*: where it remained in two difcents after him, that is, in his Son *Henry* the fift, and in his Nephew *Henry* the fixt, who was afterward deſtroyed, together with *Henry* Prince of *wales*, his onely Sonne and Heire, and confequently all that Line of *Henry Bolingbrooke* extinguifhed, by *Edward* the fourth of the Houfe of *Yorke*.

The other Son of *Iohn* of *Gaunt*, was *Iohn*, Duke The pedegree of *Somerfet*, by *Katherine Sfinsford*, his third wife: of king *Henry* which *Iohn* had iffue another *Iohn*, and he, *Margaret* the feventh. his Daughter and Heire, who being married to *Ed-*

mond

mond *Tyder*, Earle of *Richmond*, had iſſue *Henry*
Earle of *Richmond*, who after was named King *Henry* the ſeventh, whoſe Line yet endureth.

The two Daughters of *John* of *Gaunt* were married to *Portugall* and *Caſtile* : that is, *Philip* borne of *Blanch*, Heire to *Edmond Crookeback*, as hath beene ſaid, was married to *Iohn* King of *Portugall*, of whom is deſcended the King that now poſſeſſeth *Portugall*, and the other Princes which have or may make title to the ſame : and *Katherin* borne of *Conſtance*, Heire of *Caſtile*, was married back againe to *Henry* King of *Caſtile* in *Spaine*, of whom King *Philip* is alſo deſcended. So that by this, wee ſee where the remainder of the Houſe of *Lancaſter* reſteth, if the Line of King *Henry* the ſeventh were extinguiſhed : and what pretext forraine Princes may have to ſubdue us, if my Lord of *Huntington* either now, or after her Majeſties dayes, will open to them the doore, by ſhutting out the reſt of King *Henries* Line, and by drawing backe the title to the onely Houſe of *Yorke* againe : which he pretendeth to doe, upon this that I will now declare.

King *Edward* the third, albeit he had many children, yet five onely will we ſpeake of at this time : Whereof three were elder then *Iohn* of *Gaunt*, and one yonger. The firſt of the elder was named *Edward* the blacke Prince, who died before his Father, leaving one onely Sonne named *Richard*, who afterward being King, and named *Richard* the ſecond, was depoſed without iſſue, and put to death by his Coſin germain, named *Henry Bolingbrooke*, Duke of *Lancaſter*, Son to *Iohn* of *Gaunt*, as hath beene ſaid; and ſo there ended the Line of King *Edwards* firſt Sonne.

King *Edwards* ſecond Sonne, was *william* of *Hatfield*, that died without iſſue.

His

His third Sonne was *Leonell* Duke of *Clarence*, whose onely Daughter and Heire called *Philip*, was married to *Edmond Mortimer* Earle of *March* : and after that, *Anne* the Daughter and Heire of *Mortimer*, was married to *Richard Plantaginet*, Duke of *Yorke*, Son and Heire to *Edmond* of *Langley*, the first Duke of *Yorke* : which *Edmond* was the fift Son of King *Edward* the third, and younger Brother to *John* of *Gaunt*. And this *Edmond* of *Langley* may bee called the first beginner of the House of *Yorke* : even as *Edmond Crookback*, the beginner of the House of *Lancaster*.

Two Edmonds the two beginners of the two Houses of Lancaster and Yorke.

This *Edmond Langley*, then having a Sonne named *Richard*, that married *Anne Mortimer*, sole Heire to *Leonell* Duke of *Clarence*, joyned two Lines and two Titles in one : I meane the Line of *Leonell*, and of *Edmond Langley*, who were (as hath bin said) the third and the fift Sonnes to King *Edward* the third. And for this cause, the childe that was borne of this marriage, named after his Father *Richard Plantaginet*, Duke of *Yorke*, seeing himselfe strong, and the first Line of King *Edward* the thirds eldest Son to be extinguished in the death of King *Richard* the second : and seeing *william* of *Hatfield* the second Sonne dead likewise without issue : made demand of the Crowne for the House of *Yorke*, by the title of *Leonell* the third Sonne of King *Edward*. And albeit hee could not obtaine the same in his dayes, for that hee was slaine in a Battell against King *Henry* the sixt at *Wakefield* : yet his Sonne *Edward* got the same, and was called by the name of King *Edward* the fourth.

The claime and title of Yorke.

This King at his death left divers children, as namely two Sonnes, *Edward* the fift and his Brother, who after were both murdered in the Tower, as shall be shewed : and also five Daughters: to wit, *Elizabeth*,

The issue of king Edward the fourth.

Elizabeth, Cicily, Anne, Katherine, and *Briget*.
Whereof, the first was married to *Henry* the seventh.
The last became a Nunne, and the other three were
bestowed upon divers other husbands.

Hee had also two Brothers: the first was called *The Duke of*
George Duke of *Clarence*, who afterward upon his *Clarence at-*
deserts (as is to be supposed,) was put to death in *tainted by*
Callis, by commandement of the King, and his at- *Parliament.*
tainder allowed by Parliament. And this man left
behinde him a Sonne, named *Edward* Earle of
warwick, put to death afterward without issue, by
King *Henry* the seventh, and a Daughter named
Margaret, Countesse of *Salisbury*, who was married
to a meane Gentleman named *Richard Poole*, by
whom she had issue Cardinall *Poole*, that died without marriage; and *Henry Poole* that was attainted *Huntingtons*.
and executed in King *Henry* the eight his time; *title by the*
(as also her selfe was) and this *Henry Poole* left a *Duke of Cla-*
Daughter married afterward to the Earle of *Hun-* *rence.*
tington, by whom this Earle that now is maketh title
to the Crowne. And this is the effect of my Lord of
Huntingtons title.

The second Brother of King *Edward* the fourth,
was *Richard* Duke of *Glocester*, who after the Kings *King Richard*
death, caused his two Sonnes to be murdered in the *the third.*
Tower, and tooke the Kingdome to himselfe. And
afterward he being slaine by King *Henry* the seventh
at *Bosworth-field*, left no issue behind him. Wherefore King *Henry* the seventh descending as hath bin *The happy*
shewed of the House of *Lancaster*, by *John* of *Gaunts* *conjunction*
last Sonne and third Wife, and taking to Wife Lady *of the two*
Elizabeth, eldest daughter of King *Edward* the *Houses.*
fourth, of the House of *Torke*: joyned most happily
the two Families together, and made an end of all
controversies about the title.

Now King *Henry* the seventh had issue three Children:

The issue of King *Henry* the seventh.

dren : of whom remaineth posterity. First, *Henry* the eighth, of whom is descended our Soveraigne, her Majesty that now happily raigneth, and is the

The Line and Title of *Scotland* by *Margaret*, eldest Daughter to King *Henry* the 7.

last that remaineth alive of that first Line. Secondly, he had two Daughters : whereof the first named *Margaret*, was married twice ; first to *James* King of *Scotland*, from whom are directly discended the Queene of *Scotland* that now liveth, and her Sonne : and King *James* being dead, *Margaret* was married againe to *Archibald Douglas* Earle of *Anguish* : by whom shee had a Daughter named *Margaret*, which was married afterward to *Mathew Steward*, Earle of *Lenox*, whose Sonne *Charles Steward* was married to *Elizabeth Candish*, Daughter to the present Countesse of *Shrewsbury*, and by her hath left

Arbella.

his onely Heire, a little Daughter named *Arbella*, of whom you have heard some speech before. And this is touching the Line of *Scotland*, descending from the first and eldest Daughter of King *Henry* the seventh.

The Line and Title of *Suffolke* by *Mary*, second daughter to King *Henry* the 7.

The second Daughter of King *Henry* the seventh called *Mary*, was twice married also : first to the King of *France*, by whom she had no issue : and after his death to *Charles Brandon* Duke of *Suffolke*, by whom she had two Daughters ; that is, *Francis*, of which the Children of my Lord of *Hartford* do make their claime : and *Elenor*, by whom the issue of the Earle of *Darby* pretendeth right, as shall be declared. For that *Francis* the first Daughter of *Charles Brandon* by the Queene of *France*, was married to the Marquesse of *Dorset*, who after *Charles Brandons* death, was made Duke of *Suffolke* in right of his Wife, and

The issue of *Francis*, eldest Daughter to *Charles Brandon*, Duke of *Suffolke*.

was beheaded in Queene *Maries* time, for his conspiracy with my Lord of *Leycesters* Father. And she had by this man three Daughters : that is, *Jane*, that was married to my Lord of *Leycesters* Brother, and

proclaimed

proclaimed Queene after King *Edwards* death, for
which both shee and her husband were executed :
Katherine the second Daughter, who had two
Sonnes, yet living by the Earle of *Hertford* : and
Mary the third Daugter, which left no Children.

The other Daughter of *Charles Brandon* by the
Queene of France called *Elenor*, was married to
George Clifford Earle of Cumberland , who left a
Daughter by her named *Margaret*, married to the
Earle of *Darby*, which yet liveth, and hath issue.
And this is the title of the House of *Suffolke*, descended from the second Daughter of K. *Henry* the
seventh, married (as hath been shewed) to *Charles
Brandon* Duke of Suffolke. And by this, you may
see also how many there be, who do thinke their
titles to be far before that of my Lord of *Huntington*, if either right, law, reason, or consideration of
home affaires may take place in our Realm : or
if not, yet you cannot but imagine how many
great Princes and Potentates abroad , are like to
joyne and buckle with *Huntingtons* Line for the
preeminence : if once the matter fall againe to
contention by excluding the Line of King *Henry*
the seventh, which God forbid.

Truly Sir (quoth I) I well perceive that my
Lords turne is not so nigh as I had thought, whether he exclude the Line of King *Henry* , or no:
for if he exclude that , then must he enter the
Combat with forraine titlers of the House of
Lancaster : and if he exclude it not, then in all ap-
parance of reason and in Law to (as you have said)
the succession of the two Daughters of King *Henry*
the seventh (which you distinguish by the two
names of *Scotland* and *Suffolke*) must needs
bee as clearly before him and his Line ,
that decended only from *Edward* the fourth his
Brother , as the Queenes title that now reigneth

I

is

Sidenotes:

The issue of
Francis eldest
daughter to
Charles Brandon
Duke of Suffolk.

The issue of Ele-
nor second
daughter to
Charles Bran-
don.

Scholar.

Huntington be-
behind many
other titles.

is before him. For that both Scotland, Suffolke
and her Majesty do hold all by one foundation,
which is the union of both Houses and Titles
together, in King *Henry* the seventh her Majesties
Grandfather.

Gentleman.

That is true (quoth the Gentleman) and evident enough in every mans eye ; and therefore no
doubt: but as that much is meant against her Majesty, if occasion serve, as against the rest that hold
by the same title. Albeit her Majesties state (the
Lord be praised) be such at this time, as it is not
safty to pretend so much against her, as against the
rest, whatsoever be meant. And that in truth, more
should be ment against her highnes, then against
all the rest : there is this reason; for that her Majesty by her present possession letteth more their
desires, then all the rest together with their future
pretences. But as I have said, it is not safety for
them, nor yet good policy to declare openly, what
they meane against her Majesty. It is the best
way for the present to hew downe the rest ,
and to leave her Majesty for the last low and
upshot to their game. For which cause , they
will seeme to make great difference at this day,
betweene her Majesties title and the rest, that
descend in likewise from King *Henry* the seventh : avowing the one, and disallowing the
other. Albeit, my Lord of *Leicesters* Father,
preferred that of *Suffolke*, when time was, before
this of her Majesty, and compelled the whole
Realme to sweare thereunto. Such is the variable policy of men, that serve the time, or rather
that serve themselves, of all times, for their purposes.

The policy of the conspiratours for the deceiving of her Majesty.

Scholar.

I remember (quoth I) that time of the Duke,
and was present my selfe, at some of his Procla-
mations for that purpose : wherein my Lord his
Sonne

Sonne that now liveth : being then a doer, (as I
can tell he was :) I marvile how he can deale so
contrary now : preferring not onely her Majesties
title before that of *Suffolk* (whereof I wonder *Leycesters varia-
lesse because it is more gainfull to him,) but al- *bility.*
so another much further of. But you have signified the cause, in that the times are changed, and
other bargaines are in hand of more importance
for him. Wherefore leaving this to be considered by others whom it concerneth, I beseech
you, Sir, (for that I know, your worship hath
beeene much conversant among their friends and
favourers) to tell me what are the barres and
lets which they doe alledge, why the house of
Scotland and Suffolk descended of king *Henry*
the seventh his daughters, should not succeed in
the Crowne of England after her Majesty, who
ended the line of the same king by his son ; for
in my sight the matter appeareth very plaine.

They want not pretences of barres and lets a- *Gentleman.*
gainst them all (quoth the Gentleman) which I
will lay downe in order, as I have heard them
alledged. First, in the line of Scotland there are *Barres pretended*
three persons as you know, that may pretend *against the claim*
right, that is the Queen and her son by the first *of Scotland and*
marriage of *Margaret,* and *Arbella* by the second. *Suffolke.*
And against the first marriage, I heare nothing
affirmed; but against the two persons proceeding
thereof, I heare them alledge three stops, one for
that they are stangers born out of the land, & con- *Against the*
sequently incapable of inheritance within the *Queen of Scot-*
same ; another for that by a speciall testament of *land and her*
king *H.8.* authorised by 2.severall parliam. they are *sonne.*
excluded; 3. for that they are enemies to the religion now among us & therefore to be debarred.

Against the second marriage of *Margaret* with *Against Arbella.*
Archibald Douglas whereof *Arbella* is descended ;
I 2   they

they alledge, that the said *Archibald* had a former wife at the time of that marriage, which lived long after: and so neither that marriage lawfull, nor the issue therof legitimate.

The same barre they have against all the house and Line of Suffolke, for first they say, that *Charles Brandon* Duke of Suffolke, had a knowen wife alive when he married *Mary* Queen of France, and consequently, that neither the Lady *Frances* nor *Elenor*, borne of that marriage, can be lawfully borne. And this is all, I can heare them say against the succession of the Countesse of *Darby* descended of *Elenor*. But against my Lord of *Hartfords* children, that came from *Frances* the eldest daughter, I heare them alledge two or three bastardies more besides this of the first marriage. For first, they affirme that *Henry* Marquesse *Dorset*, when hee married the Lady *Frances*, had to wife the old Earl of *Arundels* sister, who lived both then and many yeares after, and had a provision out of his living to her dying day: wherby that marriage could no way be good. Secondly that the lady *Katherine*, daughter to the said Lady *Frances*, by the Marques (by whom the Earl of Hartford had his children) was lawfully married to the Earle of Pembroke that now liveth, and consequently, could have no lawfull issue by any other during his life. 3ly. that the said *Katherine* was never lawfully married to the said Earl *Hertford*, but bare him those children as his Concubine, which (as they say) is defined and registred in the Archb. of Canterburies court, upon due examination taken by order of her Majesty that now reigneth, and this is in effect so much as I have heard them all aledge, about their affars.

It is much (quoth I) that you have said, if it may be all proved. Marry yet by the way, I cannot but smile to heare my Lord of *Leycester* allow of so many bastardies now upon the issue of Lady

Against Darby.

Against the children of Hartford.

Scholar.

Frances, whom in time paſt, when *Iane* her eldeſt daughter was married to his brother, he advanced in legitimation before both the daughters of king *Henry* the eight. But to the purpoſe: I would gladly know what grounds of verity theſe allegations have, and how far in truth they may ſtoppe from inheritance: for in deed I never heard them ſo diſtinctly alledged before. **Leyceſters dealing with the houſe of Suffolk.**

Whereto anſwered the Gentleman, that our friend the Lawyer could beſt reſolve that, if it pleaſed him to ſpeake without his fee: though in ſome points alledged every other man (quoth he) that knoweth the ſtate and common government of England, may eaſily give his judgement alſo. And in the caſe of baſtardy, if the matter may be proved, there is no difficulty, but that no right to inheritance can juſtly bee pretended: as alſo (perhaps) in the caſe of forraine birth, though in this I am not ſo cunning: but yet I ſee by experience, that forrainers borne in other lands, can hardly come and claime inheritance in England, albeit, to the contrary, I have heard great and long diſputes, but ſuch as indeed paſſed my capacity. And if it might pleaſe our friend here preſent to expound the thing unto us more clearly, I for my part would gladly beſtow the hearing, and that with attention. *Gentleman.* **Baſtardy.** **Forraine birth.**

To this anſwered the Lawyer, I will gladly, ſir, tell you my minde in any thing that it ſhall pleaſe you demand: and much more in this matter, wherein by occaſion of often conference I am ſomewhat perfect. The impediments which theſe men alledge againſt the ſucceſſion of king *Henry* the 8. his ſiſters, are of two kinds, as you ſee: The one knowne and allowed in our law, as you have well ſaid, if it may be proved; and that is baſtardy: whereby they ſeek to diſable all the whole Line *Lawyer.* **Baſtardies lawful ſtops.**

I 3   and

and race of *Suffolke* : as alſo *Arbella* of the ſecond
and later houſe of Scotland. Whereof it is to ſmall
purpoſe to ſpeak any thing here : ſeeing the whole
controverſie ſtandeth upon a matter of faƈt onely
to be proved or improved by records and witneſ-
ſes. Onely this I will ſay, that ſome of theſe baſtardies, before named, are rife in many mens
mouthes, and avowed by divers that yet live : but
let other men looke to this, who have moſt intereſt therein, and may be moſt damnified by them,
if they fall out true. The other impediments,
which are alledged onely againſt the Queene of
Scots and her ſon, are in number three, as you recite them : that is forraine birth, king *Henries* teſtament, and Religion : whereof I am content to
ſay ſomewhat, ſeeing you deſire it : albeit there be
ſo much publiſhed already in bookes of divers
languages beyond the ſea, as I am informed, concerning this matter, as more cannot be ſaid. But
yet ſo much as I have heard paſſe among Lawyers my betters, in conference of theſe affaires : I
will not let to recite unto you, with this proviſo
and proteſtation alwayes, that what I ſpeake, I
ſpeak by way of recitall of other mens opinions :
not meaning my ſelfe to incurre the ſtatute of affirming or avowing any perſons title to the crown
whatſoever.

Firſt then touching forraine birth, there bee
ſome men in the world that will ſay, that it is a
common and generall rule of our law, that no
ſtranger at al may inherit any thing by any means
within the Land : which in truth I take to be ſpoken without ground, in that generall ſenſe. For I
could never yet come to the ſight of any ſuch
common or univerſall rule : and I know, that divers examples may be alledged in ſundry caſes to
the contrary : and by that which is expreſly ſet
down

The impedi-
ments againſt
Scotland three
in number.

A proteſtation.

Touching the
firſt impediment
of forraine birth.

downe in the seventh and ninth years of king
Ed. the 4. and in the eleventh and fourteenth
of *Hen.* the 4. it appeareth plainly that a stranger
may purchase lands in England, as also inherit by
his wife, if he marry an inheritrix. Wherefore
this common rule is to bee restrained from that
generality, unto proper inheritance only; in which
sense I do easily grant, that our common Law
hath beenof ancient, and is at this day, that no
person born out of the allegiance of the king of
England whose father & mother were not of the
same allegiance at the time of his birth, shall be
able to have or demand any heritage within the
same allegiance, as heire to any person. And this
rule of our common Law is gathered in these
selfsame words of a statute made in the 25. year
of king *Ed.* the third, which indeed is the onely
place of effect, that can be alledged out of our law
against the inheritance of strangers in such sense
and cases as we are now to treat of.

And albeit now the common Law of our
Country do runne thus in generall, yet will
the friends of the Scottish claime affirme,
that hereby that title is nothing let or hindred at
all towards the Crowne; and that for divers
manifest and weighty reasons, whereof the principall are these which ensue.

First, it is common and a generall rule of our
English lawes, that no rule, Axiome or Maxima
of law (be it never so generall) can touch or bind
the Crown, except expresse mention bee made
thereof in the same; for that the king and crowne
have great priviledge and prerogative above the
state and affaires of subjects, and great differences allowed in points of law.

As for example, it is a generall & common rule
of law, that the wife after the decease of her husband,

Side notes:

An Alien may purchase.

The true Maxima against Aliens.

The statute of King Edward whence the Maxima is gathered.

Reasons why the Scottish title is not letted by the Maxima against Aliens.

The first reason.

The rule of thirds.

I 4

band, shall enjoy the third of his lands: but yet the Queene shall not enjoy the third part of the Crowne, after the Kings death: as well appeareth by experience, and is to be seene by law, *Anno* 5. and 21. of *Edward* the third; and *Anno* 9. and 28. of *Henry* the sixt. Also it is a common rule, that the husband shall hold his wives lands after her death, as tenant by courtesie during his life, but yet it holdeth not in a Kingdome.

Tenant by courtesie.

In like manner, it is a generall and common rule, that if a man dye seased of Land in Feesimple, having daughters and no sonne, his lands shall be divided by equall portions among his daughters, which holdeth not in the Crowne: but rather the eldest Daughter inheriteth the whole, as if she were the issue male. So also it is a common rule of our law, that the executor shall have all the goods and chattels of the Testator, but not in the Crowne. And so in many other cases which might bee recited, it is evident that the Crowne hath priviledge above others, and cannot be subject to rule, be it never so generall, except expresse mention be made thereof in the same law: as it is in the former place and a statute alledged: but rather to the contrary (as after shall be shewed) there is expresse exception, for the prerogative of such as descend of Royall bloud.

Division among daughters.

Executors.

Their second reason is, for that the demand or title of a Crowne, cannot in true sense bee comprehended under the words of the former statute, forbidding aliens to demand heritage within the allegiance of England: and that for two respects. The one, for that the Crowne it selfe cannot be called an heritage of allegiance, or within allegiance, for that it is holden of no superiour upon earth, but immediately from God himselfe:
the

The 2 reason. The Crowne no such inheritance as is meant in the statute.

the second, for that this ſtatute treateth onely and meaneth of inheritance by deſcent, as heyre to the ſame, (for I have ſhewed before that Aliens may hold lands by purchaſe within our Dominion) and then ſay they, the Crowne is a thing incorporate, and deſcendeth not according to the common courſe of other private inheritances: but goeth by ſucceſſion, as other incorporations doe. In ſigne whereof it is evident, that albeit the King be more favoured in all his doings, then any common perſon ſhall be, yet cannot hee avoyd by law his graunts and letters patents by reaſon of his nonage (as other infants and common heires under age may doe) but alwayes be ſaid to be of full age in reſpect of his Crown even as a Prior, Parſon, Vicar, Deane, or other perſon incorporate ſhall be, which cannot by any meanes in law bee ſaid to be within age, in reſpect of their incorporations.

The Crowne a corporation.

Which thing maketh an evident difference in our caſe, from the meaning of the former ſtatute: for that a Prior, Deane, or Parſon, being Aliens and no Denizens, might alwayes in time of peace demand lands in England, in reſpect of their corporations, notwithſtanding the ſaid ſtatute or common law againſt Aliens, as appeareth by many booke caſes yet extant: as alſo by the ſtatute made in the time of King Richard the ſecond, which was after the foreſaid ſtatute of King Edward the third.

The third reaſon is, for that in the former ſtatute it ſelfe of King Edward, there are excepted expreſly from this generall rule, *Infantes du Roy*, that is, the Kings off ſpring or iſſue, as the word *Infant* doth ſignifie, both in France, Portugall, Spaine, and other Countries: and as the Latine word *Liberi* (which anſwereth the ſame) is taken com-

The 3. reaſon. The Kings iſſue excepted by name.

commonly in the civill law. Neither may we restraine the french words of that Satute *Infantes du*
Roy, to the kings children onely of the first degree
(as some doe, for that the barrennesse of our lan-
guage doth yeeld us no other word for the same)
but rather, that therby are understood, as well the
nephewes and other discendants of the king or
blood Royall, as his immediate children. For it
were both unreasonable and ridiculous to imagin
that king *Edward* by this statute, would go about
to disinherit his own nephews, if he should have
any borne out of his own allegiance (as easily he
might at that time) his sons being much abroad
from England ; and the black Prince, his eldest
son having two children borne beyond the seas :
and consequently, it is apparent, that this rule or
maxime set down againt Aliens is no way to be
stretched against the descendants of the king or
of the blood Royall.

Their fourth reason is, that the meaning of king
Edward and his children (living at such time as
this statute was made) could not be, that any of
their linage or issue might be excluded in law,
from inheritance of their right to the Crowne, by
their foraine birth wheresoever. For otherwise, it
is not credible that they would so much have dis-
persed their own blood in other Countries, as they
did, by giving their daughters to strangers, & other
meanes : as *Leonel* the kings third son was married
in Millan, and *Iohn* of Gaunt the fourth son, gave
his two daughters, *Philip* and *Katherine* to Portugall and Castile ; and his neece *Ioan* to the king
of Scots : as *Thomas* of Woodstocke also the yon-
gest brother, married his two daughters, the one
to the king of Spaine, and the other to Duke of
Briraine. Which no doubt (they being wise Princes, and so neer of the blood Royal) would never
have

Liberorum. F. de
verb. sign.

The fourth reason
The Kings mea-
ning.

The matches of
England with
foraigners.

have done; if they had imagined that hereby their
issue should have lost all claime and title to the
Crown of England : and therefore it is most evident, that no such bar was then extant or imagin'd

The fift reason is, that divers persons born out
of all English dominion and allegiance, both
before the Conquest and since, have bin admitted
to the succession of our Crown, as lawfull inhe-
ritours, without any exception against them for
their foraine birth. As before the Conquest is evident in yong *Edgar Etheling* borne in Hungarie,
and thence called home to inherit the Crowne,
by his great unckle king *Edward* the Confessor,
with full consent of the whole Realm ; the B. of
Worcester being sent as Ambassador to fetch him
home, with his father named *Edward* the out-law.

And since the Conquest, it appeareth plainly in
king *Stephen* and king *Henry* the second, both of
them borne out of English dominions, and of Parents, that at their birth, were not of the English
allegiance ; and yet were they both admitted to
the Crowne. Yong *Arthur* also Duke of Britain
by his mother *Constance* that matched with *Geffray*
king *Henry* the seconds sonne, was declared by
king *Richard* his unckle, at his departure towards
Jerusalem, and by the whole Realme, for lawfull heire apparent to the Crowne of England,
though he were borne in Britaine out of English
allegiance ; and so he was taken and judged by all
the world at that day : albeit, after king *Richards*
death, his other uncle *Iohn*, most tyrannously took
both his kingdome and his life from him. For
which notable injustice, he was detested of all
men both abroad and at home ; & most apparently scourged by God, with grievous and manifold
plagues, both upon himself and the Realm, which
yeelded to his usurpation. So that by this also it appeareth,

The fift reason.
Examples of
forainers admited

Flores hist. Anno
1066.

Pol.lib.15.Flor.
hist.1208.

K.Iohn a tyrant

peareth, what the practice of our Countrey hath beene from time to time in this case of forraine birth: which practice is the best interpreter of our common English law: which dependeth especially, and most of all, upon custome: nor can the adversary alledge any one example to the contrary.

The 6. reason.
The iudgement
and sentence of
K. Henry the
seventh.

Their sixt, is of the iudgement and sentence of King *Henry* the seventh, and of his Councell: who being together in consultation, at a certaine time about the marriage of *Margaret* his eldest daughter into Scotland: some of his Councell moved this doubt, what should ensue, if by chance the kings issue male should faile, and so the succession devolve to the heyres of the said *Margaret*, as now it doth? Whereunto that wise and most prudent Prince made answer: that if any such event should be, it could not be preiudiciall to England, being the bigger part, but rather beneficiall: for that it should draw Scotland to England: that is, the lesser to the more: even as in times past it happened in Normandy, Aquitaine, and some other Provinces. Which answer appeased all doubts and gave singular content to those of his Councell, as *Polidore* writeth, that lived at that time, and wrote the speciall matters of that reigne, by the kings owne instruction. So that hereby wee see no question made of king *Henry* or his Councellors touching forraine birth, to let the succession of Lady *Margarett* issue: which no doubt would never have beene omitted in that learned assembly, if any law at that time had beene esteemed or imagined to beare the same.

And these are six of their principallest reasons to prove, that neither by the words nor meaning of our common lawes, nor yet by custome or practice of our Realme, an Alien may bee debarred from claim of his interest to the Crowne, when

it

it falleth to him by rightull descent in blood and succession. But in the particular case of the Queen of Scots and her son, they doe adde ano her reason or two: thereby to prove them in very deed to be no Aliens: Not only in respect of their often and continuall mixture with English blood from the beginning (and especially of late, the Queens Grandmother and husband being English, and so her sonne begotten of an English father) but also for two other causes and reasons, which seeme in truth of very good importance. The first is, for that Scotland by all Englishmen (howsoever the Scots deny the same) is taken and holden as subject to England by way of Homage; which many of their kings at divers times have acknowledged: and consequently the Queene and her son being borne in Scotland are not borne out of the allegiance of England, and so no forrainers, The second cause or reason is, for that the forenamed statute of forrainers in the 25 yeare of King *Edward* the third, is intitled, *of those that are borne beyond the seas.* And in the body of the said statute, the doubt is moved of children borne out of English allegance beyond the seas: whereby cannot bee understood Scotland, for that it is a piece of the continent land within the seas. And all our old Records in England, that talke of service to bee done within these two countries, have usually these Latin words, *Infra quatuor maria,* or in French *deins les quatre mers,* that is, within the foure Seas: whereby must needs be understood as well Scotland as England, and that perhaps for the reason before mentioned, of the subjection of Scotland by way of Homage to the Crowne of England. In respect whereof it may be, that it was accounted of old but one dominion or allegiance. And consequently, no man borne therein can bee accounted

The 7. reason.
The Queene of Scots and her son no Aliens.

counted an alien to England. And this shal suffice for the first point, touching foragine Nativity.

The second impediment against the Q. of Scots, & her son, which is K. Henry the 8. his testament. For the second impediment objected, which is the testament of King *Henry* the eight, authorized by Parliament, wherby they affirm the succession of Scotland to be excluded: it is not precisely true that they are excluded, but onely that they are put back behinde the succession of the houf of *Suffolk*. For in that pretended Testament (which after shall be proved to be none indeed) King *Henry* so disposeth, that after his own children (if they shold chance to dye without issue) the Crowne shall passe to the heires of *Frances* & of *Elenor*, his neeces by his yonger sister *Mary* Queene of France ; and after them (deceasing also without issue) the succession to returne to the next heire againe. Wherby it is evident, that the succession of *Margaret* Queene of Scotland, his eldest sister, is nor excluded ; but thrust back onely from their due place and order, to expect the remainder, which may in time be left by the yonger. Whereof in mine opinion, doe ensue some considerations against the present pretenders themselves.

Forain birth no impediment in the iudgement of K. Henry the 8. First, that in King *Henries* judgement, the former pretended rule of foraine birth, was no sufficient impediment against Scotland ; for if it had bin, no doubt but that he would have named the same in his alleaged testament, and thereby have utterly excluded that succeffiõ. But there is no such thing in the testament. Secondly, if they admit The succeffion of Scotlaud next by the iudgement of the competitors. this testament, which alotteth the Crown to Scotland, next after Suffolk ; then, seeing that all the house of Suffolk (by these mens assertions) is excluded by bastardy; it must needs follow, that Scotland by their own judgement is next, & so this testament wil make against them, as indeed it doth in all points most apparantly, but only that it preferreth

ferreth the houfe of Suffolk, before that of Scotland. And therefore (I think fir) that you miftake
fomewhat about their opinion in alleaging this
teftament. For I fuppofe, that no man of my Lord
of *Huntingtons* faction, will alleage or urge the te-
ftimony of this teftament; but rather fome friend
of the houfe of *Suffolk*, in whofe favour, I take it,
that it was firft of all forged.

It may be (quoth the Gentleman) nor will I *Gentleman.*
ftand obftinatly in the contrary; for that it is hard
fometime to judge of what faction each one is,
who difcourfeth of thefe affaires. But yet I marvel
(if it were as you fay) why *Leycefters* Father after
K. *Edwards* death, made no mention therof in the
favor of *Suffolk*, in the other teftament which then
he proclaimed, as made by K. *Edward* deceafed, for
preferment of *Suffolk* before his own fifters.

The caufe of this is evident (quoth the Lawyer) *Lawyer.*
for that it made not fufficiently for his purpofe : The Duke of
which was to difinherit the two daughters of King Northumber-
Henry himfelfe, and advance the houfe of *Suffolk* lands drift.
before them both.

A notable change (quoth the Gentleman) that *Gentleman.*
a title fo much exalted of late by the Father, a-
bove all order, right, ranke and degree; fhould
now be fo much debafed by the Son, as though it
were not worthy to hold any degree, but rather to
be troden under-foot for plain baftardy. And you The mutable
fee by this, how true it is which I told you before; dealing of the
that the race of *Dudlies* are moft cunning mer- houfe of Dudley.
chants, to make their gaine of all things, men and
times. And as we have feene now two teftaments
alleaged, the one of the Kings father, and the o-
ther of the kings fonne, and both of them in prejudice of the teftators true fucceffors : fo many good
fubjects begin greatly to fear, that we may chance
to

to see shortly a third Testament of her Majesty for the tituling of *Huntington*, and extirpation of King *Henries* blood, & that before her Majesty can think of sicknesse: wherein I beseech the Lord I be no Prophet. But now, sir, to the foresaid Will and Testament of King *Henry*, I have often heard in truth, that the thing was counterfeit, or at the least not able to be proved: and that it was discovered, rejected, and defaced in Queen *Maries* time: but I would gladly understand what you Lawyers esteeme or judge thereof.

Touching this matter (quoth the Lawyer) it cannot be denied, but that in the 28. and 36 years of King *Henries* reign, upon consideration of some doubt and irresolution, which the King himselfe had shewed, to have about the order of succession in his owne children, as also for taking away all occasions of controversies in those of the next blood; the whole Parliament gave authority unto the said King, to debate and determine those matters himselfe, together with his learned councell, who best knew the lawes of the Realme, and titles that any man might have thereby: and that whatsoever succession his Majesty should declare as most right and lawfull under his letters patents sealed, or by his last Will and Testament rightfully made and signed with his owne hand: that the same should bee received for good and lawfull. Upon pretence whereof, soon after King *Henries* death, there was shewed a Will with the kings stamp at the same, and the names of divers witnesses, wherein (as hath beene said) the succession of the Crowne, after the kings owne children, is assigned to the heyres of *Frances* and *Elenore*, Neeces to the king, by his younger Sister. Which assignation of the Crown, being as it were a meer gift in prejudice

of

of the elder fifters right (as alfo of the right of
Frances and *Elenor* themfelves who were omitted
in the fame affignation, and their heires intituled
onely) was efteemed to be againft all reafon, law,
and nature, and confequently not thought to pro- *The Kings*
ceed from fo wife and fage a Prince as K. *Henrie* *Teftament*
was knowne to be : but rather, either the whole *forged.*
forged, or at leaft wife that claufe inferted by o-
ther, and the Kings ftamp fet unto it, after his
death, or when his Majefty lay now paft under-
ftanding. And hereof there wanteth not divers
moft evident reafons and proofes.

For firft, it is not probable nor credible, that King *The firft*
Henrie would ever go about, againft law and rea- *reafon.*
fon, to difinherit the line of his eldeft fifter, without any profit or intereft to himfelfe : and thereby, give moft evident occafion of Civill war and *Injuftice*
difcord within the Realm, feeing, that in fuch a cafe *and impro-*
of manifeft and apparent wrong, in fo great a *probability*
matter, the authoritie of Parlament, taketh little
effect, againft the true and lawfull inheritor : as
well appeared in the former times and contentions of *Henrie* the fixth, *Edward* the fourth, and
Richard the third : in whofe reignes, the divers
and contrarie Parliaments made and holden, a-
gainft the next inheritor, held no longer with any
man, then until the other was able to make his
owne partie good.

So likewife, in the cafe of King *Edward* the *The ex-*
third his fucceffion to *France*, in the right of his *ample of*
mother, though he were excluded by the generall *France.*
affembly and confent of their Parliaments ; yet
he efteemed not his right extinguifhed thereby :
as neither did other Kings of our Countrie that
enfued after him. And for our prefent cafe, if
nothing elfe fhould have reftrained King *Henrie*,

K   from

from such open injustice towards his eldest sister : yet this cogitation, at least, would have stayed him : that by giving example of supplanting his elder sisters Line, by vertue of a testament or pretence of Parliament ; some other might take occasion to displace his children by like pretence : as we see that Duke *Dudley* did soone after by a forged testament of King *Edward* the sixt. So ready Schollars there are to be found, which easily will learne such lessons of iniquity.

The second reason. Incongruities and indignities. Secondly, there be too many incongruities and indignities in the said pretended Will to proceed from such a Prince and learned councell as King *Henries* was. For first, what can be more ridiculous, than to give the Crowne to the heires of *Francis* and *Elenor*, and not to any of themselves? or what had they offended that their heires should enjoy the Crowne in their right, and not they themselves ? What if King *Henries* Children should have dyed, whiles Lady *Francis* had been yet alive? who should have possessed the Kingdome before her, seeing her Line was next ? and yet by this testament shee could not pretend her selfe to obtaine it. But rather having marryed *Adrian Stokes* her horse-keeper, she must have suffered her sonne by him (if she had any) to enjoy the Crown : and so *Adrian* of a Serving man and Master of Horses , should have become the great Master and Protector of *England*. Of like absurditie is that other clause also, wherein the King bindeth his owne daughters to marry by consent and direction of his counsell, or otherwise to leese the benefit of their succession : yet bindeth not his Neices daughters, to wit, the daughters of *Francis* & *Elenor* (if they had any) to any such condition.

Adrian Stokes.

Thirdly, there may bee divers causes and arguments

guments alledged in law, why this pretended will *The third* is not authenticall: if otherwise, it were certaine *reason.* that King *Henrie* had meant it: first, for that it *The pre-* is not agreeable to the mind and meaning of the *suppofed* Parliament, which intended onely to give autho-*Will is not* ritie for declaration and explication of the true *authenti-* title: and not for donation, or intricating of the *call.* fame, to the ruine of the Realme. Secondly, for that there is no lawfull and authenticall Copie extant thereof, but onely a bare inrolement in the Chancerie, which is not fufficient in fo weighty an affaire: no witneffe of the privie Councell or of Nobilitie to the fame: which had been conve- nient in fo great a cafe (for the beft of the witnef- fes therein named, is Sir *Iohn Gates*, whofe mife- rable death is well knowne:) no publike Notary, no probation of the will before any Bifhop, or any lawfull Court for that purpofe: no examination of the witneffes, or other thing orderly done, for lawfull authorizing of the matter.

But of all other things this is moft of impor- tance: that the King never fet his owne hand to *The dif-* the forefaid Will, but his ftampe was put there-*proving of* unto by others, either after his death, or when he *the Will by* was paft remembrance: as the late Lord *Paget* in *witneffes.* the beginning of Queen *Maries* dayes, being of *The Lord* the Privie Councell, firft of all other difcovered *Paget.* the fame of his owne accord, and upon meere motion of confcience, confeffing before the whole Councell, and afterward alfo before the whole Parlament, how that himfelfe was privy thereun- to, and partly alfo culpable, (being drawn thereun- to, by the inftigation and forcible authority of o- thers:) but yet afterward upon other more godly motions detefted the device: and fo of his owne free-will, very honourably went and offered the

difco-

Sir Edw.
Montague discoverie thereof to the Councell. As also did Sir
Edward Montague, Lord chiefe Iustice that had
been privy and present at the said doings, and one
William
Clarke. William Clarke, that was the man who put the
stampe unto the paper, and is ascribed among the
other pretensed witnesses, confessed the whole
premisses to be true, and purchased his pardon for
his offence therein. Whereupon Queen Marie and
her Councell, caused presently the said Inrolement, lying in the Chancerie to be cancelled, defaced and abolished.

And sithence that time in her Majesties dayes
that now liveth, about the 11. or 12. yeare of her
reigne, (if I count not amisse) by occasion of a
certaine little booke spread abroad at that time,
very secretly, for advancing of the house of Suf-
A meeting
together a-
bout this
matter of
the Nobi-
lity. folke, by pretence of this Testament: I remember well the place where the late Duke of Norfolke, the Marquesse of Winchester (which then
was Treasurer) the old Earles of Arundell and
Penbrooke that now are dead, with my Lord of
Penbrook that yet liveth, (as also my Lord of Leycester himselfe, if I bee not deceived) with divers
others, met together upon this matter: and after
long conference about the foresaid pretensed will,
and many proofes and reasons laid downe, why
it could not be true or authenticall: the old Earle
of Penbrook protesting that he was with the King
in his chamber from the first day of his sicknesse
unto his last houre, and thereby could well assure
the falsification thereof: at length it was moved,
that from that place they should goe, with the
rest of the Nobility, and proclaime the Queen of
My Lord of
Leicast. a-
gaine play-
th double. Scotland heire apparent in Cheap-side. Wherein my
Lord of Leycester (as I take it was then as forward as any man else; how bee it, now for his
profit

profit, he be turned aſide, and would turne back
again to morrow next for a greater commodity.

And albeit, for ſome cauſes to themſelves beſt
known, they proceeded not in the open publiſhing
of their determination at that time : yet my Lord
of *Penbrook* now living can beare witneſſe that
thus much is true : and that his father, the old
Earle, at that time told him openly before the o- *The old*
ther Noblemen, that he had brought him to that *Earle of*
aſſembly and place to inſtruct him in that truth, *Penbrooks*
and to charge him to witneſſe the ſame, and to *admonition*
defend it alſo with his ſword (if need required) *to the Earl*
after his death. And I know that his Lordſhip is *his ſon, yet*
of that honour and Nobility, as he cannot leave *living.*
off eaſily the remembrance or due regard of
ſo worthy an admonition. And this ſhall ſuffice for the ſecond impediment, imagined to proceed of this ſuppoſed Teſtament of King *Henrie*
the eighth.

As for the third impediment, of religion, it is *The third*
not generall to all : for that only one perſon (if I *impedi-*
be not deceived) of all the Competitors in K. *ment of re-*
Henries Line can bee touched with ſuſpition of *ligion.*
different Religion, from the preſent ſtate of *Eng-*
land. Which perſon notwithſtanding (as is well
knowne) while ſhee was in government in her
owne Realme of *Scotland*, permitted all liberty of
Conſcience, and free exerciſe of Religion to thoſe
of the contrary profeſſion and opinion, without
reſtraint. And if ſhe had not, yet doe I not ſee,
either by preſcript of law, or practiſe of theſe our
times, that diverſity of Religion, may ſtay juſt Inheritors from enjoying their due poſſeſſions, in a-
ny ſtate or degree of private men : and much leſſe
in the claime of a Kingdome : which alwayes in
this behalfe as hath been ſaid before) is preferred
in priviledge.   K 3   This

This we see by experience, in divers Countries and parts of the world at this day: as in *Germany*, where among so many Princes, and so divided in religion as they be: yet every one succeedeth to the state whereto he hath right, without resistance for his religion. The examples also of her Majesty that now is, and of her sister before, is evident; who being known to be of two different inclinations in religion, and the whole Realme divided in opinion for the same cause: yet both of them at their severall times with generall consent of all, were admitted to their lawfull inheritance: excepting onely a few * traitors against the former, who withstood her right, as also in her the right of her Maiestie that is present, and that not for Religion, (as appeared by their owne confession after) but for ambition and desire of reigne, Monsieur, the Kings brother and heire of *France*, as all the world knoweth, is well accepted, favoured, and admitted for successor of that Crowne, by all the Protestants at this day of that Country, notwithstanding his opinion in religion knowne to be different. And I doubt not, but the King of *Navarre* or Prince of *Condy*, in the contrary part would thinke themselves greatly injured by the state of *France*, which is different from them in religion at this day, if after the death of the King that now is, and his brother without issue, (if God so dispose) they should be barred from inheriting the Crowne, under pretence onely of their Religion. My Lord of *Huntington* himselfe also, is he not knowne to bee of a different religion from the present state of *England*? and that, if he were King to morrow next, he would alter the whole government, order, condition, and state of religion, now used and established within the Realme?

But

Marginal notes:

Princes of Germany.

Qu. Mary Queen Elizabeth.

**The Dudleis Monsieur.*

King of Navarre Prince of Condy.

My Lord of Huntingtons religion.

But as I said in the beginning, if one of a whole family, or of divers families be culpable, or to be touched herein; what have the rest offended thereby? will you exclude all, for the mislike of one? And to descend in order; if the first in K. *Henries* line, after her Majesty may be touched in this point, yet why should the rest be damnified thereby? The K of *Scotland* her son, that next ensueth (to speak in equity) why should he bee shut out for his religion? And are not all the other in like manner Protestants, whose discent is consequent by nature, order, and degree.

For the yong K. of Scotland *(quoth I) the truth is, that alwayes for mine own part, I have had great hope and expectation of him, not onely for the conceipt which commonly men have of such Orient youths, borne to kingdomes; but especially for that I understood from time to time, that his education was in all learning, princely exercises, and instruction of true religion, under rare and vertuous men for that purpose. Whereby I conceived hope, that he might not onely become in time an honourable and profitable neighbour unto us, for assurance of the Gospell in these parts of the world; but also (if God should deprive us of her Maiesty without issue) might be a meane by his succession to unite in Concord and Government the two Realmes together, which heretofore hath beene sought by the price of many a thousand mens bloud, and not obtained.*

Marry yet now of late (I know not by what means) there is begun in mens hearts a certaine mislike or grudge against him, for that it is given out every where that he is inclined to be a Papist, and an enemy to her Majesties proceedings, which argueth him verily of singular ingratitude

K 4   if

(margin notes:)
The title of those that ensue the Queene of Scots.

Schollar.
The yong King of Scotland

if it be true, confidering the great helpes and protection which he hath received from her Highnes ever fithens he was borne.

Gent.

And are you fo fimple (quoth the Gentleman) as to beleeve everie report that you heare of this matter? know you not, that it is expedient for my Lord of *Leycefter* and his faction, that this youth, above all other, bee held in perpetuall difgrace with her Majefty, and with this Realme? You know, that *Richard* of *Gloucefter* had never been able to have ufurped as he did, if hee had not firft perfwaded K. *Edward* the fourth, to hate his owne brother the Duke of *Clarence*, which Duke ftood in the way betweene *Richard* and the thing, which he moft of all things coveted: that is, the poffibilitie to the Crowne, and fo in this cafe is there the like device to be obferved.

The device to fet out her Majefty with the young King of Scotland.

For truly, for the yong King of *Scotlands* religion, it is evident to as many as have reafon, that it can bee no other of it felfe but inclined to the beft; both in refpect of his education, inftruction, and converfation with thofe of true religion: as alfo by his former actions, Edicts, Government, and private behaviour he hath declared. Marrie thefe men whofe profit is nothing leffe, than that he or any other of that race fhould doe well: doe not ceafe dayly by all fecret wayes, drifts, and moleftations poffible, to drive him either to miflike of our religion, or elfe to incurre the fufpition thereof, with fuch of our Realme, as otherwife would be his beft friends; or if not this, yet for very need and feare of his owne life, to make recourfe to fuch other Princes abroad, as may moft offend or miflike this ftate.

And for this caufe, they fuborne certaine bufie fellowes of their owne crew and faction, pertaining

taining to the ministerie of *Scotland*, (but unwor- *The intol-*
thy of so worthy a calling) to use such inso- *lerable pra-*
lencie towards their King and Prince , as is not *ceedings of*
onely undecent, but intolerable. For he may doe *certain Mi-*
nothing, but they will examine and discusse the *nisters in*
same in Pulpit. If hee goe but on hunting, when *Scotland*
it pleaseth them to call him to their preaching : if *against*
he make but a dinner or supper, when, or where, *their King*
or with whom they like not : if he receive but a *by subor-*
couple of horses, or other present from his friends *nation of*
or kinsemen beyond the seas : if hee salute or use *his ene-*
courteously any man, or messenger which com- *mies in*
meth from them (as you know Princes of their *England.*
nob lity and courtesie are accustomed , though
they come from their enemies , as very often
hath beene seene, and highly commended in her
Majestie of *England* :) If hee deale familiarly
with any Ambassador which liketh not them : or
finally , if hee doe say or signifie any one thing
whatsoever that pleaseth not their humour, they
wil presently as seditious Tribunes of the people,
exclaime in publicke , and stepping to the Pulpit
where the Word of the Lord onely ought to be
preached, will excite the Communalty to discon-
tentation, inveying against their Soveraigne with
such bitternes of speech, unreverend tearmes, and
insolent controlements, as is not to be spoken :
Now imagine what her Majesty and her grave
councell would do in *England*, if such proceedings
should be used by the Clergy against them.

No doubt (quoth I) but that such unquiet spirits *Scholler.*
should be punished in our Realme. And so I said
of late to their most reverend and worthy Prelate *Sir* Patrick
and Primate the Arch-bishop of *St. Andrews*, with Adamson
whom it was my luck to come acquainted in *Archbish.*
London, whither he was come by his Kings ap- *of St. An-*
poyntment *drewes.*

pointment (as he said) to treat certain affairs with
our Q. and Councell. And talking with him of
this disorder of his ministerie, he confessed the
same with much griefe of mind, and told me,
that he had preached thereof before the K. himselfe, detesting and accusing divers heads therof,
for which cause he was become very odious to
them and other of their faction, both in *Scotland*
and *England*. But he said, that as he had given
the reasons of his doings unto our Qu. so meaneth he shortly to do the same unto *Monsieur Be-
za*, and to the whole Church of *Geneva*, by sending thither the Articles of his and their doings,
protesting unto me that the proceedings and attempts of those factious and corrupt men, was
most scandalous, seditious and perilous, both to
the K. person, and to the realm; being sufficient
indeed, to alienate wholy the yong Prince from
all affection to our religion, when he shall see
the chiefe Professors thereof to behave themselves so undutifully towards him.

Gentl. That is the thing which these men, his compe-
Treasons titors, most desire (*quoth the Gentleman*) hoping
plotted a- thereby to procure him most evill will and dan-
gainst the ger, both at home and from *England*. For which
King of cause also, they have practised so many plots and
Scots. treacheries with his owne subjects against him;
hoping by that meanes to bring the one in distrust and hatred of the other, and consequently
the K. in danger of destruction by his own. And
in this machination, they have behaved themselves so dexterously, so covertly used the man-
nage and contriving hereof, and so cunningly
conveyed the execution of many things; as it
might, indeed, seem apparent to the yong K. that
the whole plot of treasons against his Realme,
                                          and

and Perſon, doth come from *England*, thereby to drive him into jealouſie of our ſtate, and our ſtate of him: and all this for their owne profit.

Neither is this any new device of my Lord of *Leiceſt.* to draw men for his own gain into danger and hatred with the ſtate, under other pretences. For I could tell you divers ſtories and ſtratagems of his cunning in this kind, and the one farre different from the other in device: but yet all to one end. *I have a friend yet living, that was towards the old Earle of* Arundel *in good credit, and by that means had occaſion to deal with the late Duke of* Norfolk *in his chiefeſt affaires before his troubles. This man is wont to report ſtrange things from the Dukes owne mouth, of my L. of* Leiceſters *moſt treacherous dealing towards him, for gaining of his bloud, as after appeared, albeit the Duke when he rep rted the ſame, miſtruſted not ſo much my Lords malice therein.* But the ſum of all, is this in effect : that *Leiceſter* having a ſecret deſire to pull down the ſaid Duke, to the end that he might have no man above himſelfe, to hinder him in that whrch he moſt deſireth, by a thouſand cunning devices drew in the Duke to the cogitation of that marriage with the Queen of *Scotland*, which afterward was the cauſe or occaſion of his ruine. And hee behaved himſelfe ſo dexterouſly in this drift, by ſetting on the Duke on the one ſide, and alſo by intrapping him on the other: as *Iudas* himſelfe never plaid his part more cunningly when hee ſupped with his Maſter, and ſet himſelf ſo neer, as he dipt his ſpoon in the ſame diſh, & durſt before others, aske who ſhould betray him ? meaning that night to doe it himſelfe, as he ſhewed ſoon after ſupper, when he came as a Captaine

Leyceſters cunning device for overthrow ing the D. of Norf.

The impudency of Iudas.

with

with a band of Conspirators, and with a courteous kiſſe delivered his perſon into the hands of them; whom hee well knevv to thirſt after his bloud.

The very like did the Earle of *Leyceſter* with the Duke of *Norfolk*, for the act of treaſon, though in the parties betrayed there vvere great difference of innocency. Namely, at one time, when her Majeſty was at *Baſing* in *Hampſhire*, and the Duke attended there to have audience, vvith great indifferency in himſelfe to follovv, or leave off his ſuit for marriage: (for that now he began to ſuſpect, her Majeſty liked not greatly thereof:) my Lord of *Leyceſter* came to him and counſelled him in any caſe to perſevere, and not to relent, aſſuring him vvith many oathes and proteſtations, that her Majeſty muſt and ſhould be brought to allovv thereof; whether ſhe vvould or no, and that himſelfe vvould ſeale that purpoſe vvith his blood. Neither was it to be ſuffered that her Maieſty ſhould have her will herein; with many other like ſpeeches to this purpoſe: which the Duke repeated againe then preſently to my ſaid friend: with often laying his hand upon his boſome and ſaying; I have here which aſſureth me ſufficiently of the fidelity of my Lord of *Leyceſter*; meaning not onely the foreſaid ſpeeches, but alſo divers letters which he had written to the Duke of that effect, as likewiſe he had done to ſome other perſon of more importance in the Realme; which matter comming afterward to light, he couſened moſt notably her Majeſty, by ſhevving her a reformed copie of the ſaid Letter, for the Letter it ſelfe.

But now how well he performed his promiſe, in dealing vvith her Majeſty for the Duke or againſt
the

The ſpeeches of Leyceſter to the Duke of Norf.

Leyceſt. couſenage of the Queene.

the Duke in this matter, her Highnesse can best tell, and the event it selfe shewed. For the Duke being admitted soon after to her Majesties speech at another place, and receiving a farre other answer than he had in hope conceived upon Leycesters promises, retyred himselfe to *London*, where the same night following hee received Letters both from *Leycester*, and Sir *Nicholas Throgmorton*, upon *Leycesters* instigation (for they were at that time both friends and of a faction) that he should presently flye into *Norfolk*, as he did, which was the last and finall complement of all *Leycest.* former devices, whereby to plunge his friend over the eares in suspition and disgrace, in such sort as he should never be able to draw himselfe out of the ditch againe, as indeed he was not, but dyed in the same.

And herein you see also the same subtile and Machivilian slight, which I mentioned before, of driving men to attempt somewhat, whereby they may incurre danger, or remaine in perpetuall suspition or disgrace. And this practice he hath long used, and doth dayly, against such as he hath will to destroy. As for example, what say you to the device he had of late, to intrap his well deserving friend, Sir *Christopher Hatton*, in the matter of *Hall* his Priest, whom hee would have had Sir *Christopher* to send away and hide, being touched and detected in the case of *Ardent*; thereby to have drawne in Sir *Christopher* himselfe, as Sir *Charles Gandish* can well declare, if it please him, being accessary to this plot, for the overthrow of Sir *Christopher*: To which intent, and most devilish drift, pertained (I doubt not) if the matter were duely examined, the late interception of letters in *Paris* from one *Aldred* of *Lyons*, then in *Rome*,

Rome, to *Henr. Vmpton*, fervant to Sir *Chriftopher*, in which letters, Sir *Chriftopher* is reported to be of fuch credit and fpeciall favour in *Rome*, as if he were the greateft Papift in *England*.

What meaneth alfo thefe pernitious late dealings againft the Earle of *Shrewsburie*, a man of the moft ancient and worthieft Nobilitie of our Realm? what meane the practifes with his neareft both in bed and bloud againft him? what meane thofe moft falfe and flanderous rumours caft abroad of late of his difloyall demeanours towards her Maiefty and his countrey, with the great prifoner committed to his charge? is all this to any other end, but onely to drive him to fome impatience, and thereby to commit or fay fomething which may open the gate unto his ruine? Divers other things could I recite of his behaviour towards other noble men of the Realm, who live abroad in their countries much injured and malecontented by his infolency: albeit in refpect of his prefent power they dare not complaine. And furely, it is ftrange to fee how litile account he maketh of all the ancient nobilitie of our Realme: how he contemneth, derideth and debafeth them; which is the fashion of all fuch as mean to ufurp, to the end they may have nene who fhall not acknowledge their firft beginning and advancement from themfelves.

Not only ufurpers (*quoth the Lawyer*) but all others who rife and mount aloft from bafe lynage, be ordinarily moft *contemptuous, contumultuous*, and *infolent* againft others of more antiquity. And this was evident in this mans father, who being a Buck of the firft head (*as you know*) was intollerable in contempt of others: as appeareth by thofe whom hee trod downe of the

Nobili-

Leycefters devices againft the Earle of Shrewfbury.

Leycefters contempt of the ancient Nobility of England.

Lawyer.

New men moft contemptuous.

Nobilitie in his time : as also by his ordinarie
jefts againft the Duke of *Somerfet* and others.
But among other times, fitting one day at his
owne table (as a Counfellor told mee that was
prefent) he took occafion to talke of the Earl of *D. Dudlies*
Arundel, whom he had then not onely removed *jeft at the*
from the Counfell , but alfo put into the Tower *Earle of*
of *London*, being (as is wel known) the firft and *Arundell.*
chiefeft Earle of the Realme. And for that the
faid Earle fhewed himfelfe fomewhat fad and
afflicted with his prefent ftate (as I marvel **not,**
feing himfelf in prifon, and within the compaffe
of fo fierce a Beares paws) it pleafed this goodly Duke to vaunt upon this Earles mifery, at his
owne Table (as I have faid) and asked the noble
men and gentlemen there prefent, what Creft
or Cognizance my L. of *Arundel* did give ? and
when every one anfwered , that hee gave the
white horfe: I thought fo (quoth the Duke) and
not without great caufe; for as the white Paulfrey when he ftandeth in the ftable, and is well
provendred, is proud and fierce, and ready to
leape on every other horfes back, ftill neying,
and prauncing, and troubling all that ftand a-
bout him : but when he is once out of his hot
ftable , and deprived a little of his eafe and fat
feeding, every boy may ride and mafter him at
his pleafure : fo is it (quoth he) with my Lord
of *Arundell*. Whereat many marvelled that
were prefent, to heare fo infolent fpeech paffe
from a man of judgement, againft a Peere of
the Realme caft into calamity.

But you would more have marvelled (quoth Gentl.
the Gentleman) if you had feene that which I
did afterward, which was the moft bafe and abject behaviour of the fame Duke to the fame
Earle

Earle of *Arundel* at *Cambridge*, and upon the way towards *London* : when this Earle was sent to apprehend and bring him up, as prisoner. If I should tell you how he fell down on his knees, how he wept, how he besought the said Earle to be a good Lord unto him, whom a little before he had so much contemned and reproached, you would have said that himselfe might as well be compared to this his white Paulfrey, as the other: Albeit in this I will excuse neither of them both, neither almost any of these great men who are so proud and insolent in their prosperous fortune, as they are easily led to contemne any man, albeit themselves bee most contemptible of all others, whensoever their fortune beginneth to change : and so will my L. of *Leicester* be, also no doubt at that day, though now in his wealth he triumph over all, and careth not whom, or how many he offend and injure.

Sir, therein I beleeve you (quoth I) for wee have had sufficient tryall already of my Lords fortitude in adversity. His base and abject behaviour in his last disgrace about his marriage, well declared what hee would doe in a matter of more importance. His fawning and flattering of them, whom he hated most : his servile speeches, his feigned and dissembled teares, are all very well knowne : Then Sir *Christopher*

Hatton must needs be enforced to receive at his hands the honourable and great office of Chamberlainship of *Chester*, for that he would by any meanes resigne the same unto him, whether he would or no : and made him provide (not without his charge) to receive the same, though his Lordship never meant it, as after wel appeared. For that the present pange being past,

it

it liked my Lord to fulfill the Italian Proverbe
of such as in dangers make vowes to Saints :
Scampato il pericolo, gabbato il santo, the danger
escaped, the Saint is deceived.

 Then, and in that necessity, no men of the
Realm were so much honoured, commended, &
served by him as the noble Chamberlaine de-
ceased, and the good Lord Treasurer yet living:
to whom, at a certaine time, he wrote a letter
in all fraud and base dissimulation, and caused
the same to be delivered with great cunning in
the sight of her Majesty ; and yet so, as to shew
a purpose that it should not be seen : to the end,
her Highnesse might rather take occasion to call
for the same and read it, as she did. For Mistris *Francis Haward* (to whom the stratagem
was committed) playing her part dexterously,
offered to deliver the same to the Lord Treasurer, neare the doore of the withdrawing
Chamber, he then comming from her Majesty :
And to draw the eye and attention of her Highnesse the more unto it, shee let fall the paper,
before it touched the treasurers hand, and by
that occasion brought her Majesty to call for the
same : Which after she had read and considered
the stile, together with the metall and constitu-
tion of him that wrote it, and to whom it was
sent, her Highnesse could not but breake forth
in laughter, with detestation of such absurd and
abject dissimulation : saying unto my Lord
Treasurer there present : my Lord believe him
not, for if he had you in like case, he would play
the Beare with you, though at this present hee
fawne upon you never so fast.

 But now Sir, I pray you goe forward in your
speech of *Scotland*, for there I remember you

            left

A pretie shift of my Lord of Leycester.

Her Maiesties speech of Leyce-ster to the Treasurer.

left off, when by occasion we fell into these digressions.

Gentl.

Well then(quoth the Gentleman) to returne againe to *Scotland* (as you move) from whence wee have digressed : most certaine and evident it is to all the world, that all the broyles, troubles, and dangers procured to the Prince in that countrey, as also the vexations of them, who any way are thought to favour that title in our owne Realme, doe proceed from the drift and complot of these conspirators. Which besides the great dangers mentioned before, both domesticall and forraine, temporall, and of religion, must needs inferre great jeopardy also to her Maiesties person and present reign, that now governeth, through the hope and heat of the aspirors ambition, inflamed and increased so much the more by the nearenesse of their desired prey.

The danger of her Majesty by oppression of the favourers of the Scottish title.

For as souldiers entred into the hope of a rich and well furnished Citie, are more fierce and furious, when they have gotten and beaten downe the Bullwarks round about : and as the greedy Burglarer that hath pierced and broken downe many walls to come to a treasure, is lesse patient of stay, stop, and delay, when he commeth in fight of that which he desireth, or perceiveth only some partition of wane skot or the like betwixt his fingers, and the cofers or monie bags: so these men when they shall see the succession of *Scotland* extinguished, together with all friends and favourers thereof, (which now are to her Majesty as Bullwarks and wals, and great obstacles to the aspirors) and when they shall see onely her Maiesties life and person, to stand betwixt them and their fierie desires (for they
make

A Similie true.

make little account of all other Competitors by King *Henries* line:) no doubt but it will bee to them a great prick and spurre to dispatch Her Majestie also: the nature of both Earles being well considered, whereof the one killed his own wife, (as hath been shewed before) onely upon a little vaine hope of marriage with a Queene, and the other being so farre blinded and borne away with the same furious fume, & most impotent itching humor of ambition, as his owne mother, when she was alive, seemed greatly to feare his fingers, if once the matter should come so neare, as her life had onely stood in his way. For which cause, the good old Countesse was wont to pray God (as I have heard divers say) that she might dye before her Majesty (which happily was granted unto her) to the end that by standing in her sonnes way (who she saw to her grief, furiously bent to weare a Crown:) there might not some dangerous extremity grow to her by that nearenesse: And if his owne mother feared this mischance, whst may her Majesty doubt at his, & his companions hands, when she onely shall be the obstacle of all their unbridled and impatient desres?

Earle of Leycester.

Earle of Huntington.

The old Countesse of Huntingtons speech of her sonne.

Cleare it is (quoth the Lawyer) that the nearenesse of aspirors to the Crowne, endangereth greatly the present possessors, as you have well proved by reason, and I could shew by divers examples, if it were need. For when *Henrie Bullingbrooke*, Duke of *Lancaster*, saw not onely *Richard* the second to be without issue, but also *Roger Mortimer*, Earle of *March*, that should have succeded in the Crowne, to bee slaine in *Ireland*: though before (as is thought) he meant not to usurpe, yet seeing the possibility and

Lawyer. Nearenesse in competitors doth incitethem to adventure. Henr. Bullingbrook after King H. the 4.

L 2　　　　near

Richard
Duke of
Glouceſter
after King
Richard
the third.

neare cut that he had, was inuited therewith to lay hands of his Soveraignes blond and dignity as he did. The like is thought of *Richard*, Duke of *Gloceſter*, that he never meant the murther of his nephewes, untill he ſaw their father dead, and themſelves in his owne hands; his brother alſo Duke of *Clarence* diſpatched, and his onely ſonne and heire Earle of *Warwick* within his owne power.

Wherefore ſeeing that it hath not pleaſed Almighty God, for cauſes to himſelfe beſt known, to leave unto this noble Realm, any iſſue by her

*The great
wiſedome
of her Ma-
jeſty in con-
ſerving the
next heires
of* Scot-
land.

moſt excellent Maieſtie, it hath been a poynt of great wiſedome in mine opinion, and of great ſafety to her Highnes perſon, ſtate, & dignity, to preſerve hitherto the line of the next Inheritors by the houſe of *Scotland*, (I meane both the mother and the ſonne) whoſe deaths hath been ſo diligently ſought by the other Competitors, and had beene long ere this atchieved, if her Majeſties owne wiſedome, and royall clemency (as is thought) had not placed ſpeciall eye upon the conſervation thereof, from time to time. Which Princely providence, ſo long as it ſhall endure, muſt needs be a great ſafety and fortreſs to her Majeſty, not onely againſt the claimes, aides, or annoyance of forraine Princes, who wil not be ſo forward to advance ſtrange titles, while ſo manifeſt heires remain at home, nor yet ſo willing (in reſpect of policy) to helpe that line to poſſeſſion of the whole Iſland: but alſo againſt practices of domeſticall aſpirers (as you have ſhewed) in whoſe affairs no doubt but theſe two branches of *Scotland* are great b ocks, as alſo ſpeciall bulwarks to her Majeſties life and perſon: ſeeing (as you ſay) theſe copartners make

ſo

so little account of the other of that line, who
should ensue by order of succession.

Marry yet of the two, I thinke the youth of *The K. of*
Scotland be of much more importance for their *Scotlands*
purpose, to bee made away, both for that hee *destruction*
may have issue, and is like in time to be of more *of more im-*
ability, for defence of his owne inheritance: as *portance to*
also for that he being once dispatched, his mo- *the conspi-*
ther should soone ensue by one slight or other, *rators, then*
which they would devise unwitting to her Ma- *his mothers*
jesty: albeit, I must needes confesse that her
Highnesse hath used most singular prudence for
prevention thereof, in placing her restraint with
so noble, strong, and worthy a Peere of our *The Earle*
Realme, as the Earle of *Shrewsburie* is, whose *of Salisbu-*
fidelity and constancy being nothing plyable to *ry disgra-*
the others faction, giveth them little contenta- *ced by the*
tion. And for that cause the world seeth how *competi-*
many sundry and divers devices they have used, *tors.*
and do use dayly to slander and disgrace him, and
thereby to pull from him his charge committed.

To this the Gentleman answered nothing at all, Gentl.
but stood still musing with himselfe, as though hee
had conceived some deep matter in his head: and
after a little pause he began to say as followeth

I cannot truly but much marvaile, when I do *The vigi-*
compare some things of this time and govern- *lant eye*
ment, with the doings of former Princes, Pro- *that her*
genitors to her Majesty. Namely of *Henrie* the *Maiesties*
7. and *Henrie* the 8. who had so vigilant an eye *ancestors*
to the laterall line of King *Edward* the 4. by *had to the*
his brother of *Clarence*, as they thought it ne- *coleterall*
cessary, not only to prevent all evident dangers *line.*
that might ensue that way, but even the possibi-
lities of all perill: as may well appear by the
execution of *Ed.* Earl of *Warwick* before named

Son

Son and heire to the said Duke of *Clarence*, and of *Margaret* his sister Countesse of *Salisbury*, with the Lord *Henry Montague* her sonne, by whose Daughter the Earle of *Huntington* now claimeth. All which were executed for avoyding of inconveniencies, and that at such times, when no imminent danger could be much doubted by that Line, especially by the latter. And yet now when one of the same house and Line, of more ability and ambition, than ever any of his Ancestors were, maketh open title and claime to the Crowne, with plots, packs, and preparations to most manifest usurpation, against all order, all law, and all rightfull succession ? and against a special statute provided in that behalfe: yet is he permitted, borne out, favoured, and friended therein : and no man so hardy, as in defence of her Majestie and the Realme to controle him for the same.

persons executed of the house of Clarece.

It may be that her Majestie is brought into the same opinion of my Lord of *Huntingtons* fidelity, as *Iulius Cæsar* was of *Marcus Brutus*, his dearest obliged friend : of whose ambitious practises, and aspiring, when *Cæsar* was advertised by his carefull friends ; he answered, that hee well knew *Brutus* to be ambitious, but I am sure (quoth he) that my *Brutus* will never attempt any thing for the Empire while *Cæsar* liveth : and after my death let him shift for the same among others, as he can. But what ensued? Surely I am loath to tell the event for ominations sake, but yet all the world knoweth that ere many moneths passed, this most noble and Clement Emperour was pittifully murthered y the same *Brutus* and his partners in the publique Senate, when least of all he expected such

The example of Iulius Cæsars destruction.

such treason. So dangerous a thing it is to be secure in a matter of so great sequell, or to trust them with a mans life, who may pretend preferment or interest by his death.

Wherefore, would God her Majestie in this case might be induced to have such due care and regard of her own estate and royall person, as the weighty moment of the matter requireth: which containeth the blisse and calamity of so noble and worthy a kingdome as this.

I know right well, that most excellent natures are alwayes furthest off from diffidence in such people as proves love, and are most bounden by dutie: and so it is evident in her Majestie. But yet surely, this confidence so commendable in other men, is scarce allowable oftentimes in the person of a Prince: for that it goeth accompanyed with so great perill, as is inevitable to him that will not suspect principally when dangers are foretold or presaged, (as commonly by Gods appoyntment they are, for the speciall hand he holdeth over Princes affaires) or when there is probable conjecture, or just surmise of the same. *Too much confidence verie perillous in a Prince.*

We know that the forenamed Emperor *Cæsar*, had not onely the warning given him of the inclination and intent of *Brutus* to usurpation, but even the very day when hee was going towards the place of his appoynted destiny, there was given up into his hands a detection of the whole treason, with request to read the same presently, which he upon confidence omitted to doe. Wee read also of *Alexander* the great, how hee was not onely forbidden by a learned man to enter into *Babylon* (whither he was then going) for that there was treason meant against him in the place, but also that he was foretold of *Antipaters* mischievous *The example of Alexander the great, how hee was foretold his danger.*

L 4   chievous

chievous meaning against him in particular. But the yong Prince having so well deserved of *Antipater*, could not be brought to mistrust the man that was so deare unto him: and by that meanes was poysoned in a banquet by three sons of *Antipater*, which were of most credit and confidence in the Kings Chamber.

Schollar. Here, truly, my heart did somewhat tremble with feare, horror, and detestation of such events. And I said unto the Gentleman: I beseech you Sir, to talke no more of these matters; for I cannot well abide to heare them named: hoping in the Lord that there is no cause, nor ever shall be, to doubt the like in *England*: especially from these men, **Late executions.** who are so much bound to her Majesty, and so forward in seeking out, and pursuing all such as may be thought to be dangerous to her Majesties person, as by the sundry late executions wee have have seen, and by the punishments every way of Papists we may perceive.

Gentl. Truth it is (quoth the Gentleman) that justice hath bin done upon divers of late, which contenteth me greatly, for the terrour and restraint of others, of what sect or religion soever they be: And it is most necessary (doubtles) for the compressing of parties, that great vigilance be used in that behalfe. But when I consider, that only one kind of men are touched herein: and that all speech, regard, doubt, distrust, and watch is of them alone, without reflection of eye upon other mens doings or designements: when I see the double diligence and vehemency of certaine instruments, which I like not, bent wholly to raise wonder and admiration of the people, feare, terrour, and attention to the doings, sayings, and meanings of one part or faction alone, and of that namely and only which these

these conspirators esteem for most dangerous and *Fraud to* opposite to themselves : I am (beleeve me) often *be feared* tempted to suspect fraud and false measure : and *in pursuing* that these men deale, as wolves by nature in other *one part or* Countries are wont to do : Which going together *faction on-* in great numbers to assaile a flocke of sheep by *ly.* night, doe set some one or two of their company *The com-* upon the wind side of the fold a far off, who par- *parison of* ly by their sent and other bruteling, which of pur- *Wolves* pose they make, may draw the dogs and shep- *and Rebels.* heards to pursue them alone, whiles the other doe enter and slay the whole flock. Or as rebels that meaning to surprize a Town, to turne away the Inhabitants from considering of the danger, and from defence of that place, where they intend to enter, doe set on fire some other parts of the Towne further off, and doe sound a false alarme at some gate, where is meant least danger.

Which art was used cunningly by *Richard* D. *Richard* of *Yorke* in the time of King *Henrie* the sixt, *Duke of* when he to cover his owne intent, brought all the *Yorke.* Realme in doubt of the doings of *Edmond* Duke of *Somerset*, his enemy. But *Iohn* of *Northumber-* *D. Dudly.* *land*, father to my Lord of *Leycester*, used the same art much more skilfully, when hee put all *England* in a maze and musing of the Protector, and of his friends : as though nothing could be safe about the yong King, untill they were sup- pressed : and consequently, all brought into his *A good rule* owne authority, without obstacle. I speake not *of policy.* this to excuse Papists, or to wish them any way spared wherein they offend : but onely to signifie that in a Countrey, where so potent factions bee, it is not safe, to suffer the one to make it selfe so puissant by pursuit of the other : as afterwards the Prince must remaine at the devotion of the stronger :

stronger : but rather as in a body molested and troubled with contrarie humours, if all cannot be purged, the best Physick is without all doubt to reduce and hold them at such an equality, as destruction may not be feared of the predominant.

To this said the Lawyer laughing, yea marry Sir, I would to God your opinion might prevaile in this matter ; for then should wee bee in other tearmes then now we are. I was, not long since, in company of a certaine honourable Lady of the Court, who, after some speech passed by Gentlemen that were present, of some apprehended, and some executed, and such like affaires , brake into a great complaint of the present time, and therewith (I assure you) moved all the hearers to griefe (as women you know are potent in stirring of affections) and caused them all to wish that her Majesty had beene nigh to have heard her words.

The speech of a certaine Lady of the Court. I doe well remember (quoth she) the first dosen yeares of her Highnesse reigne, how happy, pleasant and quiet they were, with all manner of comfort and consolation. There was no mention then of factions in religion, neither was any man much noted or rejected for that cause: so otherwise his conversation were civill and courteous. No suspition of treason, no talke of bloudshed, no complaint of troubles, miseries, or vexations, All was peace, all was love, all was joy, all was delight. Her Majestie (I am sure) took more Recreation at that time in one day , than shee doth now in a whole week : and wee that served her Highnesse, enjoyed more contentation in a weeke, than we can now in divers yeares. For now, there are so many suspitions every where, for this thing, and for that, as we cannot tell whom to trust. So many melancholick in the Court, that seem malecontencontented, so many complayning or suing for their friends that are in trouble : others slip over the Sea, or retire themselves upon the suddaine : so many tales brought us of this or that danger; of this man suspected, of that man sent for up, and such like unpleasant, and unsavorie stuffe ; as we can never almost bee merry one whole day together.

Wherefore (quoth this Lady) wee that are of her Majesties traine and speciall service, and doe not onely feele these things in our selves, but much more in the grief of her most excellent Majesty whom we see dayly molested herewith (being one of the best natures, I am sure, that ever noble Princesse was indued withall:) wee cannot but mone, to behold contentions advanced so far forth as they are : and we could wish most heartily that for the time to come these matters might passe with such peace, friendship, and tranquillity, as they doe in other Countryes, where difference in religion breaketh not the band of good fellowship, or fidelity. And with this in a smiling manner she brake off, asking pardon of the company, if she had spoken her opinion over boldly, like a woman.

More moderation wished in matters of faction.

To whom answered a Courtier that sate next her : Madame, your Ladiship hath said nothing in this behalfe, that is not dayly debated amongst us, in our common speech in Court as you know. Your desire also herein is a publick desire, if it might be brought to passe : for there is no man so simple, that seeth not how perilous these contentions and divisions among us may bee in the end. And I have heard divers Gentlemen that be learned, discourse at large upon this argument : alleaging old examples of the *Athenians, Lacedemonians,*

The speech of a Courtier.

demonians, Carthigenians, and *Romans*, who received notable dammages, and destruction also in
the end, by their divisions and factions among
themselves, and specially from them of their own
Cities and Countries, who upon factions lived a-
broad with Forrainers : and thereby were always
as fire-brands, to carry home the flame of Warre
upon their Countrey.

 The like they also shewed by the long experience of all the great Cities and States of *Italy* :
which by their factions and forucites, were in
continuall gar-boyle, bloud-shed and miserie.
Whereof our owne countrey hath also tasted her
part, by the odious contention between the houses of *Lancaster* and *Yorke* : wherein it is marvailous to consider, what trouble a few men oftentimes, departing out of the Realme, were able to
worke by the part of their faction remaining at
home: (which commonly encreaseth toward
them that are absent)& by the readines of forrain
Princes, to receive alwayes, and comfort such as
are discontented in another state : to the end, that
by their meanes, they might hold an Ore in their
neighbours boat : Which Princes that are nigh
borderers, doe alwayes above all other things
most covet and desire.

 This was that Courtiers speech and reason,
whereby I perceived, that aswell among them in
Court, as among us in the Realme and Country
abroad, the present inconvenience and dangerous
sequell of this our home dissention, is espyed, and
consequently most English hearts inclined to wish
the remedy or prevention thereof , by some reasonable moderation , or re-union among our
selves. For that the prosecution of these differences to extremitie, cannot but after many wounds
          and

and exulcerations bring matters finally to rage, fury, and moſt deadly deſperation.

Whereas on the other ſide, if any ſweet qualification, or ſmall tolleration among us were admitted : there is no doubt, but that affaires would paſſe in our Realme with more quietneſſe, ſafety and publike weale of the ſame, then it is like it will doe long : and men would eaſily be brought, that have Engliſh bowel's, to joyne in the preſervation of their Countrey from ruine, bloudſhed, and forraine oppreſſion, which deſparation of factions is wont to procure.

I am of your opinion (quoth the Gentleman) Gentl. in that, for I have ſeene the experience thereof, and all the world beholdeth the ſame at this day, in all the Countries of *Germanie, Polonia, Bœm-* *Examples* *land,* and *Hungarie :* where a little bearing of *of tollera-* the one with the other, hath wrought them much *tion in mat* eaſe, and continued them a peace, whereof all *Eu-* *ters of reli-* *rope* beſides hath admiration and envie. The firſt *gion.* 12 years alſo of her Majeſties reign, whereof your *Germany.* Lady of the Court diſcourſed of before, can well bee a witneſſe of the ſame : wherein the commiſeration and lenity that was uſed towards thoſe of the weaker ſort, with a certaine ſweet diligence for their gaining, by good means was the cauſe of much peace, contentation, and other benefit to the whole body.

Wee ſee in *France,* that by over much preſſing *The breach* of one part onely, a fire was inkindled not *& reunion* many yeares ſince, like to have conſumed and *again in* deſtroyed the whole : had not a neceſſary mol- *France.* lification been thought upon by the wiſeſt of that Kings Councell full contrary to the will and inclination of ſome great perſonages, who meant perhaps to have gained more by the other : and

and fince that time we fee what peace, wealth, and re-union hath enfued in that Country that was fo broken, diffevered, and wafted before. And all this, by yeelding a litt'e in that thing, which no force can mafter, but exulcerate rather, and make worfe: I meane the confcience and judgement of men in matters of Religion.

Flanders. The like alfo I could name you in *Flanders,* where after all thefe broyles and miferies of fo many yeares warres (caufed principally by too much ftreyning in fuch affaires at the beginning) albeit the King bee never fo ftrict-laced, in yeelding to publike liberty, and free exercife on both parts: yet is he defcended to this at length (and that upon force of reafon) to abftaine from the purfuit and fearch of mens confciences, not only in the townes, which upon compofition hee receiveth, but alfo where he hath recovered by force, as in *Torney,* and other places: where I am informed that no man is fearched, demanded, or molefted for his opinion or confcience, nor any act of Papiftry or contrary religion required at their hands, but are permitted to live quietly to God and themfelves, at home in their owne houfes: fo they performe otherwife their outward obedience and duties to their Prince and Country. Which only qualification, tollerance, and moderation in our Realme (if I bee not deceived, with many more that be of my opinion) would content all divifions, factions, and parties among us, for their continuance in peace: bee they Papifts, Puritans, Familians: or of whatfoever nice difference or fection befides, and would be fufficient to retaine all parties within a temperate obedience to the Magiftrate and government, for confervation of their Country: which were of no fmall importance

tance to the contentation of her Majesty, and the weale publick of the whole kingdome.

But what should I talke of this thing which is *Moderati-* so contrary to the desires and designements of our *on impug-* puissant Conspirators ? What should *Cicero* the *ned by the* Senator use perswasions to Captaine *Cateline,* and *conspira.* his crew, that quietnesse and order were better *Cicero.* than hurliburlies ? Is it possible that our aspirors *Cateline.* will ever permit any such thing, cause, or matter, to be treated in our state, as may tend to the stability of her Majesties present government ? No surely, it standeth nothing with their wisedome or policy, especially at this instant, when they have such opportunity of following their owne actions in Her Majesties name, under the vizard and pretext of her defence and safety : having sowed in every mans head so many imaginations of the dangers present both abroad and at home : from *scotland, Flanders, Spaine,* and *Ire-* land : so man conspiracies, so many intended *The Con-* murthers, and others so many contrived or con- *spirators* ceived mischiefes : as my Lord of *Leicester* assu- *opportuni-* reth himselfe that the troubled water cannot be *tie.* cleared againe in short space, nor his baits and lines laid therein, easily espyed : but rather, that hereby, ere long, he will catch the fish he gapeth so greedily after : and in the meane time , for the pursuit of these crimes, and other that he dayly will finde out, himselfe must remaine perpetuall Dictator.

But what meaneth this so much inculcating of troubles, treasons, murthers, and invasions ? I like not surely these ominous speeches. And as I am out of doubt, that *Leicester* the caster of these shadowes, doth looke to play his part first in these troublesome affaires : so doe I heartily feare, that

unlesse

unleſſe the tyranny of this *Leiceſtrian* fury bee
ſpeedily ſtopped , that ſuch miſerie to Prince
and people (which the Lord for his mercies
ſake turne from us) as never greater fell before to
our miſerable Countrey, is far nearer hand than
is expected or ſuſpected.

And therefore for the prevention of theſe cala-
mities , to tell you plainly mine opinion (good
Sirs) and therewith to draw to an end of this our
conference (for it waxeth late:) I would thinke
it the moſt neceſſarie poynt of all for her Majeſty
to call his Lordſhip to account among other, and
to ſee what other men could ſay againſt him , at
length, after ſo many yeares of his ſole accuſing,
and purſuing of others. I know,and am very well
aſſured , that no one act which her Majeſtie hath
done ſince her comming to the Crowne (as ſhee
hath done right many moſt highly to be commended) nor any that lightly her Majeſty may doe
hereafter, can be of more utility to Her ſelfe, and
to the Realme,or, more gratefull to her faithfull
and zealous ſubjects than this noble act of Iuſtice
would be, for tryall of this mans deſerts towards
his Countrey.

I ſay it would be profitable to her Majeſty, and
to the Realme , not onely in reſpect of the many dangers before mentioned, hereby to be avoy-
ded,which are like to enſue moſt certainly , if his
courſes bee ſtill permitted : but alſo for that her
Majeſty ſhall by this , deliver Her ſelfe from that
generall grudge and griefe of mind,with great diſlike, which many ſubiects, otherwiſe moſt faithfull, have conceived againſt the exceſsive favour
ſhewed to this man ſo many yeares , without de-
ſert or reaſon.Which favour he having uſed to the
hurt, annoyance, and oppreſſion both of infinite

*Leyceſter
to be called
to account.*

ſeverall

severall persons, and the whole common-wealth
(as hath bin said:) the griefe and resentment
thereof, doth redound commonly in such cases
not only upon the person delinquent alone, but
also upon the Soveraigne, by whose favour & authority he offers such iniuries, though never so
much against the others intér,d. sire or meaning.

And hereof we have examples of sundry Princes, in all ages and Countries, whose exorbitant
favour to some wicked subiect that abused the
same, hath bin the cause of great danger and ruine ; the sins of the favourite being returned and
revenged upon the favourer. As in the Historie
of the *Grecians* is declared , by occasion of the
pittifull murther of that wise and victorious P. *The death*
Philip of *Macedony* , who albeit , that he were *K Philip*
well assured to have given no offence of himself *of Mace-*
to any of his subiects, & consequently feared no *donie, and*
thing, but conversed openly and confidently a- *cause there*
mong them : yet, for that hee had favoured too *of.*
much one like *Attalus*, a proud and insolent
Courtier, and had born him out in certain of his
wickednes, or at least not punished the same after it was detected and complained upon : the
parties grieved accounting the crime more proper and heinous on the part of him, who by
office should do iustice, & protect other, than of
the perpetrator, who followeth his own passion and sensuality, let pass *Attalus*, & made their
revenge upon the bloud & life of the K himself,
by one *Pausanias*, suborned for that purpose, in *Pausanias.*
the marriage day of the Kings owne daughter.

Great store of like examples may be repeated,
out of the stories of other countries; nothing being more usuall or frequent among all nations,
than the afflictions of realms and kingdoms, and
M the

the overthrow of Princes and great Potentates themselves, by their too much affection towards some unworthy particular persons : a thing indeed so common and ordinary, as it may well seem to be the speciall Rock of all other, whereat Kings & Princes doe make their shipwracks.

For if we look into the states and Monarchies all Christendome, and consider the ruines that have bin of any Princes or Ruler within the same : we shall find this poynt to have bin a great and principall part of the cause thereof : and in our owne state and countrey, the matter is too evident. For whereas since the Conquest we number principally, three just and lawfull Kings, to have come to confusion, by alienation of their subjects : that is, *Edward* the second, *Rich.* the second, and *Henrie* the sixt : this only point of too much favour towards wicked persons, was the chiefest cause of destruction in all three. As in the first, the excessive favour towards *Peter Gaveston,* and two of the *Spencers.* In the second, the like extraordinarie, and indiscreet affection towards *Robert Vere,* Eurle of *Oxford,* and Marquesse of *Dublin,* and *Thomas Mowbray,* two most turbulent and wicked men, that set the K. against his own Vncles & the nobility. In the third (being a simple and holy man) albeit no great exorbitant affection was seene towards any, yet his wife Queen *Margarets* too much favour and eredit (by him not controled, towards the Marquesse of Suffolke, that after was made Duke, by whose instinct and wicked Counsell, she made away first the noble Duke of *Gloucester,* and afterward committed other things in great prejudice of the Realme, and suffered the said most impious and sinfull

Kings of England overthrown by too much favouring of some particular men.

K. Edw. 2.

K. Rich. 2.

K. Henr. 6.

finfull Duke to range and make havock of all
fort of fubjects at his pleafure (much after the
fathion of the Earle of *Leicefter* now , though
yet not in fo high and extreame a degree: (this I
fay was the principall and originall caufe, both
before God and man, (as *Polidore* well noteth) *Pol.lib.*23
of all the calamity and extreme defolation, *hift.Angl.*
which after enfued both to the King, Queene,
and their onely child, with the utter extirpation
of their family.

And fo likewife now to fpeak in our particular cafe, if there be any grudge or griefe at this
day, any miflike, repining, complaint or mur-
mure againft her Majefties government, in the
hearts of her true and faithfull fubjects, who
wifh amendment of that which is amiffe , and
not the overthrow of that which is well : (as I
trow it were no wifedome to imagine there
were none at all :) I dare avouch upon Confcience, that either all, or the greateft part thereof, proceedeth from this man; who by the favor of her Majefty fo afflicteth her people as never did before him, either *Gavefton*, *Spencer*, *Vere*,
or *Mowbray* or any other mifchievous tirant, that
abufed moft his Princes favour within our
Realme of *England* Whereby it is evident how
profitable a thing it fhould bee to the whole
Realme , how honourable to her Majefty , and
how gratefull to all her fubjects, if this man at
length might be called to his account.

Sir (quoth the Lawyer) you alleage great rea- Lawyer.
fon, and verily I am of opinion, that if her Majefty knew but the tenth part of this, which you
have here fpoken, as alfo her good fubjects de-
fires and complaint in this behalfe : fhe would
well fhew , that her Highneffe feareth not to

M 2 per-

permit iustice to passe upon *Leicester*, or any other within her Realme, for satisfaction of her people, whatsoever some men may think and report to the contrary, or howsoever otherwise of her owne milde disposition towards the person, she have borne with him hitherto. For so we see that wise Princes can doe at times convenient for peace and tranquillity, and publike weale: though contrary to their owne particular and peculiar inclination.

As to goe no further then to the last example named and alleaged by your selfe before: though Queen *Margaret* the wife of K. *Henrie* the sixt, had favoured most unfortunately many yeares together, *William* Duke of *Suffolk* (as hath bin said) whereby he committed manifold outrages, and afflicted the Realme by sundry meanes: yet she being a woman of great prudence, when she saw the whole Communalty demand iustice upon him for his demerits, albeit she liked and loved the man still : yet for satisfaction of the people, upon so generall a complaint, shee was content first to commit him to prison, and afterward to banish him the Realme : but the providence of God would not permit him so to escape : for that he being incountred, and taken upon the sea in his passage, he was beheaded in the ship, and so received some part of condigne punishment for his most wicked, loose, and licentious life.

And to seeke no more examples in this case, & we know into what favour and speciall grace Sir *Edmond Dudley*, my Lord of *Leycesters* good Grandfather was crept, with King *Henry* the seventh, in the latter end of his reigne : and what intollerable wickednesse and mischiefe he wrought

The punishment of William Duke of Suffolk.

wrought againſt the whole Realme, and againſt
infinite particular perſons of the ſame, by the
polings and oppreſſions which hee practiſed:
wherby though the King received great temporall commodity at that time, (as her Majeſty *The puniſh*
doth nothing at all by the preſent extortions of *ment of*
his Nephew:) yet for juſtice ſake, and for meere Edmond
compaſſion towards his afflicted ſubiects, that Dudley.
complained grievouſly of this iniquity : that
moſt vertuous and wiſe Prince King *Henrie* was
content to put from him this lewd inſtrument,
and devilliſh ſuggeſtor of new exactions: whom
his ſonne *Henrie* that enſued in the Crown, cau-
ſed preſently before all other buſines, to be called publickly to account , and for his deſerts to
leeſe his head : So as where the intereſt of a
whole Realme, or common cauſe of many, taketh place : the private favour of any one cannot
ſtay a wiſe & godly Prince, (ſuch as al the world
knoweth her Maieſty to be) from permitting iuſtice to have her free paſſage.

Truely it ſhould not (quoth the Gentleman) Gentl.
for to that end were Princes firſt elected , and *The cauſes*
upon that conſideration doe ſubiects both pay *why Prin-*
them tribute and obedience ; to bee defended *ces are cho-*
by them from iniuries and oppreſſions , and to *ſen, and do*
ſee lawes executed, and iuſtice exerciſed, upon *receive o-*
and towards all men with indifferency. And *bedience.*
as for our particular caſe of my Lord of *Ley-*
ceſter, I doe not ſee in right and equity how her
Maieſty may deny this lawfull deſire and petition of her people. For if her highneſſe doe permit and command the Lawes dayly to paſſe upon thieves and murderers without exception,
and that for one fact onely, as by experience we
ſee ; how then can it be denyed in this man,

M 3   who

who in both kinds hath committed more enormous acts, then may be well recounted.

Leycesters Thefts. As in the first, of theft, not onely by spoyling and oppressing almost infinite private men : but also whole Towns, Villages, Corporations, and Countries, by robbing the Realme with inordinate licences, by deceiving the Crown with racking, changing and imbezeling the Lands, by abusing his Prince and Soveraigne in selling his favour both at home and abroad : with taking bribes for matter of justice, grace, request, supplication, or whatsoever sute else may depend upon the Court, or of the Princes authority : with setting at sale, and making open market of whatsoever her Majesty can give, doe, or procure, be it spirituall or temporall. In which sort of traffick he committeth more theft oftentimes in one day than all the way-keepers, cut-purses, couseners, pirates, burglares, or other of that art in a whole yeare, within the Realme

Leycesters murthers. And as for the second, which is murther, you have heard before somewhat said and proved : but yet nothing to that which is thought to have bin in secret committed upon divers occasions at divers times, in sundry persons, of different calling in both sexes, by most variable means of killing, poysoning, charming, inchanting, conjuring, and the like, according to the diversity of men, places, opportunities, and instruments for the same. By all which meanes, I think he hath more bloud lying upon his head at this day, crying vengeance against him at Gods hands, & her Majesty, than ever had private man in our Country before, were he never so wicked.

Whereto now, if we adde his other good behaviour, as his intollerable licentiousnesse in all filthy kinde

M

kind and manner of carnality, with all sort of *A heap of*
Wives, Friends, and Kinsewomen: if wee add his *Leycesters*
iniuries aod dishonours, done hereby to infinite: if *enormities*
we adde his treasons, treacheries, and conspiracies *that would*
about the Crowne; his disloyall behaviour, and ha- *be ready at*
tred against her Majesty, his ordinarie lying, and *the day of*
common perjuring himselfe in all matters for his *his triall.*
gain, both great and smal; his rapes and most violent extortions upon the poore; his abusing of the
Parliament and other places of justice, with the
Nobility and whole Communalty besides; if we add
also his open injuries which bee offereth duly to
Religion, and the Minister; thereof, by tithing
them, and turning all to his owne gaine; together
with his manifest and known tyranny practised towards all estates abroad, through out all Shires of
the kingdome; his dispoyling of both the Universities, and discouraging of infinite notable wits
there, from seeking perfection of knowledge and
learning, (which otherwise were like to become
notable) especially in Gods word (which giveth life
unto the soule,) by defrauding them of the price
and reward proposed for their travail in that kind,
through his insatiable Simoniacall contracts: if I
say, we should lay together all these enormities before her Majesty, and thousands more in particular, which might and would be gathered, if his day
of his triall were but in hope to be granted. I do not
see in equity and reason, how her Highnesse sitt rg
in throne, and at the royall sterne, as shee doth,
could denie her Subiects this most lawfull request;
considering, that every one of these crimes apart,
requireth justice of his owne nature; and much
more all together ought to obtaine the same, at the
hands of any good and godly Magistrate in the
World.

Schollar.
Her Ma-
iesties ten-
der heart
towards
the realme.

No doubt (quoth I but that these considerations must needs weigh much with any zealous
Prince, and much more with her most excell.nt
Majesty whose tender heart towards her Realm
and Subjects, is very well known of all men. It
is not to be thought also but that her Highnesse
hath intelligence of divers of hese matters alleaged, though not perhaps of all. But what
would you have her Majesty to doe? perhaps the
consultation of this affaire, is not, what were
convenient, but what is expedient: not, what
ought to bee done in justice, but what may bee
done in safety. You have described my Lord before to be a great man, strongly furnished and
fortified for all events. What if it be not secure to
bark at the Bear that is so wel britched? I speak
unto you, but that which I heare in *Cambridge*
and other places where I have passed: where e-
very mans opinion is, that her Majesty standeth
not in free choyse to doe what her selfe best liketh in that case, at this day.

Gentl.
Leycesters
desire that
men should
thnike her
Maiesty
to stand in
feare of
him.

I know (said the Gentleman) that *Leicesters*
friends give it out every where that her *Maiesty*
now, is their good Lords prisoner, and that shee
either will or must be directed by him for the
time to come, except she will do worse: Which
thing his Lordship is well contented should bee
spread abroad, and believed for two causes: the
one to hold the people thereby more in awe of
himself, than of their Soveraign: and secondly to
draw her Majesty indeed by degrees to fear him.
For considering with himselfe what hee hath
done: and that it is impossible in truth that ever
her Majesty should lo   trust him
after so many   weth are
com   thinketh
                                 that

that he hath no way of sure standing, but by terror and opinion of his puissant greatnesse; wherby he would hold her Majesty and the Realme in thraldome, as his father did in his time before him. And then, for that he wel remembreth the true saying, *Malus custos diuturnitatis, metus:* he must provide shortly, that those which feare him, be not able to hurt him: and consequently you know what must follow, by the example of K. *Edward*, who feared Duke *Dudley* extreamly for that he had cut off his two Vncles heads, and the Duke took order that he should never live to revenge the same. For it is a setled rule of *Machiavel*, which the *Dudlies* doe observe: *That when you have once done a great injury, there must you never forgive.*

Cicero in Officio.

A rule of Machivell observed by the Dudlies

But I will tell you (my friends) and I will tell you no untruth, for that I know what I speak herein, and am privie to the state of my Lord in this behalfe, and of mens opinions and affections towards him within the Realme. Most certaine it is, that hee is strong by the present favour of the Prince (as hath bin shewed before) in respect wherof, he is admitted also as chief patron of the *Huntington* faction, though neither loved, nor greatly trusted of the same: but let her Majesty once turn her countenance aside from him in good earnest, and speak but the word only, *that iustice shall take place against him;* and I will undertake with gaging of both my life and little lands that God hath given me, that without stur or trouble, or any danger in the world, the Beare shall be taken to her Majesties hand, and fast chained to a stake, with mouzell, cord, collar, and ring, and all other things necessary: so that her Majesty shal bait him at her pleasure, without all danger of byting, breaking loose, or any other inconvenience whatsoever.

Leyceßer strong onely by her Maiesties favour.

An offer made for taking and tying the Beare.

For

For (Sirs) you must not think, that this man holdeth any thing abroad in the Realme but by violence, and that onely upon her Majesties favour and countenance towards him. He hath not any thing of his owne, either from his ancestors, or of himselfe, to stay upon, in mens hearts or conceits: he hath not ancient Nobility, as other of our realm have, wherby mens affections are greatly moved. His father *John Dudley* was the first noble of his line; who raised and made himselfe big by supplanting of other, and by setting debate among the Nobilitie. as also his grandfather *Edmond*, a most wicked Promoter, and wretched Petifogger, enriched himselfe by other mens ruines: both of them condemned Traitors, though different in quality, the one being a cousener, and the other a tyrant, and both of their vices conjoyned, collected, and comprised (with many more additions) in this man (or beast rather) which is *Robert*, the third of their kin and kind. So that from his ancestors, this Lord receiveth neither honour nor honesty, but onely succession of treason and infamy.

And yet in himselfe hath he much lesse of good, wherewith to procure himselfe loye or credit among men, than these ancestors of his had; hee being a man wholy abandoned of humane vertue, and devoted to wickednes, which maketh men edible both to God and man. In his father (no doubt) there were to be seen many excellent good parts, if they had been joyned with faith, honesty, moderation and loyalty. For all the world know that he was very wise, valiant, magnanimous, liberall, and assured friendly where he once promised: of all which vertues my Lord his son hath neither strew nor shadow, but onely a certaine false repre-

Leicester what hee receiveth from his ancestors.

The comparison of Leycester with his father.

representation of the first, being craftie and subtile to deceive, and ingenious to wickednesse. For as for valour, he hath as much as hath a mouse: his magnanimity is base sordidity: his liberality rapine: his friendship plaine fraud, holding onely for his gaine, and no otherwise, though it were bound with a thousand oathes; of which he maketh as great account, as hens doe of cackling, but onely for his commodity: using them specially and in greatest number, when most he meaneth to deceive. Namely, if he sweare solemnly by his *George*, or by the eternall God, then be sure it is a false lye: for these are observations in the Court: and sometimes in his owne lodging; in like case his manner is to take up and sweare by the Bible, whereby a Gentleman of good account, and one that seemeth to follow him, (as many do that like him but a little) protested to me of his knowledge, that in a very short space, hee observed him wittingly and willingly to be forsworn sixteen times.

This man therefore so contemptible by his ancestors, so odible of himselfe, so plunged, overwhelmed and defamed in all vice, so envyed in the Court, so detested in the Country, and not trusted of his owne and dearest friends, nay (which I am privie to) so misliked and hated of his owne servants about him, for his beastly life, nigardy, and Atheisme (being never seene yet to say one private prayer within his chamber in his life) as they desire nothing in this world so much as his ruine, and that they may be the first, to lay hands upon him for revenge. This man (I say) so broken both within & without, is it possible that her Majesty and her wise Councell should feare? I can never believe it, or if it be so, it is Gods permission without all cause, for punishment of our sins: for

The weaknesse of Leycester if her Majisty turne but her countenace from him.

that

that this man, if he once perceive indeed that they feare him, will handle them accordingly, and play the Beare indeed: which inconvenience I hope they will have care to prevent, and so I leave it to God, and them, craving pardon of my Lord of *Leicester* for my boldnes, if I have been too plain with him. And so I pray you let us goe to supper, for I see my servant expecting yonder at the Gallery doore to call us downe.

Lawyer.
The end and departure from the Gallerie.

To that, said the Lawyer, I am content with all my heart, and I would it had beene sooner, for that I am afraid, left any by chance have overheard us here since night. For my owne part, I must say, that I have not been at such a conference this seven years, nor meane to bee hereafter, if I may escape well with this; whereof I am sure I shall dreame this fortnight, and thinke oftner of my Lord of *Leicester*, than ever I had intended: God amend him and me both. But if ever I heare at other hands of these matters hereafter, I shall surely be quake britch, and thinke every bush a theefe. And with that, came up the Mistris of the house to fetch us down to supper, and so all was husht; saving that at supper a gentleman or two began again to speak of my Lord, and that so conformable to some of our former speech (as indeed it is the common talke at tables every where) that the old Lawyer began to shrink and be appaled, and to cast dry looks upon the Gentleman our friend, doubting lest something h id been discovered of our conference. But indeed it was not so.

Pia et utilis Meditatio, desumpta ex libro Iobi, Cap. 20.

Hoc scio a principio, ex quo positus est homo super terram, quod laus impiorum brevis sit, et gaudium hypocritæ ad instar puncti. Si ascenderit usq; ad cœlum superbia ejus, et caput ejus nubes tetigerit: quasi sterquilinium in fine perdetur, et qui eum viderant, dicent ubi est? velut somnium avolans non invenietur, transiet sicut visio nocturna. Oculus qui eum viderat, non videbit, neq; ultra intuebitur eum locus suus. Filii eius atterentur egestate, & manus illius reddent ei laborem suum. Ossa eius implebuntur vitiis adolescentiæ ejus, & cum eo in pulvere dormient. Panis eius in utero illius vertetur in fel aspidum intrinsecus. Divitias quas devoravit, evomet, et de ventre illius extrahet eas Deus. Caput aspidum surget, & occidet eum lingua vipræ. Luet quæ fecit omnia, nec tamen consumetur. Iuxta multitudinem adinventionum suarum, sic et sustinebit. Quoniá côfringens nudabit pauperes: domum rapuit, & non ædificavit eam, nec est satiatus venter eius, & cum habuerit quæ concupierit possidere non poterit. Non remansit de cibo eius, & propterea non permanebit de bonis eius. Cũ satiatus fuerit, arctabitur, æstuabit, & omnis dolor irruet super eum. Vtinam impleatur venter eius, ut immittat in eũ (Deus) in ã furoris sui, & pluat super illum bellam suum. Fugiet arma ferrea, & irruet in arcum æreum. Gladius eductus & egrediens de vagina sua, & fulgurans in amaritudine sua: Omnes tenebræ absconditæ sunt in occultis eius. Devorabit eum ignis qui non succenditur, affligetur relictus in tabernaculo suo. Apertum erit germen domus illius, detrahetur in die furoris dei. Hæc est pars hominis impii à deo, & hæreditas verborum ejus à domino.

✠✠✠✠✠✠✠✠✠✠✠✠✠✠✠✠✠✠✠✠✠✠✠✠✠

A Godly and profitable Meditation, taken out of the 20. Chapter of the Booke of Job.

The wic-
ked mans
pomp.

THis I know from the first, that man was pla-ced upon earth, that the praise (or applause) given to wicked men, endureth but a little, and the joy of an hypocrite is but for a moment.

His joy.
His pride.
His fall.

Though his pride were so great as to mount to heaven, and his head should touch the skyes, yet in the end shall hee come to perdition as a dung-hill, and they who beheld him (in glory before) shall say, where is he? he shall be found as a fly-ing dreame, and, as a phantasie by night shall fade away. The eye that beheld him before, shall no more see him, nor yet shall his place (of honour) ever more behold him. His children shall be worne

His chil-
dren.
His old age

out with beggerie, and his owne hands shall re-turne upon him his sorrow. His (old) bones shal be replenished with the vices of his youth, and

His bread.

they shall sleep with him in his grave. His bread in his belly shal be turned inwardly into the gaule

His resti-
tution.

of Serpents. The riches which hee hath devoured he shall vomit forth againe, and God shall pull them forth of his belly. He shall suck the head of Cocatrices, and the (venemous) tongues of adders

His punish-
ment.

shall slay him. He shall sustaine due punishment for all the wickednes that he hath committed, nor yet shall he have end or consummation thereof. Hee shall suffer according to the multitude of all

His wic-
kednesse.

his wicked inventions. For that by violence hee hath spoyled the poore, made havock of his house,

and

and not builded the fame. His womb is never fa-
tisfied,& yet when he hath that which he defired,
he fhall not bee able to poffeffe the fame. There
remaineth no part of his meat (for the poore:)
and therefore there fhall remaine nothing of his
goods. When his belly is full then fhall he begin *His griefe.*
to be ftraitned,then fhall he fweat, and all kinde
of forrow fhall rufh upon him. I would his belly *His affli-*
were once full, that God might fend out upon *ction.*
him the rage of his fury, and raine upon him his
war. He fhall flye away from Iron weapons,and
run upon a bow of braffe. A drawne fword comming out of his skabard fhall flafh as lightning
in his bitterneffe. All darkneffe lye hidden for *His dam-*
him in fecret: the fire that needeth no kindling *nation.*
fhall devoure him, and hee fhall be tormented a-
lone in his tabernacle. The off-fpring of his *His pofte-*
houfe fhall be made open,and pulled down, *rity.*
in the day of Gods fury. This is the
portion of a wicked man from
God, and this is the inheritance of his fubftance
from the Lord.

F I N I S.

LEICESTER'S
GHOST.

Printed, *Anno Dom.* MDCXLI.

LEICESTER'S
GHOST.

I That sometimes shin'd like the orient Sunne,
 Though Fortunes subject, yet a puissant Lord,
 Am now an object to be gaz'd upon,
An abject rather fit to be deplor'd
Dejected now that whilome was ador'd :
    Affected once, suspected since of many
    Rejected now, respected scarce of any.

My Spirit hovering in the foggie aire
Since it did passe the frozen Stygian flood,
Vnto great *Britaines* Empire did repaire;
Where of ELIZA's death I understood,
And that the heavens carefull of Englands good
    Rais'd up a King, who crowned with loves peace
    Brought in new Ioyes & made old griefes to cease.

Thus from the concave vaults of starlesse night
Where neither sunne nor moone vouchsafe to shine;
My wretched Ghost at length is come to light
By charters granted from the powers divine
Snake-eating envie, ô doe not repine
    At honours-shadow, doe not bite the dead,
    My pride is past, my pompe from th'earth is fled.

My Princely birth, my high enobled state
My somtime-dreadfull frownes now none regard;
My great good-turnes to many done of late
With gratefull hearts, now few or none reward
My fame is blotted out, my honour scar'd ;
    My monuments defac'd, my reliques torne
    Yea, vassiles doe my Excellency scorne.

Ah

Ah filly peafants, as each Greeian boy,
Would brave ſtout *Hector* being dead and cold,
That whilome was the piller of old Troy.
Whoſe preſence living they durſt ſcarce behold,
Now ſince you ſee me dead you grow ſo bold,
  As to controle my acts, whoſe lookes did daunt
  The proudeſt Peeres that liv'd in *Troynovant.*

A time there was, when ſtately Beares could clime,
And in that time, was I a ſtately Beare ;
Who climb'd ſo faſt and in a little time,
That my high mounting other beaſts did feare
My fortunes, by their downfals I did reare :
  I now rejoyce, whilſt others I made mourne,
  And ſerv'd the time to make time ſerve my turne.

I was the off-ſpring of a Princely Syre
He too well knew by his clime-falling pride
Like *Dedalus* hee taught me to aſpire ;
Wee both did flie: he fell, I did but ſlide ;
Like in attempts, yet unlike chance we tryed :
  Hee by a Queene did dye, and as that chanc'd,
  I by a Queene did live, and was advanc'd.

For Lady *Iane* by him a Queene proclaim'd
Was ſoone ſuppreſt, Queene *Mary* got the Crowne,
Which as her proper right ſhe boldly claim'd,
My Father ſtriv'd in vaine to keepe her downe,
And for that loſt his life, I my renowne,
  Till ſacred *Cynthia* to the Kingdome came,
  That gave new life to my late dying fame.

That Peereleſſe Queene of happie memory
That late like *Debora* the Kingdome ſwaid,
Now triumphs in the Iaſper coloured ſkie
With ſtarre-embrodered veſture rich array'd,
Shee, ſhee reſtor'd my honours then decay'd
  When treaſon did attaint my Fathers bloud,
  And drown'd our Princely race in *Lethes* floud.

Then

Then *Iupiter* was in my Horoscope
And *Ciathia* bleſt me with her faire aspect,
What might not then my youth and courage hope
When me my Soveraignes favour did protect,
O what may not a Princeſſe grace effect
  When Majeſtie on hopeleſſe men doth ſmile
  Whoſe joyes did ſeeme to periſh in exile.

Even when Queene *Maries* tragick Raigne did end
My comick ſortunes in their prime begun
That time when *Ciathia's* brightneſſe did extend
To lighten this darke Land whoſe ſplendant Sunne
Was in Eclipſe and ſorrowes ſtreame did runne
  I like the glorious day-ſtarre did appeare
  With faire upriſe, to grace this Hemiſpheare.

Since *Brute* firſt ſway'd all this united Land
No Subject firmer held his Soveraignes grace,
My will imperiall for a Law did ſtand,
Such was my Princes pleaſure, ſuch my place,
As Momus durſt not offer me diſgrace;
  What man did ſmile when *Leiſters* brow did frowne
  Whoſe wit could guide, though never get the Crown

Whilſt in this glorious Ocean I did ſwim
To high preferment divers men I brought,
Which ſince have ſought my Honours Lamp to dim,
Yea ſuch as I before advanc'd of nought
Againſt my perſon treacheries have wrought,
  Thus honours doe oft-times good manners change,
  And men grown rich to anciét friends grow ſtrange.

I grieve to thinke, I did ſuch men advance
And raiſe their baſe lines to a ſtately pitch
Vnder the ſhadow of my countenance
The ſubſtance of the Earth did make them rich,
What fury did their ſences thus bewitch,
  Or was it ſome ill Spirit that poſſeſt them ?
  To ſeeke my ruine, whoſe large bounty bleſt them.
                        Thus

Thus they in vaine my downefall did conspire
Like dogs that at the Moone doe fondly barke
And did but burne themselves like *Ætna's* fire,
Or like grim Owles did wonder in the darke
Contem'd of me that mounted like the Larke,
  Or that rare bird that builds her nest on high
  In Cedar Trees whose tops affront the skie.

When I commanded who durst countermand
Were not meane subiects, subject to my beck,
What man of worth my pleasure did with-stand,
What simple swaines could doe, I did not wreake
I gave the mate to those that gave me check
  By the Queenes helpe and threatning lookes
  I rul'd the pawnes, the Bishops, Knights, & Rooks.

Thus did I play at Chesse and wonne the game
Having the queene my puissance to support,
The Bishops for ambition did me blame
The pawnes affirm'd I wan by much extort
TheRooks &Knights foud draughts to mar my sport,
  Had not some stopt me with their timely checks,
  I might have given them check without their necks.

My braine had wit, my tongue was eloquent
Fit to discourse or tell a Courtly tale
My presence portly brave Magnificent,
My words imperious, stout, substantiall
My gestures loving, kind, Heroicall;
My thoughts ambitious, proud, and full of ire,
My deeds were good or bad as times require.

Some of my foes that bare me deadly hate,
That had to them chiefe Offices assign'd,
And were my fellow Consuls in the State
Iealous still of my aspiring mind
Gave me this praise though otherwise vnkind,
  That I was wondrous politique and wise,
  A States-man that knew how to temporise.

Some

Some others tooke me for a zealous man
Becaufe good Preachers I did patronize,
And many thought me a Precifian
But God doth know, I never was precife
I feem'd devout in godly exercife :
 And by Religious fhew confirm'd my might
 But who durft fay, I was an hypocrite.

As *Numa* when he firft did feeke to draw
The Roman people underneath his yoke,
Touching Religion he ordain'd a Law
And feyned he with Nimph *Egeria* fpoke
That him to this good motion did provoke :
 Whereby as if it were with heavens confent
 He brought his men to civill government.

So when I came in high affaires to deale
Of found Religion I did make a fhow
And by pretence of hot and fervent zeale
In wealth and faction I more ftrong did grow
For this by practice I did plainly know ;
 That men are apt to yeeld to any motion
 Made by a man that is of pure devotion.

Yet could I ftraine my Confcience for a need,
For though I feem'd an earneft Proteftant,
For gaine I favour'd Papift fo indeed,
Some held me for a newter, and I grant
To ferve my turne I would turne Puritant :
 Thus by Religion, honour fome doe winne
 And this faire cloke oft covers filthy finne.

Like as the ayre-fucking-Chamelion
Can him transforme to any hue fave white ;
So men can turne to any fafhion
Save to that forme which is fincere and right,
For though he may delude the peoples fight,
 It is in vaine before God to diffemble
 Whofe power the Divels know, & knowing trembl

Wa

Was I the onely man that hath offended
In making holinesse a cloake for sinne ?
The Frenchmen for religions sake pretended
Their civill Warres of late time did begin,
But yet ambition chiefly drew them in,
  Yea mad ambition, and desire of gaine
  Makes endlesse broyles betwixt the States & Spain.

Of promises, I was so prodigall,
So kind, well spoken, and so liberall,
That to some great Divine as it might fall
Perhaps I promised a Bishoprick,
But in performance I was nothing quick ;
  Thus with faire words, mens humours oft I fed
  Whilst hope this while a good opinion bred.

To learned Schollers I was something franck
Not for the love that I to learning bore,
But either to get praise or pick a thanke
Of such as could the Muses aide implore
To consecrate my name for evermore ;
  For he is blest that so befriended dyes
  Whose praise the Muses will immortalize.

You that desire to have your fame survive
When you within your graves intomb'd shall lye,
Cherish those sacred Sisters while you live
For they be daughters of Dame memory
Of the thundring Monarch of the sky :
  They have the gift to register with pen
  Th'eternall fame or infamy of men.

The Students of the Vniversity
Oxford whereof I was the Chancellor,
That Nurse of science and Philosophy
Knowing the greatnesse of my wit and power
Did honour me as the faire springing flower;
  That in the Princesse favour highly grew
  Whom she with showers of gold did of bedew.

          Ar

At my command both *Dee* and *Allen* tended
By Magick Art my pleasure to fulfill
These to my service their best studies bended,
And why they durst not disobey my will,
Yea whatsoever was of secret skill
In Oxford or in Cambridge to be sold
I bought for love, for feare, or else for gold.

Doubtlesse the most renown'd Philosophers
As *Plato* and *Pithagoras* have sought
To learne the Hierogliphick Characters
And secrets which by Magick skill are wrought,
Such as th'Egyptians, Iewes, and Chaldees taught :
Th'art's not ill if men doe not abuse it,
No fault so bad, but some men will excuse it.

Lopus and *Iulio* were my chiefe Physitians,
Men that were cunning in the Art to kill
Good Schollers but of passing ill conditions,
Such as could ridde mens lives yet no blood spill,
Yea and with such dexterity and skill
Could give a dram of poyson that could slay
At end of the yeare, the moneth, the weeke or day.

I never did these wicked men imploy
To wrong my Prince or my true loving friend
But false deceitfull wretches to destroy
And bring them to an vnexpected end
Let them looke to it that did most offend,
Whose names are Regiftred in Pluto's fcroules,
For I will never answer for their soules.

Knights and Esquires the best in every shire
Did waite on me in England up and downe,
And some among them did my Livery weare
My smiles did seeme to promise them renowne,
But dismall haps insu'd when I did frowne
As when the starre Arcturus doth appeare
Of raging Tempests Sea-men stand in feare.

As

As for the Souldiers and the men of warre
At home in service some I did retaine,
Others I sent abroad not very farre
At my commandment to returne againe,
These I with cost did secretly maintaine
  That if ought chanced otherwise then well,
  I might haue sent my foes to heauen or hell.

Likewise I brought the Lawyers in some awe,
The worthy students of the Innes of court,
That then applied them to the common Law,
Did yeeld to me in matters of import,
Although sometimes I did the Lawe extort,
  And whether right or wrong, my cause once heard,
  To plead against me made great Lords afeard.

So the Lord *Barkley*, lost good lands by me,
Whereof perchance at first he did not dreame,
Might many times doth overcome the right,
It is in vaine to strive against the streame,
When he that is chiefe subiect in the Realme,
  Vpon his Princes favour rests him bold,
  He cannot or he will not be controld.

Thus by the Queene my puissance was upheld,
And for my foes I euer was too strong,
The grace I had from her all feare expeld,
I might wrong others, but not suffer wrong,
So many men did unto me belong,
  Which on my favour chiefely did depend,
  And for my sake both goods, and land would spend.

The best esteemed Nobles of the land.
On whose support the publique state relied,
Were linckt with me in friendships faithfull band,
Or else in kindred nerely were allied,
Their perfect loues and constant hearts I tried,
  The inferior sort at our devotion stood
  Ready to execute what we thought good.

The

The Earle of Warwicke my owne loving brother
My sisters Husband th'Earle of Huntington,
The bounteous Earle of Bedford was another
Of my best friends belov'd of every one
Sir *Henry Sidneys* power in *Wales* well knowne :
   And there the Earle of Pembroke chiefe of all
   Of kinne my friend what ever thence might fall

In *Barwick* my wives Vncle had chiefe power
The Lord of Hunsdon my assured friend,
In Ireland the Lord *Grey* was Governour,
Gernsey and Iersey, likewise did depend
Vpon such men as did my will attend :
   Hopton my man Lieutenant of the Tower
   Was prompt to doe me service at an houre.

Sir *Edward Horsey* in the Isle of Wight
And noble Sir *George Cary* next bore sway,
Men of great courage and no little might
To take my part in any doubtfull fray
In London the Recorder *Fleetwood* lay :
   That often us'd good words that might incense
   The Citizens to stand in my defence.

The Prentises did likewise take my part
As I in private quarrels oft have tryde,
So that I had the very head and heart
The Court and City leaning on my side,
With flattery some, others with gifts I plyd ,
   And some with threats, stern looks & angry words.
   I wonne to my defence with Clubs and Swords.

Thus I by wisedome and fine pollicie,
Maintain'd the reputation of my life,
Drawing to me the flowre of Chivalrie
To succour me at need in civill strife
Men that lov'd change in every place were rife :
   And all the realme was w my power possest (best.
   Think what this might have wrought but judge the

Like

Like *Claudius Marcellus* drawne through Rome
In his faire chariot which with Trophees deckt,
Crowned with Garlands by the Senates doome,
Whom they five times their Conful did elect
That from their foes he might their lives protect:
   When he with conqueft did his Country greet
   Loaden with fpoyles lay proftrate at his feet.

So did I ride in tryumph through chiefe townes
As if I had beene Vice-roy of this Land, (crownes
My face well grac'd with fmiles, my purfe with
Holding the reynes of honour in my hand,
I managed the ftate, I did command:
   My lookes with humble majefty repleat,
   Made fome men wifh me a Kings royall feat.

Thus waxt I popular to purchafe fame
To me the common peoples knees did bow,
I could my humour ftill fo fitly frame
To entertaine all men to outward fhew
With inward love, for few my heart did know:
   And that I might not feeme puft up with pride
   Bare-headed oft through Cities I did ride.

While fome cry'd out, God fave you gracious Lord,
Lord how they did my fame hyperbolize
My words and geftures did fo well accord
As with their hearts I feem'd to fimpathize,
I charm'd their eares and did inchant their eyes:
   Thus I was reckoned their chiefe Potentate
   No poller but a piller of the ftate.

Then I was call'd the life and th'heart o'th'Court
And fome I wot wifht I had beene the head,
I had fo great a trayne and fuch a port,
As did the pompe of *Mortimer* exceed,
Who as in th'Englifh Chronicles we read,
   When fecond *Edward* loft his Kingly rights
   Was waited on at once with nine-fcore Knights.

That

That Earle of March and *Roger Mortimer*,
Rul'd the young King, queene mother, and the Peeres
I *Robert Dudley* Earle of Leicester,
Did sway in court and all the English steeres,
His rule was short, mine flourisht many yeares.
  He did his life with ignominy loose,
  I lived and triumpht o're my proudest foes.

As the Image of great *Alexander* dead,
Made king *Cassander* tremble at the sight,
Spying the figure of his Royall head,
Whose presence sometime did the world affright,
Or like as Cæsars Monarchising spright,
  Pursued false *Brutus* at *Philippes* field,
  Till he that slew his Liege himselfe was kild.

So view yee petty Lords my Princely ghost,
I speake to you whose hearts be full of gall,
I whilst I lived was honour'd of the most,
And either fear'd for love of great and small,
Or lov'd for feare of such as wisht my fall,
  Behold my shadow representing state,
  Whose person sometime did your pride abate.

Weigh what I was, knights, gentlemen, and Peeres,
Whē my death threatning frowns did make you quake
As yet they have not passed many yeares,
Since I your plumes pluckt, lofty crest's did shake
Then tell me Sirs, for old acquaintance sake,
  Wax yee not pale to heare of *Leisters* name,
  Or to backebite me blush ye not for shame.

You say in dealings that I was unjust,
As if true Iustice ballance yee could guide,
Had I dealt justly I had turnd to dust
Long before this, your corps swolne vp with pride,
Which now surviving doe my acts deride,
  My fame yet liues though death abridgd my daies,
  Some of you di'd that over-liu'd your prayse.

Ar

Are there not some among you Parasites,
Time-servers, and observers of no measure,
Prince-pleasers, people-pleasers, hypocrites,
Damb'd Machiavilians giuen to lust and pleasure,
Church-robbers, beggers of the Princes treasure,
 Truce-breakers, Pirats, Athiests, Sicophants,
 Can equity dwell heere where conscience wants.

And yet you thinke none iustly deales but you,
Diuine Astrea vp to heauen is fled,
And turnd to Libra, there looke vp and view
Her ballance in the zodiacke figured,
Iust Aristides once was banished,
 Where liues his match whom enuy did pursue
 Because men thought he was to iust and true.

Yee say, ambition harbourd in my braine,
I say ambition is no heynous sinne
To men of state, do stately thoughts pertaine,
By baser thoughts what honour can he win,
Who euer did a great exploit begin,
 Before ambition moued him to the deed
 And hope of honour, urg'd him to proceed.

Themistocles had neuer put to flight,
Zerxzes huge host, nor tam'd the Persians pride,
Nor sad King *Tarsus* got by martiall fight,
The Romane spoyles with conquest on his side,
It first ambition had not beene their guide,
 Had not this humor their stout hearts allure,
 To high attempts their fame had beene obscure.

The Eagle doth disdaine to catch poore flyes,
The Lyon with the Ape doth scorne to play,
The Dolphin doth the whirlpoole low dispise,
Thus if Birds, Beasts, and Fishes beare such sway,
If they would teach vnderlings to obey,
 Much more should men whom reason doth adorne,
 Be noble minded and base fortunes scorne.

Admit I could diffemble wittily,
This is no grievous finne in men of ftate ;
Diffembling is a point of policie
Plaine dealing now growes ftale and out of date :
Wherefore I oft conceal'd my private hate
   Till I might find fit time though long I ftay'd
   To wreake the wrath that in my heart I layd.

Th'old Proverbe is, plaine dealing is a jewell,
And he that ufeth it a Begger dyes,
The world is now adayes become fo cruell
That Courtiers doe plaine Cuntry-men defpife,
Quicke wits and cunning heads doe quickly rife.
   And to be plaine, yee muft not plainly deale
   That office feeke in Court or Common-weale.

Now *Ariftippus* is in more requeft
That knew the way to pleafe a Monarchs mind,
Then that poore cynicke fwad that us'd to jeft
At every idle knave that he could find,
To unkind friends yee muft not be too kind :
   This is a maxime which to you I give,
   Men muft diffemble or they cannot live.

Yee fay, I was a coward in the field,
I fay it fits not fuch a noble wight
To whom his Countrey doth the title yeeld
Of Lord-Lieutenant with full power and might
To venture his owne perfon in the fight :
   Let others dye, which as our vaffailes ferve
   While heaven for better haps our hopes preferve.

How foone did Englands joy in France diminifh
When th'Earle of Salisbury at Orleance
By Gun-fhot ftroke, his honour'd life did finifh ;
When *Talbot* that did oftentimes advance
The Englifh enfignes in difgrace of France,
   Was at the laft invironed and flaine
   Whofe name the French-mens terror doth remaine
               And

And what a fatall wound did Rome receive
By *Craffus* death whom faithleffe Parthians flew,
How did the Senate for *Flaminius* grieve
And for *Æmilius* death, and his ftout crew,
Whom *Haniball* at Cannes did fubdue :
 Cut off an arme, yet life the heart may cherifh
 Cut of the head and every part will perifh.

Ipocrates th'Athenian us'd to fay,
Vaunt-curters are like hands to battell preft
The men of armes are feet whereon to ftay,
The footmen as the ftomach and the breft,
The captaine as the head above the reft :
 The head once crafed troubleth all the parts,
 The Generall flaine doth kill ten thoufand hearts.

Therefore a Lord Lieutenant fhould take care
That he in fafety doe himfelfe repofe
And fhould not hazard life at every dare,
But watch and ward, fo *Fabius* tir'd his foes
When rafh *Minutius* did the conqueft lofe :
 If fuch in open danger will intrude
 It is fond rafhneffe and not fortitude.

Yee fay, I was lafcivious in my love
And that I tempted many a gallant Dame,
Not fo content, but I did alfo prove
To winne their handmaids if I lik'd the game,
Why firs yee know, love kindles fuch a flame
 As if we may believe what Poets pen
 It doth inchant the hearts of Gods and men.

Iove lov'd the daughter of a jealous fire
Danae a maid immured within a tower,
Yet to accomplifh th'end of his defire
He metamorphiz'd to a golden fhower
Fell in the lap of his faire Paramour :
 And being tearm'd a god did not difdaine
 To turne to man, to beaft, and fhowre of raine.

Deare

Deere Lords,when Cupid throwes his fiery darts
Doth none of them your tender bodies hit,
Doth *Cytherea* never charme your hearts,
Nor beauty try your quinteſſentiall wit
Perhaps you will ſay no, fie 'tis unfit,
  Now by my Garter,and my *George* to boot,
  The blind God ſurely hits,if he doth ſhoote.

Whereas ye doe objeċt my Magick charmes,
I ſought to winne faire dames to my deſire,
'Tis better ſo then ſtrive by force of Armes
For forced love will quickly backe retire
If faire meanes cannot winne what we require :
  Some ſecret tricks and ſleights muſt be deviſed
  That love may even from Hell be exerciſed.

To you dull wit it ſeemes impoſſible
By drinkes or charmes this worke to paſſe to bring,
Know then that *Giges* were inviſible
By turning the ſigill of his Ring
Toward his palme and thereby ſlew theKing,
  Lay with his wife of any man unſeene
  Laſtly did raigne by marrying with the queene.

King *Salomon* for Magick naturall
Was held a cunning man by ſome Divines,
He wrote a booke of Science naturall
To bind ill Spirits in their darke confines
He had great ſtore of wives and Concubines,
  Yet was a Sacred King, this I inferre
  The wiſeſt man that now doth live may erre.

Alſo yee ſay, that when I waxed old
When age and time miſpent had made me dry,
For ancient,held in carnall Luſt is cold,
Natures defeċt with Art I did ſupply
And that did helpe this imbecility,
  I uſ'd ſtrong drinks and Oyntments of great price,
  Whoſe taſte or touch might make dead fleſh ariſe

T

To this I answer : that those fine extractions,
Drams and electuaries finely made,
Serv'd not so much to helpe veneriall actions,
As for to comfort nature that's decaid :
Which being with indifferent judgment weigh'd,
  In noble men may be allowed I trust,
  As tending to their health, not to their lust.

What if I drinke nothing but liquid gold,
Lactrina, christal, pearle resolv'd in wine,
Such as th'Egyptians full cups did hold,
When *Cleopatra* with her Lord did dine;
A trifle, care not, for the cost was mine ?
  What if I gave Hippomenes to drinke
  To some fair Dames, at smal faults you must winke?

Ye say I was a traytor to the Queene,
And that when *Monsieur* was in greatest grace,
I being out of favour, mov'd with spleene,
To see a Frenchman frolique in the place,
Forth toward Barwick then did post apace,
  Minding to raise up a rebellious rout,
  To take my part in what I went about.

That I was then a traytor I deny,
But I confesse that I was *Monsieurs* foe,
And sought to breake the league of amity,
Which then betwixt my Prince and him did grow,
Doubting Religion might be changed so,
  Or that our Lawes and customes were in danger,
  To be corrupt or altered by a stranger:

Therefore I did a faction strong maintaine,
Against the Earle of *Suffex*, a stout Lord
On *Monsieurs* side, and then Lord Chamberlain,
Who sought to make that nuptiall accord,
Which none may breake, witnesse the sacred Word:
  But thus it chanced, that he striv'd in vaine
  To knit that knot which heaven did not ordaine.

Thus

Thus did ye mif-interpret my conceits,
That for difloyalty my deeds did blame,
Yet many men have laid their fecret baits,
T'intrap me in fuch fnares to work my fhame,
Whom I in time fufficiently did tame,
    And by my Soveraignes favour bore them downe,
    Proving my felfe true Liegeman to the Crowne.

Thinke yee I could forget my Soveraigne Lady,
That was to me fo gracious and fo kinde ?
How many triumphs for her glory made I ?
O I could never blot out of my minde,
What Characters of grace in her have fhin'd.
    But fome of you, which were by her prefer'd,
    Have with her bones almoft her name inter'd.

When fhe was gone, which of you all did weep ?
What mournfull fong did *Philomela* fing ?
Alas ! when fhe in deaths cold bed did fleep,
Which of you all her dolefull knell did ring ?
How long will yee now love your crowned King,
    If you fo foon forget your old Queen dead,
    Which foure and fourty yeares hath governed ?

Yee fay, I fought by murder to afpire,
And by ftrong poyfon many men to flay,
Which as ye thought might croffe my high defire,
And cloud my long expected golden day,
Perhaps I laid fome blocks out of my way,
    Which hindred me from comming to the Bower,
    Where *Cynthia* fhin'd like lamps in *Pharohs* tower.

Alas ! I came not of a Tygers kinde,
My hands with bloud I hated to defile ;
But when by good experience I did finde,
How fome with fained love did me beguile,
Perchance all pitty then I did exile ;
    And as it were againft my will, was preft
    To feek their deaths that did my life deteft.

                      Lo

Lo then, attend to heare a dolefull tale
Of those whose death yee doe suppose I wrought,
Yet wish I that the world beleeve not all
That hath of me by envious men been wrought,
But when I for a Kingly fortune sought,
  O pardon me, my selfe I might forget,
  And cast downe some, my state aloft to set.

My first wife fell downe from a paire of staires,
And brake her neck, and so at Comner dy'd;
Whilst her true servants led with small affaires,
Unto a Faire at Abingdon did ride,
This dismall hap did to my wife betide;
  Whether yee call it chance or destiny,
  Too true it is, she d d untimely dye.

O had I now a showre of teares to shed,
Lockt in the empty circles of my eyes,
All could I shed in mourning for the dead,
That lost a spouse so young, so faire, so wise,
So faire a corps so foule a coarse now lies,
  My hope t'have married with a famous Queene,
  Drave pitty back, and kept my teares unseene.

What man so fond that would not lose a Pearle
To finde a Diamond, leave brasse for gold;
Or who would not forsake a gallant girle,
To win a Queen, great men in awe to hold,
To rule the state, and of none be control'd?
  O but the steps that lead unto a throne,
  Are dangerous for men to tread upon.

The Cardinall *Chatillion* was my foe,
Whose death peradventure did compact,
Because he let Queen *Elizebeth* to know
My false report given of a former act,
How I with her had made a precontract.
  And the great Princes hope I bar'd thereby,
  That sought to marry with her Majesty.

              The

The Prelate had bin better held his tongue,
And kist his holy Fathers feet in Rome:
A Masse the sooner for his soule was sung;
But he might thanke me, had he staid at home,
Or late or never he to heaven had come:
  Therefore I sent him nimbly from the coasts,
  Perhaps to supper with the Lord of hosts.

When death by hap my first wives neck had crackt,
And that my suit unto the Queene ill sped,
It chanced that I made a post contract,
And did in sort the Lady *Sheffeild* wed,
Of whom I had two goodly children bred:
  For the Lord *Sheffeild* died as I was sure;
  Of a Catarre, which physicke could not cure.

Some thinke the rhume was artificiall,
Which this good Lord before his end did take:
Tush, what I gave to her was naturall,
My plighted troth yet some amends did make,
Though her at length, unkinde I did forsake;
  She must not blame me, for a higher reach
  Made my sure promise finde a sudden breach.

The valiant Earle whom absent I did wrong,
In breaking Hymeneus holy band;
In Ireland did protract the time too long,
Whilst some in England ingled under hand,
And at his coming homeward to this land
  He dyed with poyson, as they say, infected,
  Not without cause, for vengeance I suspected:

Because this fact notorious scandall bred,
And for I did his gallant wife abuse;
To salve this sore when this brave Lord was dead,
I for my selfe did this faire Lady chuse,
And flesh is fraile, deare Lady me excuse;
  It was pure love that made me undertake,
  This haplesse recontract with thee to make.

Now

Now in Joves pallace that good Lord doth sup,
And drinke full bowles of Nector in the skie.
Hunnies his page, that tasted of that cup,
Did onely loose his haire, and did not dye;
True-noble Earle, thy fame to heaven doth flye.
   He doth repent his fault, and pardon crave,
   That marr'd thy bed and too soon made thy grave:

Thou didst behinde thee leave a matchlesse Sonne,
A peerelesse paterne for all princely peeres,
Whose sparks of glory in my time begun,
Kindled with hope, flam'd highly in few yeeres,
But death him struck, and drown'd this land in teares;
   His Sonne doth live true image of him dead,
   To grace thissoil, where showers of tears were shed.

They were to blame that said the Queen should marry
With me, her Horf-keeper, for so they call'd me.
But thou *Throgmarton* which this tale didst carry
From France to England, hast more sharply gall'd me,
Sith my good Queene in office high extold me;
   For I was Master of her Highnesse Horse,
   I scorne thy words, which did my hate inforce.

But tell me then, how didst thou like thy fare,
When I to supper last did thee invite?
If I did rid thee of a world of care,
By giving thee a Salet, gentle Knight,
With gastly lookes doe not my soule affright:
   Leiter I was, whom England once did dread,
   But now I am like thee *Throgmarton*, dead.

My Lord of Suffex was too cholerick,
That call'd me traitor and a traitors sonne;
But I serv'd him a fine Italian trick;
Had not I done so, I had bin undone;
Now marke the end, what conquest hath he won?
   A litle scruple that to him I sent,
   Did purge his choler, till his life was spent.

          He

He was a gallant Noble man indeed ;
O but his life did ſtill my life decreaſe:
Therefore I ſent him with convenient ſpeed,
To reſt amongſt his anceſtors in peace :
My rage was pacifi'd at his deceaſe.
    And now I come t'imbrace his love too late,
    Him did I love, whom living I did hate.

I came to viſit as I chanc'd to walke
My Lady of Lenox, whom I found not well,
I took her by the hand, had private talke,
And ſo departed, a ſhort tale to tell :
When I was gone, into a flux ſhe fell,
    That never ceaſt her company to keep,
    Till it had brought her to a ſenſleſſe ſleep.

I dream'd ſhe had not many dayes to live ;
And this my dreame did ſhortly fall out true,
So as her Ghoſtly Father I did give
Some comfort to her ſoule : for well I knew
That ſhe would ſhortly bid the world adiew.
    Some ſay I gave ſuch phyſick as did ſpill her;
    But I ſuppoſe that meere conceit did kill her.

Some will object perhaps, I did pretend
To meet the Earle of Ormond on a day,
In ſingle fight our quarrell for to end ;
But did command my ſervant *Killygray*,
To lye in ambuſh that ſtout Lord to ſlay.
    But heaven did not conſent to work his ſpoile,
    That was the glory of the Iriſh ſoile.

Perhaps I doubted that I was too weake,
And loath I was he ſhould the conqueſt win :
If in this cauſe I did my promiſe breake,
I hope men will not count it for a ſin ;
Is it not good to ſleep in a whole skin ?
    When *Hannibal* could not prevaile by blowes,
    He uſed ſtratagems to kill his foes.

If I the death of Monſieur *Simiers* ſought,
When he from France Ambaſſadour was ſent,
I had juſt cauſe to ſeeke it as I thought ;
For towards me he bore no good intent ;
Had he not fled betimes, perhaps I ment
   T'have ſent him in embaſſage for my pleaſure
   To the black king that keeps Avernus treaſure.

For when no man about the Court durſt ſpeak,
That I the Lady *Lettice* married,
This pratling Frenchman firſt the ice did breake,
And to the Qu'ene the fact diſcovered ;
Which not without juſt cauſe the anger bred :
   Thus th'ape did play his part control'd of none,
   When he eſpi'd the Beare from home was gone.

One *Salvadore* an Italian borne,
Having once watcht with me till mid'ſt of night,
Was found ſlaine in his bed the next day morne :
Alas poore man I rue his wofull plight,
That did in nothing but in ſinne delight :
   Had he to honeſt actions bent his wit,
   He might have longer liv'd and ſcap'd this fit.

But what reward ſhould ſuch a man expect,
Whom gold to any lewdneſſe could entice,
Ones turne once ſerv'd, why ſhould we not reject
So vilde an inſtrument of damned vice ?
What if he were diſpatched in a- trice ?
   Was it not better this mans blood to ſpill,
   Then let him live the world with ſinne to fill ?

I doubted leſt that *Doughty* would bewray
My counſell, and with others party take ;
Wherefore, the ſooner him to rid away,
I ſent him forth to ſea with Captaine *Drake*,
Who knew how t'entertain him for my ſake ;
   Before he went his lot by me was caſt,
   His death was plotted, and perform'd in haſt.

He

He hoped well ; but I did so difpofe,
That he at Port St. *Iulian* loft his head,
Having no time permitted to difclofe
The inward griefes that in his heart were bred:
We need not feare the biting of the dead :
　　Now let him goe tranfported to the feas,
　　And tell my fecrets to th'Antipodes.

My fervant *Gates* did fpeed as ill or worfe,
To whom I did my clofe intents impart,
And at his need with money ftuft his purfe,
And wil'd him ftill take courage at his heart ;
Yet in the end he felt the deadly fmart :
　　He was inveigled by fome fubtle witted,
　　To rob; fo he was taken and committed.

Of pardon I did put him ftill in hope,
When he of felony was guilty found,
And fo condemn'd,till his laft friend the Pope
Did him uphold from falling to the ground.
What hope of grace where vice did fo abound.
　　He was beguil'd like birds that ufe to gape
　　At *Zeuxes* table for a painted grape.

Yet I did to the man no injury,
And gave him time and leafure to repent,
And well he knew he had deferv'd to dye,
Therefore all future mifchiefe to prevent,
I let him flip away with my confent :
　　For his reprivall, like a crafty Fox,
　　I fent no pardon but an empty Box.

Elfe as unfaithfull *Banefter* betraid
The Duke of Buckingham his Mafter deare,
When he of *Richards* tyranny afraid,
Fled to his fervants houfe for fuccour there:

So

So might my man for gaine, or forc'd for feare,
Have brought my corps with shame unto my grave,
By too much trusting on a paltry knave.

Me seems at me great Norfolkes Duke doth frowne,
Because he thinkes I did his death contrive,
Perswading some he aimed at the Crowne,
And that by royall match he meant to strive.
A kingdome to his Lordship to revive.
  Alas good Duke! he was too meek and milde,
  And I too faithlesse that his trust beguil'd.

For that I found his humour first was bent
To take the Scots captived Queen to wife,
I egg'd him on to follow his intent,
That by this meanes I might abridge his life,
And she a crowned Queen to stint all strife,
  First finding Scotland lost, to England fled,
  Where she in hope of succour lost head.

O blessed Spirits, live yee evermore
In heavenly Sion, where your maker reignes,
And give me leave my fortunes to deplore,
That am fast fetterd with sins iron chaines.
Mans most sweet joys are mixt with some foul pains.
  And doth he live of high or low degree,
  In life or death that can from woe be free?

Ah now my tongue growes weary to recite
Such massacres as have been here exprest,
Whose sad remembrance doth afflict my spright,
Me thinkes I see legions of soules to rest
In *Abrahams* bosome, and my selfe opprest.
  The burden of my sinnes doe weigh me downe,
  At me the fiends doe laugh, and Angels frowne.

My

My crimes I grant were geat and man ifold,
Yet not fo heynous as men make report,
But flattering Parafites are growne fo bold
That they of Princes matters make a fport,
To pleafe the humors of the vulgar fort:
   And that poore peevifh giddiheaded crue,
   Are prone to credit any tale untrue.

Let thofe that live endeavour to live well,
Left after death like mine their guilt remaine ;
Let no man thinke there is no Heaven or Hell,
Or with the impious Sadduces maintaine
That after death no flefh fhall rife againe:
   Let no man truft on Fortunes fickle wheele;
   The guerdon due for fine I partly feele.

Know that the Prince of heavenly Saraphins,
When he 'gainft his Creator did rebell,
Was tumbled downe for his prefumptuous finne ;
Sathan that once was bleft like lightning fell
From the higheft heaven, to the deepeft hell :
   And all thofe Angells that his part did take,
   Have now their portion in the burning lake.

Of mighty heapes of treafure I could vant,
For I reapt profit out of every thing,
I could the Prince and peoples hearts inchant,
With my faire words and fmoothfac'd flattering,
And out of droffe pure gold I oft did wring:
   For though the meanes to win be oft unmeet,
   The fmell of lucre ever fmelleth fweet.

So I fomtimes had very much good hap
Great fuites of my dread Soveraigne to obtaine,
Prodigall fortune powr'd down from her lap,
Angels of gold as thick as drops in raine.
Such was my luck to finde the golden veine ;
   Likewife with me it feemed nothing ftrange,
   Both rents and lands oft with my Prince to change.

I

I had another way t'inrich my felfe
By geting licences for me alone,
For Wine, Oyle, Velvet, Cloath, and fuch like pelfe,
By licences to alienation,
By raifing rents, and by oppreffion :
 By claiming Forrefts, Paftures, Commons, Woods,
 And forfeiture of lands, of life and goods.

By this ftrong courfe alfo I greatly thrived
In falling out with my deere Soveraigne,
For I the Plot fo cunningly contrived,
That reconcilement foone was made againe,
And by this meanes great gifts I did obtaine :
 For that I might my bags the better fill,
 I beg'd great fuites as pledge of new goodwill.

Befides fomtimes I did encreafe my ftore,
By benefit that I from Oxford tooke,
Electing heads of houfes heretofore,
I lov'd their money, and they lov'd their booke,
Some poorer though more learned I forfooke :
 For in thofe daies your charity was cold,
 Little was done for love, but much for gold.

Doubtleffe my Father was a valiant Peere
In *Edward* the fixt daies when he was fent,
Gainft Rebells that did rife in Norfolke fhire.
And after that when he to Scotland went,
Under the Lord Protectors Regiment ;
 By notable exploits againft the Scot,
 Eternall glory to himfelfe he got.

Truly ambition was his greateft fault,
Which commonly in noble hearts is bred,
He thought the never could his ftate exalt
Till the good Duke of Sumerfet was dead,
Who by my Fathers meanes did lofe his head :
 So ill the race of *Dudlies* could endure
 The *Seymors* lives which did their fame obfcure.

When

When once King *Edward* at the butt had shot,
My Father sayd, your Grace shoots neere the mark,
The King repli'd, but not so neere I wot,
As when you shot my Vncles head off quite :
The duke my Father knew the King said right,
  And that he ment this matter to debate
  If ere hee liv'd to come to mans estate.

It seemes my Father in times past had been
A skillfull Archer, though no learned clerke,
So strange a chance as this is seldome seen,
I doe suppose he shot not in the dark,
That could so quickly hit so faire a mark :
  Nor have I mist my aime, nor worse have sped,
  When I shot off the Duke of Norfolks head.

Now when the Duke of Somerset was dead,
My Father to the French did Bulloigne sell,
As pleased him the King he governed,
And from the privy counsell did depell
Th'earles of Southampton, and of Arundell :
  Thus whilst he ruled and controuled all,
  The wise young King extreamly sick did fall.

Who having languisht long, of life depriyed,
Not without poison as it was suspected ;
The counsell through my Fathers meanes contriyed
That Suffolks Daugther should be Queen elected,
The Sisters of King *Edward* were rejected :
  My brother *Guilford* to *Iane Gray* was wedded,
  Too high preferr'd that was so soone beheaded.

This Lady *Iane* that once was tearmed Queeen,
Greater in fame then fortune, was put downe,
Had not King *Henries* Daughters living been,
Might for her vertues have deserv'd a Crowne ;
Fortune at once on her did smile and frowne :
  Her wedding garment for a Princes meet
  Was quickly changed for a winding sheet.

For I was iump of *Julius Cesars* minde
That could no one superior Lord endure,
Nay I to guide my Soveraigne was inclin'd,
And bring the common people to my lure,
Accounting that my fortune was obscure,
   And that I lived in a wofull plight
   If any one eclipst my glorious light.

The love to reigne makes many men respect
Neither their friend, their kindred, nor their vow,
The love to reigne makes many men neglect
The duty which to God and man they ow,
From out this fountaine many mischeifes flow:
   Hereof examples many may be read
   In Chronicles of th'English Princes dead.

This humor made King *Harrold* break his oath
Made unto *William* Duke of Normandy:
This made King *Rufus* and young *Beauclark* both
Their elder Brother *Robert* to defie,
And *Stephen* to forget his loialty
   To *Mawd* the Empresse, and to hold in scorne
   The faithfull oath which he to her had sworne.

This made yonng *Henry* crowned by his sire,
Against his Father Warfare to maintaine:
This made King *Iohn* the kingdome to aspire,
Which to his Nephew *Arthur* did pertaine,
And him in prison hardly to retaine:
   And this made *Bullingbrook* t'usurp the Crowne,
   Putting his lawfull Soveraigne *Richard* downe.

This made *Edward* the fourth at his returne
From Burgundy, when he to Yorke was come,
To break the oath which he had lately sworne,
And rule the Realme in good King *Henries* roome:
This made the Tyrant *Richard* eke to doome
   His Nephewes death, and rid away his wife,
   And so in bloud to end his wretched life.

A

A prety plot in practice I did put,
Either to take a Queene without delay,
Or when the cards were shuffled and well cut,
To chuse the King and cast the knaves away ;
He should be cunning that great game would play ;
   Ill luck hath he that no good game can make,
   When Princes play and crownes lye at the stake.

First I assayed Queene *Elizabeth* to wed,
Whom divers Princes courted, but in vaine ;
When in this course unluckily I sped,
I sought the Scots Queenes mariage to obtaine ;
But when I reapt no profit for my paine,
   I sought to match Denbigh my tender childe
   To Dame *Arbella*, but I was beguil'd.

Even as *Octavius* with *Marke Anthony*,
And *Lepidus* the Roman Empire shar'd,
That of the world then held the soveraignty,
So I a new Triumverat prepar'd,
If death a while yong Denbighs life had spar'd,
   The grandame, uncle and the father in law,
   Might thus have brought all England under awe.

In the low Countries did my fame soare high,
When I was sent Lievtenant generall,
The Queenes proud foes I stoutly did deny,
And made them to some composition fall,
There I maintained port majesticall ;
   In pompe and triumph many dayes I spent,
   From noble then my name grew excellent,

Then was my heart in height of his desire,
My minde puft up with surquedry and pride :
The vulgar sort my glory did admire,
Even as the Romans *Ave Cæsar* cri'd,
When the Emperour to the Senat house did ride ;
   So did the Flemings with due reverence,
   Like thunder say, God save your Excellence.

Few Subjects before me obtain'd this ftile,
Unleffe they were as Viceroyes of this land :
The name of Lordfhip feem'd too bafe and vile,
To me that govern'd fuch a royall band,
And had a Princes abfolute command :
   Who did not of my puiffance ftand in awe,
   That might put him to death by martiall law ?

Loe, what a title hath my honour got,
And Excellency added to my name ?
Can this injurious world fo quickly blot
A name fo great out of records of fame,
Covering my glory with a vale of fhame ?
   Or will it now contemne me being dead,
   Whom living even with feare it honoured ?

The towne of Densborough I did befiege,
Which did on compofition fhortly yeeld :
I did good fervice to my gracious liege,
Till by ill councellours I was beguil'd :
For fuch as were my Captains in the field,
   To whom at length chiefe charge I did commit,
   Seduced me to many things unfit.

When Sir *Iohn Norris* counfell I refufed,
Whofe perfect skill in feats of armes I knew,
By *Rowland Yorkes* device I was abufed,
Whereon fome loffe foone after did enfue ;
Deventer towne and Zutphen fconce I rue,
   By *Yorke* and *Stanley* without many blowes,
   Were rendred to the mercy of the foes.

And that which to my heart might more griefe ftrike,
Happened the death of that renowned Knight,
My Nephew *Sidney*, neere Colefton dike
Receav'd his deadly wound through fortunes fpight,
I fent no frefh fupply to him in fight ;
   I was not farre off with a mighty hoft :
   So with his loffe of life fome fame I loft.

The

The Court in him lost a brave Courtier ;
The Countrey lost a guide, their faults to mend ;
The Campe did loose an expert Souldier ;
The City lost an honourable friend :
The Schooles a patron, their right to defend :
  The Court,the Countrey,the Schools & City,
   For *Sidneys* death still sing a mournfull dity.

Now while my princely glory did abound,
Like rich *Lucullus* I great feasts did make,
And was for hospitality renown'd :
The use of armes I quickly did forsake ;
An easier taske I ment to undertake :
  I tooke no joyes in wounds and broken pates,
   But to carouse and banquet with the States.

Not *Heliogabalus*,whose dainty fare,
Did all the Roman Emperours feast exceed
In cost and rarenesse, might with mine compare,
Though he on braines of Ostriches did feed
And Phenicopteines,and that instead
  Of oyle he us'd his lamps with balme to fill :
   Such was the pleasure of this tyrants will.

To me Count *Egmounts* daughter did resort,
Of such brave Dames as Flanders still did yeeld ;
That it did rather seeme I came to court
A gallant Lady,then to pitch a field ;
For I did lay aside the sword and shield :
  At cards and dice I spent the vacant dayes,
   And made great feasts,instead of martiall fraies

But whilst in games and love my time I spent,
Seeming secure,as though I car'd for nought :
My messengers abroad I daily sent,
As instruments of my still working thought,
Whereby my purpose oft to passe I brought,
  And compasse what before I did devise,
   At such a time as no man will surmise.

Thus

Thus great attempts I oft did enterprise,
Like a Magician that with some fine wile
Dazles the sight of the spectators eyes,
And with illusions doth their sense beguile,
Such policies my cunning did compile,
   That I before mans eyes did cast a mist,
   While I perform'd such matters as I list.

Ye that like apes doe imitate my deeds,
Hoping thereby like favour to obtaine;
Know that so high a spirit never breeds
In a blunt peasant, or vannurtured swaine,
But in my heart imperious thoughts did reigne:
   No flegmatick dull milk-sop can aspire,
   But one compact of th'element of fire.

He daily must devise some stratagem,
He must be rich, stout, liberall, and wise,
The humours of base men he must contemne,
He must be gracious in the peoples eyes,
He should be furnisht with rare qualities,
   With learning, judgement, policy and wit,
   And such like parts as for the time are fit.

For every forward fellow is not borne
To be a *Scipio* or a *Maximus*,
Unlesse that wisedome doth his state adorne,
Or valour make his life more glorious,
Though he be base of birth like *Marius*,
   Yet he by vertues aid aloft may come,
   Like him that was seven times Consull in Rome.

Ventidius name at first was meane and base,
Till he the Parthians host had overthrowne,
And *Cicero* came not of noble race,
Borne at Arpinia a poore country towne,
Yet he made armes give place unto the gowne.
   And Rome by his great wisdome freed from spoile,
   Call'd him the father of their native soile.

        C   Pet.

Perhaps young Courtiers learne something to sing,
To skip or dance before their Mistris face,
To touch like *Orpheus* some inchanting string,
To run at tilt,to jet with stately pace,
Or by some fine discourse to purchase grace;
    But cannot manage the affaires of State,
    Which best belongs to each great Potentate.

Listen to me ye lusty Souldiers,
That in such favour high attempt to grow,
Experience bred in me this manly yeares,
Hath taught me cunning which you doe not know;
Some precepts here I doe intend to show :
    And if my Syren song please not great Peeres,
    Then may they with *Ulysses* stop their eares.

Trust not a friend that is new reconcil'd,
In loves faire shew he may hide foule deceit,
By him ye unawares may be beguil'd,
Reveale to none your matters of great waight,
If any chance to know your lewd conceit,
    Suspected to bewray your bad intent,
    He ought to suffer death and banishment.

Caligula the scourge of famous Rome,
Wisht all the Romanes had onely one head,
That when he list to give their fatall doome,
He might with one great blow strike all them dead,
So should he never need their hate to dread :
    Even such a mischiefe I wisht to my foes,
    That many men might perish with few blowes.

But unto those that doe your favour seeke,
And by your helpe hope their low states to raise,
You must be courteous,bountifull,and meeke :
Cæsar by clemency won greatest praise,
And was esteem'd the mirrour of his dayes.
    For it belongs to men of great estate,
    To spare the poore,and rich mens mindes abate.

                         It's

It's ill to be a rub upon that ground
Whereas the Prince the alley meanes to fweep,
Their owne conceits they fondly doe confound,
That into high attempts doe boldly creep,
And with their fhallow pates doe wade fo deep,
   To hinder what their Soveraigne doth intend,
   Or to controule what they cannot amend.

Califthenes much torment did fuftaine,
Becaufe great *Alexanders* pride he checkt,
Grave *Seneca* choofing his death was flaine
By *Nero's* doome, whofe faults he did correct:
Ufe not too fharpe rebukes, but have refpect
   Unto the perfons, when great men doe evill,
   The vengeance leave to God, or to the devill.

Be not too haughty, pride procureth hate,
And meane mens hate may turne to your difgrace,
Nor too familiar be in high eftate,
For that will breed contempt among the bafe,
Obferve a meane which winneth man much grace:
   Speake well to all, truft none, ufe well your foes,
   For this may purchafe love where hatred growes.

And if that you doe feare your friend fhould chance
To mount too highly in the Princes grace,
His praife to heaven then ftick not to advance,
Say that the charge he beareth is too bafe,
And that his worth deferves farre better place,
   So may you by this praife rid him away,
   And fo fupply his place another day.

Say he will prove a terror in the field,
This private life doth much obfcure his fame,
More fit to beare great *Ajax* fevenfold fhield,
Then like *Sardanapalus* court a dame,
He idlely lives at home, it is a fhame.
   His very prefence may his foes appall,
   Let him be fent Lieutenant Generall.

Now

Now if he chance to perish in some fight,
It was not your worke, but the chance of warres,
Or thus you may excuse your selves by sleight,
Blaming the influence of the angry starres,
That thus by death his future fortune barres,
  And (sighing) we are sory, you may say,
  That this brave man would cast himselfe away.

But if in feats of armes he have no skill,
If he be learned, wise, and eloquent,
By praising him thus may you have your will,
Procure him in ambassage to be sent
Far off, lest he returne incontinent,
  As to the mighty Cham, or Prester Iohn,
  And triumph in his roome when he is gone.

Let no man think I exercis'd the ghost
Of this great Peere that sleepeth in the dust,
Or conjur'd up his spirit to this coast,
To presse him with despaire, or praise unjust:
I am not partiall, but give him his due,
And to his soule I wish eternall health:
Ne doe I think all written tales are true,
That are inserted in his Commonwealth:
What others wrote before, I do survive,
But am not like to those incenst with hate,
And as I plainly write, so doe I strive
To write the truth, not wronging his estate:
  Of whom it may be said, and censur'd well,
  He both in vice and vertue did excell.

Iamq́, opus exegi,
Deus dedit his quoque finem.

FINIS.

Non omnia possumus omnes